AF361493

Paul Pelliot (1878–1945)

His Life and Works—A Bibliography

Indiana University Oriental Series
Denis Sinor, Editor
Volume IX

Paul Pelliot (1878–1945)

His Life and Works — a Bibliography

COMPILED BY

Hartmut Walravens

Indiana University
Research Institute for Inner Asian Studies
Bloomington, Indiana
2001

Library of Congress Control Number: 00-105779
ISBN: 0-933070-47-0

Paul Pelliot (1878–1945)

Contents

Compiler's Note

Paul Pelliot's work has had a tremendous impact on the development of East and Central Asian Studies. His thorough command of the respective languages, his field work in Sinkiang, his enormous collections and his extensive and authoritative publications demand attention and respect even today. Therefore, it is quite surprising not to find a comprehensive list of Pelliot's publications.

The present list is meant to fill the gap. A chronological seemed preferable to a sorting by subject, or formal criteria, like books, articles and reviews. Many of Pelliot's reviews are essays in their own rights, and thus the usual criteria would often not fit.

Every effort has been made to base the description of the items on the originals. Fortunately, only few titles were not available, and in these cases even the Musée Guimet and the Bibliothèque nationale de France were not able to help. Titles not seen are marked accordingly.

Especially in reviews the bibliographic data are given in various ways. As far as possible the presentation has been standardised.

The statement of authorship is reproduced as in the originals. When a paper is signed «P. Pelliot» the bibliographic record reproduces this in the same way, without the addition «signed».

The translation system for Chinese is Wade/Giles, except when it is part of a French title. The Russian Cyrillic x has been rendered x in order to avoid the awkward «kh» or «ch».

While the indexes of names and titles are comprehensive, the subject index is a supplementary register of selected keywords. A real subject index would be a major research project in its own right.

Berlin, spring 2000   Hartmut Walravens

ABBREVIATIONS

BEFEO	Bulletin de l'Ecole française d'Extrême-Orient
BMFEA	Bulletin of the Museum of Far Eastern Antiquities
BN	Bibliothèque nationale de France, Paris
IAN	Izvestija Akademii Nauk
JA	Journal asiatique
JNCBRAS	Journal of the North China Branch of the Royal Asiatic Society
JRAS	Journal of the Royal Asiatic Society
Lalou	M. Lalou: L'œuvre de M. le Prof. Paul Pelliot. *Bibliographie bouddhique* 4/5.1934,1–29
OLZ	Orientalistische Literaturzeitung
OZ	Ostasiatische Zeitschrift
rev.	review
TP	T'oung Pao
ZDMG	Zeitschrift der Deutschen Morgenländischen Gesellschaft

PAUL PELLIOT†
(May 28th 1878 – October 26th 1945)

After the cruel losses caused by the war the death of Paul Pelliot is the worst diasaster that could befall Far Eastern scholarship. He was a Master, second to none, in practically every field of Sinological studies in their widest sense. Equipped with an astounding memory, great critical acumen, analytical power, indefatigable energy and love of research, minute accuracy and ability to combine and make use of the smallest facts, the strictest logic and a scrupulous respect for truth, he stood entrenched in a firm and secure knowledge of Chinese books whenever he made his excursions into the most diverse fields of sinology. He was equally well-read in practically everything written in whatever language relating to Chinese studies. As his researches expanded and embraced all Central Asia his store-house of information became immense. He seemed at all times to have full access to it and the wide range of his information enabled him to draw comparative material from many sources. Not only was he in the first rank in all departments of sinological studies proper, bibliography, linguistics, textual cristicism, historical research, archaeology, history of art, history of religions etc., but he was equally eminent as Mongolist and Iranist, studying by preference, though by no means exclusively, the problems of China's relations with the outside world, whether in ancient or in modern times.

How did Pelliot become the scholar he was? I shall in these few pages briefly attempt to trace his development. Born in 1878, after his studies in Paris with masters like Sylvain Lévi, Chavannes and Cordier, he arrived early in 1900 in Hanoï, as «pensionnaire» of that excellent institution, then just founded, the Ecole française d'Extrême-Orient. After a first mission to Hué, in Annam[1] he was by decree of February 15th 1900,[2] of the Governor-General of Indo-China, sent to China, in order to, as the Director of the School, M. Louis Finot, explains,[3] «se perfectionner dans la pratique de la langue chinoise». He arrived in Peking in good time for the siege of the

---

1   *BEFEO* II,116.
2   *BEFEO* I,75.
3   *Ibid.*, 74.

Legations and was already so proficient in the use of the language that, during a semi-armistice, he risked a very daring excursion into the enemy lines, penetrating even to Jung-lu's headquarters where he was able to paint a roseate picture of the condition of the besieged.[4] He had collected a fairly complete library of Chinese books relating to Indo-China, the East Indies and the Chinese provinces bordering on Tongking, which unfortunately was lost when, in the night of June 13th, the house of the student-interpreters of the French Legation was destroyed by fire.[5] After the delivery of the legations he was able to acquire a number of paintings and rare books, among which were two volumes of the Yung-lo-ta-tien.[6] He received the Légion d'honneur for his conduct during the siege.

In 1901 he returned to Hanoï, where, by decree of February 6th he was made Proefssor of Chinese at the Ecole.[7] The same year he returned to Peking and the next couple of years, apart from another mission to Hué and a home-leave to France in 1901 he dvided his time between sojourns in China, collecting books,[8] and Hanoï. There was held, from December 3–8 1902, the «Premier congrès international des Etudes d'Extrême-Orient», for which he acted as Secretary-General.[9]

In the meantime he had begun to publish. It is characteristic that his first article should be a review, and that this review should be one of a catalogue of Chinese books, viz. Courant's *Catalogue des livres chinois, coréens, japonais* etc. of the Bibliothèque nationale, of which the first instalment had just appeared in 1900. His second article evidences his interest in geographical matters: it is a review of Cl. Madrolle, *Hai-nan et la côte continentale voisine*. In this Marco Polo is mentioned in passing, and à

---

4   The best account of this adventure of «der allzeit ungestüme Pelliot» may be found in Theodor Ritter von Winterhalder: *Kämpfe in China.* 1902,pp.317-319.

5   *BEFEO* II,116.

6   *Ibid.*

7   *BEFEO* II,118.

8   Among these books were such interesting items as «deux séries de vocabulaires bilingues, chinois-tibétain, chinois-lolo et chinois-payi du Sseu-Tchouen et du Yunnan, qui .... remontent au XVIII siècle; ... une série en grand format des gravures exécutées en Europe au XVIIIe siècle et représentent les victoires de l'Empereur K'ien-long en Asie centrale.» BEFEO III,541. One sees how old Pelliot's interest in these engravings was when in 1920 (T'oung Pao XX,pp.183-274) he published his long article *Les «conquêtes de l'empereur de la Chine»!*

9   *Ibid.*

propos of unnecessary excursions by the author, the wish is expressed that there should be, in such books «un peu plus de sobriété, et de precision!»[10] In the second volume of the *Bulletin* this trickle of contributions becomes a stream, in the third and forth they gush forth like a torrent. He admires Hoang's *Tableau chronologique de la dynastie mandchoue-chinoise Ta-ts'ing* («voilà de bon et utile travail»),[11] he criticizes Schlegel, who in the first volume[12] is still treated with gloves on, for his *Geographical Notes*[13] emphasizing the need of phonetic exactness in all attempts to identify historical geographical names,[14] and he also published his first original work, a translation of Chou Ta-kuan's 周達觀 *Chen-la feng-t'u-chi* 真臘風土記.[15]

This first «essai» is at once a «coup de maître»; it has all the qualities that are going to distinguish his work for forty years: the same exactness, the same strict method, the same astonishingly wide information, the same cirtical spirit, and the same ease and clarity of treatment that could only proceed from a perfectly clear and logical mind, in full possession of the facts and sure of itself. The copious notes, as usual, are not the least important part of the article. In this same second volume he begins the first of his invaluable «Notes de bibliographie chinosie»[16] in which he gives a detailed analysis of the contents of the *Ku-yi ts'ung-shu* 古逸叢書 published in Japan.[17] These «Notes» were continued in volume IX of that excellent Bulletin, one article being concerned with publications on «Le droit

---

10   *BEFEO* I,147.
11   BEFEO II,88.
12   *BEFEO* I,277.
13   Published in *T'oung Pao* 1901.
14   *BEFEO* 94-96.
15   *Ibid.*, 123-177.
16   *Ibid.*, 315-340.
17   The texts were collected by Yang Shou-ching 楊守敬(1839-1915) who in the early eighties was in Japan as secretary to the Chinese minister in Japan, Li Shu-ch'ang 黎庶昌 (1837-18897). Yang's notes on these books were published in 1901 under the title *Jih-pen-fang-shu-chih* 日本訪書志 in 16 chüan. Through Li Shu-ch'ang's good offices part of this collection was publiushed at Tôkyô in 1882-1884 as the *Ku-yi-ts'ung-shu*. On Li Shu-ch'ang cf. now Hummel: *Eminent Chinese of the Ch'ing period*, pp.483-484, where another work by Li, mentioned by Pelliot, l.c. p. 316, *Li Hsing-shih ts'ung-kao* 黎星使叢稿, containing useful information on Japanese reprints of old Chinese books is omitted.

chinois»[18] and the third, long one, in two instalments, with an analysis of
«L'œuvre de Lou Sin-yuan» (陸心源).[19]

Concrete problemes, exact solutions, a wide reading in Chinese books
grouped around a certain problem. Could anything be more formative for a
young and eager mind? He had a horror of vague speculations. In reviewing
Nel's biography of Philastre, the translator of the *Yi-ching*, he exclaims:
«Pour moi, j'ai peine à comprendre la sorte de prédilection qu'ont certains
savants pour les textes peu intelligibles.»[20] A review of Henri Cordier's
Histoire des relations de la Chine avec les pussances occidentales draws
from him a strong protest against the mutilation of Chinese names, so
frequent in that books. «J'attache pour ma part une grosse importance à
cette question de forme. Estropier un nom chinois est aussi grave que
d'estropier un nom européen.»[21] This review demonstrates at the same time
that such a political history should utilize the numerous Chinese publications
of that period, of which an excellent bibliography is given.[22] Some more
articles should be noted in thjis volume. One is a brief study[23] on Le
Bhaisjyaguru or Yao-shih-liu-li-kuang-ju-lai 藥師瑠璃光如來, his first on
a purely Buddhistic subject (except some remarks on the festival
«Avalambana» in his criticism of Schlegel in *BEFEO* II,192). The second is
a review[24] of J.J. M. de Groot's contribution to the *Mitt. d. Sem. f. orient.
Spr. zu Berlin* (V1, 103-151), entitled: «Is there religious liberty in China?»
Another article,[25] reviewing de Groot's *Sectarianism and religious
persecution in China I*, gives a mass of new and interesting information on
Chinese sects. And in an important note[26] on Les Mo-ni et le Houa-hou-
king he brings to light some more facts about this religion of the «Mo-ni»
which would continue to fascinate him in later years, and he gives the
history of that curious text, the *Hua-hu-ching* 化胡經, associating Lao-tze

---

18   *BEFEO* IX,123-152.
19   *Ibid.*, 211-249,424-469. On Lu Hsin-yüan cf. Hummel, *op. cit.*, pp.545-547.
20   *BEFEO* III,472.
21   *Ibid.*, 685.
22   *Ibid.*, 683-689.
23   *Ibid.*, 33-37.
24   *Ibid.*, 102-108.
25   *Ibid.*, 304-317.
26   *Ibid.*, 318-327.

with the origin of Buddhism. Later, in Tun-huang, he was to discover two chapters of this important text.[27]

In these last-named articles he deals for the first time with the history of Chinese religions. His life-long interest in the work of the Jesuit missionaries in China appears from a long review of Cordier's *L'imprimerie sino-européenne en China*.[28] Nevertheless, during this time his principal interest was centred round the historical-geographical problems of the South coast and China's early maritime relations with the West. In Vol. III he published a long article on *Le Fou-nan*[29], establishing the location of this ancient country on the site of the historical Cambodia, supplanted later, aroung 600 A.D. by Chen-la 真臘, originally a vassal state. Volume IV of the *Bulletin* contains his famous *Deux itinéraires de Chine en Inde à la fin du VIIIe siècle*, a work of nearly 300 pages, the largest consecutive study he ever wrote. The translation takes only a few pages, but, as he explains himself,[30] it has only been a pretext, in order to pass in review a number of related problems concerning which many old errors seemed to have obtained a certain «droit de cité». Not only did he successfully introduce method and order into a host of questions which his predecessors had often treated in an too lackadaisical manner, but he also presented many new and ingenious solutions. The article ends: «Quand les travaux des autres ou les miens propres ne me paraîtront pas conciliables avec certaines de mes idées présentes, je dirai sans ambages que je me suis trompé. Puissé-je n'avoir pas à me rétracter trop souvent!» After more than forty years the article remains as fundamental as it was when it first appeared.

In the same volume of the *BEFEO*[31] were published the results of his mission to Hué in 1903, in collaboration with father Cadière, missionary in Annam who had conceived the plan of that work. It is entitled: *Première étude sur les sources annamites de l'histoire d'Annam*. It is primarily a

---

27 *BEFEO* VIII,516. They were published in the *Tun-huang shih-shih-yi-shu* 敦煌石室遺書 (1909) and the *Shih-shih-pi-pao* 石室祕寶(1910); cf. JA 1913,pp. 116 fll.
28 *BEFEO* IIII,108-116.
29 *BEFEO* III,248-303.
30 *BEFEO* IV,363.
31 *Ibid.*, 617-671.

bibliographical study which lays the foundation for the study of Annamese history.

Fou-nan, Deux itinéraires, Annam, – it seemed that the young and brillant scholar was entirely wrapped up in problems somehow connected with Indo-China. But there is a prophetic note in the same volume of the *BEFEO* showing his real ambition. He reviews Yule-Cordier's edition of Marco Polo[32] and, after a number of corrections, he writes: «Le livre de Marco Polo sera encore pendant longtemps un fructueux champ d'études. Il est bon que de temps en temps quelqu'un se charge de réunir le résultat de ses propres recherches et celles des autres.» Here is sketched, in a few words, a large part of his life's programme and while these words were being printed, he had already begun the preparations that would lead him on Marco Polo's tracks: – in Central Asia.

On July 9th 1904 he sailed «en mission» to France.[33] All that transpires at first is that he will represent the Ecole at the 14th International Congress of Orientalists to be held at Algiers during the Easter vacation 1905. His contributions to the *BEFEO* continue: in a review of Bushell's *Chinese art* he discusses archaeological problems for the first time,[34] and also for the first time, he reviews a Russian book by Prince Oukhtomskii on Lamaïsm. Douglas' *Supplementary catalogue of Chinese books and manuscripts in the British Museum* is castigated,[35] some books on travel on the Yang-tze are reviewed,[36] and in an important review[37] of Watters' *On Yüan Chwang's travels in India* the rules of Chinese phonetics are systematically applied to the identification of Central Asiatic names.[38]

A notice[39] in the *Bulletin* betrays the fact that he has been in St. Petersburg where he received a number of books from the Academy of Sciences as a present for the Ecole. Not until p. 478 of Vol. V of the

---

32   *BEFEO* IV,768-772.
33   *Ibid.*, 490, 804.
34   *BEFEO* V,211-217.
35   *Ibid.*, 219-224.
36   *Ibid.*, 224, 226-228.
37   *Ibid.*, 423-457.
38   As a beautiful example of the scrupulous strictness of his method one should read the discussion on p. 424-430 on the romanisation of the second character of the name Hsüan-tsang.
39   *Ibid.*, 239-241.

Bulletin are we told that Pelliot has been charged with a scientific mission to Central Asia and for that purpose his leave of absence has been prolongued by two years. M. Senart's address[40] to the public session of the five Academies on October 5th 1905, entitled «Un nouveau champ d'exploration archéologique: le Turkestan chinois» is printed as well as Pelliot's own speech to the Comité de l'Asie française held on December 1st 1905.

The Russians, the Germans, the Swedes and the British had, in the closingy ears of the 19th century, explored certain parts of Turkestan. The surprising archaeological discoveries resulting from these missions had caused a sensation in the scholarly world and an international association had been founded for the exploration of Central Asia, of which the headquarters were at St. Petersburg. France had, so far, not been represented in the field, but a French committee had been formed in connection with this international association, and its preseident, M. Senart, had taken the initiative for a mission to Central Asia. The Institut, the Ministère de l'Instruction publique, the Museum of Natural History, the geographical societies all joined in the enterprise of which the direction had been confided to Pelliot.[41] For studies of natural history and geography he was to be seconded by Dr. Louis Vaillant, aide major de 1e classe de l'armée coloniale, and Mr. Charles Nouette was attached to the mission as special photographer.[42]

The mission started from Paris on June 15th 1906 and ended in Peking in October 1908. It is out of the question here to retrace its itinerary and summarize its results. One should read Pelliot's address delivered at the solemn reception given to him on his return to Paris by the Comité de l'Asie française and the Société de Géographie in the great amphitheatre of the Sorbonne, to an audience of more than 4000 invited guests, on December 10th 1909.[43] Or that before the Académie des Inscriptions et belles-Lettres on February 25th 1910.[44] Or better still the letter to M. Senart, written in the first flush of the discovery of the hoard of Mss. at Tun-huang: *Une*

---

40   *Ibid.*, 492-497.
41   *Ibid.*, 498-499.
42   *BEFEO* VI,482.
43   *BEFEO* X,274-281.
44   *Ibid.*, 655-660.

bibliothèque mediévale retrouvée au Kansou.[45] Those three weeks, on his haunches in the badly lit cave, surrounded by Mss. «dans un hâchis de langues» as he once said,[46] examining with lightning rapidity every single one of 15,000 scrolls in order to decide what to take and what to leave, must have been the happiest of his life and with justifiable pride I have heard him say, many years later,[47] that there was only one text which he regretted to have overlooked. I think he referred to the scroll on Manichaeism published by Lo Chen-yü.[48]

«Depuis près de deux ans que je vis loin des livres, j'ai beaucoup oublié» he writes in closing this letter.[49] Nobody, in reading this account of his finds, would suspect weakness of memory. Rarely was anybody better equipped than he was for the particular work to be done at Tun-huang. The results of his excavations at Tumchuq (between Kashgar and Kucha), and in the region west of Kucha, at Duldur-âqur, are no less remarkable, but, as a Sinologue, I naturally insist on Tun-huang. In an important review[50] of Chavannes' study «Les pays d'occident d'après le Wei-lio» (*T'oung Pao* VI), he had rightly complained: «Nous n'avons autant dire pas d'anciens manuscrits chinois» and he had stressed the necessity of having comparative text material and different editions.[51] Here, with one stroke, by his finds and those of Sir Aurel Stein, this situation was completely revolutionised. As he says himself: «A mon sens, ces manuscrits apportent en Sinologie deux nouveautés. D'abord, le manuscrit chinois était une catégorie à peu près inconnue dans nos bibliothèques. Sans doute, il existe des manuscrits en Chine, et d'importants; mais les bibliophiles indigènes les recherchent, et nous-mêmes étions trop peu au courant de l'imprimé pour nous mettre en quête de l'inédit ... Mais aujourd'hui nous nous apercevons que la tradition manuscrite ou imprimée n'a pas été impeccable, et qu'il faut faire, en chinois comme ailleurs, de la critique de textes. Pour cette œuvre, les

---

45   *BEFEO* VIII,501-525.
46   In an after-dinner speech at the International Orientalists Congress, held at Leyden, September 1931.
47   In a lecture at The Hague, 1930.
48   In the *Kuo-hsüeh-ts'ung-k'an* 國學叢刊 II, cf. *JA* 1911, pp. 500 fll.
49   *BEFEO* VIII,528.
50   *BEFEO* VI, 366.
51   *Ibid.*, 361-367.

manuscrits du Ts'ien-fo-tong, religieux ou profanes, nous seront d'une grande utilité. Non seulement ils vaudront pour les textes qu'ils contiennent, mais, en nous montrant les formes en usage à l'époque des T'ang dans l'écriture régulière ou cursive, ils nous permettront souvent de donner la raison d'altérations insoupçonnées ou qui nous paraissent inexplicables. La seconde nouveauté est que, pour la première fois en sinologie, nous pourrons travailler en quelque sorte sur pièces d'archives. J'entends par là que la science indigène nous a toujours mis en face de résultats. Ces résultats, nous pouvions les admettre ou les rejeter en opposant les livres les uns aux autres, mais toujours des livres, écrits après coup; nous ne disposions jamais de documents originaux, indépendants, et qui n'eussent pas été destinés à la publicité. Cette fois, nous pourrons voir pas des notes privées, pas des actes, pas des correspondances, ce qu'était en fait, dans une province reculée de la Chine, du VIIe au Xe siècle, la vie réelle, vie religieuse ou vie civile, que nous ne connaissions jusqu'ici qu'en ses traits généraux et d'après des écrits dogmatiques ....» The paintings, moreover, opened an entirely new chapter in the study of the history of art.[52]

With this journey, Pelliot's formative years are closed. To his former qualifications he had added that of the great specialist of Central Asia. He acquired a practical knowledge of Eastern Turkish at Tashkend while waiting for his luggage[53] and in the 6th volume of the *Bulletin* he was already able to publish a Kashgar text.[54] Mongol, of which a few years ealier he had confessed ignorance,[55] seems to have followed pretty soon and as the years went by he became more and more engrossed in Mongol studies, as the readers of the *T'oung Pao* well know. Persian and Uigur, Sogdian and Toharian, Jučen or Hsi-hsia, Tibetan and Sanskrit he could handle whenever his roving studies made it desirable. He became a Marco Polo of the spirit, equipped with all the knowledge of languages, religions and books that Marco Polo himself had lacked. He threw himself into the study of the foreign religions introduced into China: Nestorianism, Mani-

---

52   Cf. the different volumes published in *Mission Pelliot en Asie Centrale*. For a summary of the results of Pelliot's mission and bibliographical information down to 1921 cf. P. Demiéville, *BEFEO* XXI 1, pp. 366-374.

53   *BEFEO* X,275.

54   *BEFEO* VI,255-260.

55   *BEFEO* III,651.

chaeism, Mazdeism. I only mention his important publication, in cooperation with Chavannes on *Un traité manichéen retrouvé en Chine*.[56] He
became deeply involved in studies on Buddhism.[57] Already in his review[58]
of Chavannes' article on Les pays d'occident, quoted before, he had made
penetrating remarks on the relationship of early Buddhism[59] and Taoism, a
problem to which he would return more then once, as for example in his
Autour d'une traduction sanscrite du Tao-tö-king.[60] He emphasised the
necessity of studying the Chinese religions in their historical development:
«Bouddhisme, Taoisme, et pourrais-je ajouter, Confucéisme ont toujours
été pris dans l'abstrait, à part des réalités vivantes qui donnent aux systèmes
leur valeur occasionnelle et leur portée. Les philosophies, les religions sont
nées, ont évolué et dépérissent dans des conditions données de temps et de
milieu. Ce sont ces conditions qu'il faut connaître, et pour leur intelligence,
un petit fait correctement établi vaut de longs raisonnements. Nous avons eu
beaucoup de dilettants ...»[61]

In 1911 Pelliot was appointed Professor at the Collège de France in a
chair for the languages and the history of Central Asia. In 1921 he became
Membre de l'Institut. Many honours were showered on him, memberships
of foreign academies, honorary doctor's degrees, chairmanships of learned
societies. He travelled a great deal, visiting all the important libraries and
archives abroad. His production went on uninterruptedly, at first chiefly in
the *Journal asiatique*,[62] from 1920 on, when he succeeded Chavannes as

---

56   *JA* 1911,499-617; 1913,99-199,261-394.

57   An excellent analysis by Mlle Marcelle Lalou of Pelliot's Buddhistic studies up to
1928 will be found in *Bibliographie Bouddhique*, IV-V, pp.1-22: Rétrospective,
L'œuvre du Professeur Paul Pelliot. From 1928-1933 on see the annual *Bibl.
Bouddh.*

58   *BEFEO* VI,379.

59   In his review he mentions Mou-tze 牟子several times, and in a note on p.390 he
states that he had completed a translation of this important work, that so far had
been entirely unnotioced. His annotation however was not yet finished. It was
published several years later in the *T'oung Pao* XIX,255-433.

60   *T'oung Pao* XIII,350-430.

61   *BEFEO* VI,400.

62   One very important exception is his long article on «Le Chou-king en caractères
anciens et le Chang chou che wen» in the *Mémoires concernant l'Asie orientale*. II,
123-177 (1916) with its fundamental discussion of the *Chin-wen* and *Ku-wen*
problem.

editor of the *T'oung Pao*, mainly in this journal, of which, after Cordier's death in 1925, for ten years he carried the responsibility alone. Only the first world war brought a stagnation of several years in his production. Part of that time he served in Peking as military attaché of the French Legation and he took part in the allied expedition to Siberia. He must have made as good a soldier as he was a scholar. In his bearing there was something martial, he moved easily among people, free from that shyness that often characterises scholars who are more at home in their closet than in a drawing-room, and he spoke well and fluently in several languages.

For more than forty years his influence on our studies has been immense. I shall not attempt to enumerate more of his important articles. Every one of them deserves reading and rereading. His innumerable book-reviews were sometimes more important than the books discussed. «The gentle art of making enemies», he once observed to me with a smile. At times he was perhaps over-critical and his insistence on exactness in the smallest details gave him the undeserved reputation of being a stickler. Yet he taught a younger generation what exact work should be, and he himself gave a high example of that scientific probity, that scrupulous respect of facts, that passionate search for all available data, that had been too much lacking in the old-fashioned dilettantism that is not yet dead. Was it his horror of the «à peu près» that kept him from ever attempting a larger synthesis? He wrote like many Chinese scholars, *sui-pi* 隨筆 There always remained so much spade-work to be done, so many facts to be ascertained and the field of his interest was so wide, that the task seemed too Herculean. Probably his mind was more analytic than synthetic, more critical than creative, and the host of facts on any given subject which he could marshall at any time was never coordinated in a more permanent form. In so far the very extent of his information defeated its ultimate purpose: the burden of knowledge which he carried was too heavy to allow his fancy free play with it in a major composition.

Pelliot lived through the invasion and the occupation and, after a period in the «zône non-occupée» he returned to Paris and, unshaken, resumed his work. The last issues of this journal [*T'oung Pao*] and some of the supplementary volumes bear witness to part of his activity. In the spring of 1945 he went to the U. S. as a delegate to the Congress of the Institute of Pacific Relations at Hot Springs Va. he seemed in excellent form and gave several lectures. Some months after his return to France he went to a hospital to be operated for a complaint, as he wrote to me in a dictated letter of September 19th «rien d'organique ni de caractère malin, mais quelque chose d'assez tenace». His illness however proved fatal and on October 26th he passed away unexpectedly, only 67 years old. Our deepest sympathy goes out to his widow, Madame Pelliot.

Without him Sinology is left like an orphan. He was its watchful guardian, guring, chiding, encouraging, and forever setting an example. His rôle was unique and irreplaceable. His works live after him and will continue to influence our studies. It is imperative that his countless articles be collected so that his entire œuvre should become more easily accessible.

It is also fervently hoped that the *Onomasticon* in the great Marco Polo edition which he prepared jointly with professor A. C. Moule will soon be published and the many *Inedita*, left by him, will appear without too much delay.

Pelliot's death means the end of an era. A heavy burden falls on us, his younger contemporaries. We have decided to continue the *T'oung Pao*; professor Paul Demiéville, the successor at the Collège de France of Maspero, whose tragic death fills us equally with great sadness, had kindly consented to act as co-editor. Our task will not be an easy one in this world of post-war ruins. Yet we believe that more than ever Sinological studies have their importance; the cooperation between Chinese and Western scholarship, so ardently advocated by Pelliot,[63] is now happily a fact. We for our part shall carry on to the measure of our strength.[64]

J. J. L. Duyvendak

---

63   *BEFEO* X, 659.
64   While this article was in the press, I received through the kindness of professor Demiéville, the proofs of a commemorative volume in honour of Pelliot, in which are printed obituaries by MM. Edmond Faral, Jean Filliozat, Louis Vaillant, Paul Demiéville, J. Deny, L. Hambis. From this I have borrowed one or two factual details on Pelliot's life.

Denis Sinor
Indiana University

I have recently visited the studies of two Sinologists, one of whom was in his mid-thirties, the other in his mid-forties. Both had on display pictures of Paul Pelliot who had died more than half a century ago, before these scholars were born. It is a fact that his many publications are still widely used and that his extraordinary personality still seems to arouse interest and command respect. As a matter of fact his oeuvre is still very much read and, in sheer volume, his posthumous publications exceed those that appeared during his lifetime.

I have three reasons for putting to paper these reminiscences. I am the only scholar still alive who knew him well. Secondly, in the whole hagiology dealing with Pelliot, no mention is made of his foibles. Thirdly, and quite rightly, they emphasize mostly his work on the Dunhuang manuscripts and his contribution to Sinology. As it were, they all speak of the young Pelliot and few remarks are made on his last years and on his contributions to Altaic studies. It is on this period of his life and on his contribution to this field of study that I shall focus my attention. I venture to present him here from an unusual angle. Reminiscences such as these carry the risk of containing too much that concerns the narrator; I am not sure that I could entirely avoid this pitfall.

My relationship with Pelliot was of short duration, barely six years, from August 1939 to his death on October 26, 1945. In more than one way, those were fateful times, very hard on all of us living in German-occupied France. I first met Pelliot in early August 1939 when, with modest support given by the Hungarian Ministry of Education, I arrived in Paris, ostensibly to prepare for my PhD examination but, in fact, to get to know and study with Pelliot. Of my two teachers in Budapest, one, Louis Ligeti, had himself worked for three years with Pelliot, the other, the great Turcologist Gyula Németh, bid me farewell with the parting words that in the person of Pelliot I was going to meet a man «with limitless know-

---

1   Revised and enlarged version of two papers read respectively on July 7 1997 at the 35th International Congress of Asian and North African Studies held in Budapest and on April 6, 1998 at the 208th meeting of the American Oriental Society held in New Orleans

ledge». As a matter of fact I had been in touch with Pelliot at an earlier date. At the age of 19 I sent him for publication an atrociously bad article, the receipt of which he never acknowledged, but which, for reasons unfathomable, he published in the *T'oung Pao*. In later years I never mustered the courage to ask him how this could happen; I dreaded the thought that he might recognize in me the perpetrator of that sorry effort.[2]

Aged 23, early in August 1939, I arrived in Paris, and soon after, formally dressed with hat and gloves, I called on him. The reception I received was, to put it mildly, something of an anticlimax. Wearing pyjamas, he opened the door of his apartment, situated Avenue Foch on the top floor of the Musée Dennery, would not let me pass the antechamber and informed me that in October when he was to begin his classes at the Collège de France. I could attend those. Not exactly a warm welcome, which compared most unfavorably with those which, in 1937 and 1938, I experienced in Berlin from Erich Haenisch or Otto Franke. By the way, in the course of time, this first impression needed no revision. Kindness, friendliness at first sight, were not Pelliot's dominant traits of character.

Pelliot was a solitary man and scholar, he created no school, had no institute of his own, and was not surrounded with an adoring and helpful group of students. Contrary to the current practice, when junior professors of small colleges rely on the services of research assistants, Pelliot had none, not even a secretary, at least not in France (perhaps he had someone Chinese working for him when he was in Hanoi). He wrote all his works himself, in a small not very legible hand. It seems he never owned a typewriter. In the last years of his life I was officially his assistant for Altaic Studies at the Institut des Hautes Etudes Chinoises, but this was a courtesy title, given for me to include on my resumé so to speak. He never once asked me to perform any scholarly task for him. My principal duties, if they may be so called, consisted of providing him with cigarettes, in those war years difficult to come by. He was almost a chain smoker. Shortly before his death - he was already hospitalized - as I was visiting him, I was received by a very agitated Mme. Pelliot, clamoring for cigarettes. I had none and pointed out that not long ago I had brought enough to last for a good while. «Je sais Sinor» - came her reply - «mais c'est terrible, je pensais qu'il allait mourir et je les ai toutes fumées moi-même.»

In the strict, traditional sense of the word, Pelliot had few pupils. From among those who persevered in research the names of Louis Ligeti,

---

2   For reasons quite understandable, I will refrain from giving the exact reference for this article.

Francis Woodman Cleaves, Louis Hambis, Rolf Stein, Louis Bazin, and my own come to mind. I regret if, accidentally, I have omitted a name or two, but, be it as it may, it was a very small band. Without any doubt, Hambis - whose role was almost that of a research-assistant - was closest to him; but more will be said about this later.

Soon after our first brief meeting, but not because of it, World War II broke out and, after a period of administrative hesitation, the Collège de France opened its doors. Because of his age, Pelliot could not be mobilized and he found unacceptable such war-time duties that had been offered to him. He could not see himself in a hierarchy in which his place was not on the top. So, to my great luck, he resumed his courses. These were of two types: one addressed to humans, i.e. to a wider public, the other intended for his students. In his courses of the latter type he paid no consideration whatsoever to the level of knowledge we may have had. I vividly remember the occasion when, in opening his course, he announced that it would be based on the Kirghiz chapter of the *T'ang shu*. The fact that some of the handful of auditors (including myself) could not read Chinese did not bother him. By the time of the next lesson I had learned, all on my own, how to use a Chinese dictionary, and had a vague idea of the contents of the first few lines to which he added his superb commentaries, veritable dazzling fireworks. If by any chance an outsider ventured into one of his lectures (the Collège de France lectures were open to everyone, the motto of the institution being *Docet omnia*), he went out of his way to become even more technical. When the unwary human had taken to flight, Pelliot remarked with some satisfaction, «On est de nouveau entre nous».

He was a fascinating speaker with a pleasant voice and, however technical the matter may have been, the presentation was made in a beautiful, clear French style, with no «ahhs» or «ers». He used notes but no prepared text. He allowed interruptions, questions and quite often he addressed one of us with the formula «Monsieur X nous dira sans doute...». In answering one took upon oneself a considerable risk. It was not enough to make an intelligent comment or to provide some information he may not have had, but it also had to be done in faultless French. He had zero tolerance for mistakes in French grammar and his reactions to linguistic mistakes were quite often plainly rude. In this respect I was lucky, having spent years in a French-speaking Swiss boarding school, all in all, I could express myself correctly.

Modesty was not Pelliot's strongest point. In fact he had none. Accordingly, he would not tolerate contradiction and would dislike people who, in his view, could have intruded into what he considered his own territory. He simply was not interested in training young Sinologists. Rolf Stein found asylum with the formidable Marcel Granet. Robert des Retours, an aristocrat, was autonomous, and with his manners and fortune impressed Pelliot. As for Louis Hambis, he diligently prepared draft translations of scores of Chinese texts of the Yuan period which then served as basis for the display in the commentaries of Pelliot's immense learning. As for me, who had no intention to remain permanently in France, my diagnosis was quite unequivocal. If it was out of the question to challenge any of Pelliot's views, the very solid scholarly education (should I say boot-camp experience?) which I had acquired in Hungary every now and then allowed me to cite data mainly in the Turkic and Finno-Ugric field, which, quite surprisingly, were unknown to Pelliot and yet relevant to his interests. Towards me he could be astonishingly generous, to the point of inaccuracy, in his recommendations. In a letter of reference written on 11 July 1942 he wrote that I had arrived in Paris «solidement préparé pour le turc» and in another letter (1 October 1942) he even went further and indulged in gross exaggeration: «M.Sinor, familier des langues finno-ougriennes, connaît également bien le turc dans toutes ses formes et dans tous les temps.» It should be noted that such praise, going well beyond the limits of truth and necessity, assigned me a place beyond the borders of Sinology. Pelliot supported only those whose interest lay outside his private hunting ground. I see this much clearer now then at that distant time and I am certain that this attitude of his was more instinctive than deliberate. As could be expected, a young student in Sinology could not measure up to Pelliot and, thus, was of no interest to the «Maître».

Pelliot very much disliked people who appeared to intrude on his own Inner Asian territory. Let me cite a few examples. For him, Sven Hedin was a mere ignorant traveler, and he could never muster a kind word for Sir Aurel Stein who had the audacity of discovering the treasures of Dunhuang before him. He was ready to give Stein credit for entrusting Chavannes with the task of editing some of the texts he himself was unable to read. He could never forgive Erich Haenisch for publishing and translating the *Secret history of the Mongols*, tidbits of which had appeared in Pelliot's papers and in his courses for many years. As we know, Pelliot's partial translation of this important text[3] was published posthumously and, let us face it, all in all it is no better than that of Haenisch. Yet it should be remembered that, probably dissatisfied with his own work, Pelliot never published it. In the œuvre of Otto Franke Pelliot could detect only the mistakes made in the reconstruction of foreign names and not the merit of writing a historical synthesis.

His favorite scholars (of course all dead) were Sir Henry Yule, Joseph Marquart, Berthold Laufer, and Bretschneider. He often referred to the «robuste bon sens» of Yule with whom he shared a fondness for early travelers. Yule's *Cathay and the Way Thither*, his studies on Marco Polo, and last but not least his *Hobson - Jobson* were constantly cited and ameliorations, if any, were offered in a tone of respect and affection. As for the intolerable Marquart, Pelliot, as all of us, stood in awe before the breadth of his knowledge.[4]

Among the German scholars of the Turfan expeditions, his favorite was Albert von Le Coq (perhaps because of his French ancestry); he respected F. W. K. Müller and was fond of retelling the adventures of Grünwedel with a high-class prostitute in St. Petersburg. As just said, he completely ignored Otto Franke but was objective enough to let Wolfgang Eberhard's pioneering *Kultur und Siedlung der Randvölker Chinas* appear as a supplement to the *T'oung Pao*. True, Eberhard was then in voluntary exile in Turkey and the book, just like *Hobson-Jobson*, was for Pelliot a rich mine of information. Among his *bêtes noires* the Sinologist J. J. M. De Groot held pride of place. As far as Hungarian orientalists were concerned, he almost never referred to the formidable Ligeti - I guess he considered him a clone of himself - but, for example, spoke with deep respect about the lesser-known Nándor Fettich, for the simple but valid reason that Fettich had archeological data on the Avars formerly unknown to Pelliot. Among the living scholars, he often mentioned, and always with respect and affection, the Rev. A. C. Moule - with whom he collaborated on the Marco Polo text - and Cardinal Eugène Tisserand. In later years I was received with open arms in Cambridge by the former, in the Vatican by the latter.

---

3   *Histoire secrète des Mongols. Restitution du texte mongol et traduction française des chapitres I a VI.* Paris: Maisonneuve, 1949.

4   Let me cite what he wrote about him in his «A propos des Comans»: «...au milieu d'hypothèses si aventurées que l'auteur les abandonne lui-même à mi-route, jaillissent les éclairs d'une véritable divination. Mais l'ordre des livres de M. Marquart n'existe que dans la tete encyclopedique de M. Marquart lui-même...» (p. 25)

In the face of the occupying Germans - we are now in 1940 - Pelliot was uncompromising and I had to take great care not to allow my relative objectivity to appear in our conversations. When the German Islamist and specialist of Mongol history in Islamic lands, Berthold Spuler, wished to visit him - I heard the story from Spuler himself - Pelliot let him know that he would be willing to meet him «quand nous aurons gagné la guerre», a war which he did not for a moment consider ended with the armistice signed by Pétain. In a letter in my possession, meant to be a sort of certificate, he writes as follows: «Je suis moi-même un résistant de la première heure, et les points de vue de M. Sinor ont toujours concordé avec les miens.» I cannot possibly tell whether Pelliot has ever done anything against the Germans but he certainly never hesitated to show his contempt towards the officials of the Vichy Government. There was the much talked-about incident when he refused to shake the extended hand of a minister of that government. More significantly, he would not ask for the permission of the Vichy Government required for the Société Asiatique to continue its meetings during the Occupation. Thus all of our meetings were technically speaking illegal and I was impressed to note that no member of the society betrayed this activity. Pelliot was once arrested for a short period; but I now cannot tell whether this was by the Vichy police or by the Germans.

Once again his view towards me was overly generous, and, for a short while, let me shift here the emphasis from Pelliot to Sinor. In June 1940 I was neither surprised nor sentimentally affected by France's collapse. I was and felt Hungarian to the point that in June 1940 I became deputy director of the Institut des Etudes Hongroises in Paris whose director was not ready to risk staying in a city facing a German assault. On 30 August 1940, as a result of the Second Verdict of Vienna one part of Transylvania was returned by Romania to Hungary whence it had been detached in 1920 in the Treaty of Trianon. I felt it my duty to celebrate the event in a reception given in the Institute but I was faced with the delicate question, whether I should invite Germans, and notably the Director of the German Institute in Paris. On the one hand, the Verdict which I welcomed was passed under German pressure, on the other, I instinctively recoiled at the idea of having victors and vanquished face each other at what was to be a dignified but celebratory occasion. So: no Germans were invited to the reception. My decision, based on tact rather than on political considerations, proved to be one of lasting consequences. Some 50 to 60 people came to the reception (the first in my life I had to give), including my French teachers, such as Demiéville, René Grousset, the Turcologist Jean Deny and, of course Pelliot. I was only 24 at that time and felt moved and grateful for their presence. The Hungarian Consul General made a short speech, I made a short speech, we sang the gloomy Hungarian National Anthem immediately followed by the stirring sounds of the Marseillaise played on a gramophone. The effect was stunning. What for me was a self-evident courtesy towards the host country, was for the French there present a defiant assertion of their sovereignty: the playing of the *Marseillaise* had been strictly forbidden by the German occupant. Grousset had tears in his eyes and embraced me, while a very serious Pelliot shook my hand for a long time; he had devoted his life to scholarship but first and foremost he was just French. Without being aware of it, on that afternoon I crossed my Rubicon and entered France.

A good-looking, elegant man with a slightly military comportment, Pelliot was liked by women and, in turn, appreciated feminine charm. He also valued elegant company and good food - the key to his close relationship with Hambis, a generous though not disinterested host in whose country home in Ligugé I myself spent some happy days. I have no information on Pelliot's family background but he might have come from a modest petit-bourgeois family whence his genius catapulted him into the highest French circles where he moved with ease yet without losing the enjoyment they could offer. I somehow sensed this and in the Spring of 1940, with some trepidation, I dared to invite Pelliot for dinner. True, it was not to some obscure student hide-out but to the Chinese Embassy to which I had access through an attaché of the Chinese mission who happened to be my girl-friend. At any function given at the embassy, Chinese ladies were supposed to wear national dress but I managed to convince her to disregard this rule. In her dress of *haute-couture* she looked quite spectacular, and I must leave it to the judgement of my readers to decide whether it was pure coincidence that soon after that dinner, on May 10, co-sponsored by Pelliot and Grousset, I was elected a member of the Société asiatique.

I remember, some years before his lamented death, the formidable scholar Francis Woodman Cleaves of Harvard telling me that during his years attending Pelliot's courses he had never had any personal conversation with him. Such was also Ligeti's experience who, as far as I could gather, never had any social contact with Pelliot. Neither of them had social skills and they could not sense that Pelliot enjoyed the good life, that he was wide open to adventures even of the kind where men's lives were at risk. His courage during the Boxer Rebellion had made him famous and he endorsed with enthusiasm my decision to join the Free French Forces. He also showed considerable interest in my venture into the fur-coat business, one that sustained me in those difficult years. I may have been awe-stricken by Pelliot's knowledge but lacked any shyness in social intercourse.

In October 1942 when, as a consequence of that playing of the *Marseillaise* two years earlier, to escape arrest I had to leave Paris, I invited for a farewell dinner Pelliot and the Consul General of Hungary (somewhat snobbish, Pelliot enjoyed the company of diplomats). It was a very moving occasion. My wife and I intended to cross illegally into what was called the *zone libre*, i.e. the south of France, not yet occupied by the Germans, with the intention of continuing for Argentina where my father-in-law lived. It so happened that by the time we arrived in Marseille so had the Germans, who now occupied the whole of France. There was no point in staying there, and by mid-March 1943 I was back in Paris where Pelliot received me with open arms. By that time the war had taken a bad turn for the Germans and one could foresee the final outcome of the conflict. One day, abruptly, Pelliot asked me what I intended to do with my life once the war was over. Quite frankly, preoccupied with the triple task of dodging arrest, finding food and working on my next article, I had no plans for the more distant future and I told him so. I will never forget that moment. Standing in his study with no trace of any smile or benevolence, he told me peremptorily: «Vous devez rester en France. Je m'occuperai de vous.» It was an order and a promise, Pelliot the «grand mandarin», giving orders, making decisions. In a few seconds he changed the course of my life.

It was my good fortune that late in his life, when I knew him, Pelliot was more and more attracted to Inner Asian history and to Altaic studies. In a not very respectful way I would describe his approach as leech-scholarship. He read one work, attached himself to it and produced a masterpiece which, very often, did little to improve on what was the essential merit of the original but served as vehicle to carry the reader into uncharted territories. John F. Baddeley's *Russia, Mongolia and China* (1919) inspired *Notes critiques d'histoire kalmouke*,[5] Spuler's *Die Goldene Horde. Die Mongolen in Russland 1223-1502*[6] produced *Notes*

---

5   Paris: Maisonneuve 1960, 2 vols. 235 pp. The text was written in 1920 but Pelliot
      never put the finishing touches to it.
6   Leipzig: Harrassowitz 1943. 556 pp.

sur l'histoire de la Horde d'Or suivi de quelques noms turcs d'hommes et de peuples finissant en ‹ar›.[7] But even many of his articles such as «A propos des Comans»[8] (already mentioned), «Notes sur le Turkestan de M.W. Barthold»[9] , or «Notes sur la légende d'Uγuz kaghan en écriture ouigoure»[10] are but *addenda* or vastly improved versions of works written by others. His chef-d'oeuvre in Altaic linguistics «Les mots à h- initiale aujourd'hui amuie, dans le mongol des XIIIe et XIVe siècle»[11] is, in fact, an elaboration of an idea of G. J. Ramstedt.[12] When he assigned to Louis Hambis the translation of two chapters of the *Yüan-shih* or of the *Sheng-wu ch'in-cheng-lu*[13] he did so to create a trellis which he could then cover with the vine of his own commentaries; it can truly be said that at least three quarters of the text of these books was the work of Pelliot. On occasion, Pelliot himself admitted that he was guilty of «overkill» in his remarks. On p.197 (!) of his «Le Hoja et le Sayyid Husain de l'Histoire des Ming»[14] he allowed himself to muse «Le présent mémoire paraîtra bien long pour un sujet assez mince.»

Pelliot tended to avoid the constraints faced by the translator who is obliged to face all the difficulties presented by the text and cannot pick out only those passages he was interested in and ready to solve. He was less secure in Mongol, Turkic or Latin than in Chinese. As already mentioned, his translation of the *Secret History of the Mongols* remained a torso and, as far as I can see, the only longer Turkic text he fully translated was *La version ouïgoure de l'histoire des princes Kalyānaṃkara and Pāpaṃkara.*[15]

---

7   Paris: Maisonneuve 1949, 292 pp.; also published posthumously.

8   *Journal asiatique* 1921,I, pp.125-178. A review of sorts of J. Marquart: «Über das Volkstum der Komanen.» *Abh. der königl. Gesellschaft der Wissenschaften zu Göttingen.* N.F. 13 .1912/1914, 25-238.

9   *T'oung Pao* 27.1930,12-36.

10   T'oung Pao 27.1930,247-358.

11   *Journal asiatique* 1925, I, 193-263.

12   Zur Geschichte des labialen Spiranten im Mongolischen. *Festschrift Vilhelm Thomsen zur Vollendung des siebzigsten Lebensjahres.* Leipzig 1912, 182-187. Thus Pelliot wrote a seventy page commentary on a five-page article.

13   *Le chapitre CVII du Yuan che.* T'oung Pao supplément au vol.38.1945; *Le chapitre CVIII du Yuan che.* Leiden: Brill, 1954. Paul Pelliot, Louis Hambis: *Histoire des campagnes de Gengis khan. Cheng-wou ts'in-tcheng lou.* Leiden: Brill, 1954.

14   *T'oung Pao* 38.1948, 81-292.

15   *T'oung Pao* 15.1914, 225-272. This translation was the product of Pelliot's dissatisfaction with a previous attempt to read and translate the text: C. Huart: Le conte bouddhique des deux frères, en langue turque et en caractères ouïgours. *Journal asiatique* 1914, I, 1-57. It so happens that Pelliot's reading and translation was not

Rightly distrustful of any theory claiming to explain how the world was working, he could never bring himself to write a synthesis. Pelliot was certainly no historian and lacked the essential virtue necessary for such a vocation: he was unable, or unwilling, to distinguish between the important and the unimportant. Once - and this is really my favorite personal anecdote about Pelliot - I mustered all my courage and confronted him with the question: «Maître» (this was the way we, the few chosen, addressed him) «why do you waste your time, and why do you use your fantastic knowledge to clarify matters of no consequence?» I was afraid that the sky would split, lightning would strike me down and I would be cast into eternal darkness, but nothing of the sort happened. Pelliot looked at me and cheerfully answered: «Ça m'amuse, Sinor, ça m'amuse»! Here was the key to his manifold activities: he did what he liked.

His vast knowledge of all subjects oriental (at that time we were not ashamed of using this term; I am still not) made him the ideal president of the Société asiatique. No sooner had the presenting of a paper started than Pelliot appeared to fall asleep; no sooner was it over, than he made pertinent remarks on the subject just treated. As a young man I had no problem in having my papers published, I never had to send them to any periodical for approval. Not without some apprehension I handed them to Pelliot and, a few days later, he informed me of his decision to having them published in the *T'oung Pao* or in the *Journal asiatique*. He was quite liberal in his editorial decisions and would accept an article even though he disagreed on some point with the author. In the last footnote of his posthumous *Notes sur l'histoire de la Horde d'Or* he reproached me «aux moins deux erreurs assez graves» of which, so he felt, I had been guilty in an article which he had accepted for publication in the *Journal asiatique*. In accepting my manuscript (which perhaps he did not bother to read) he did not raise these questions. Stylistic corrections were seldom made by Pelliot but he disliked wishy-washy «diplomatically» expressed views. One had to state one's opinion in a straightforward manner. This went so far that he did not tolerate the use of the «majestic plural» nous, - so commonly used by French scholars - but made me write the singular form, *je*. For better or for worse, in my works written in French I remained faithful to this practice.

---

superior on all points to that of Huart, and the text received a new, complete treatment by James Russell Hamilton: *Le conte bouddhique du bon et du mauvais prince en version ouïgoure*. Paris: Klincksieck, 1971.

He was a prince, «un grand mandarin», as we used to call him, and, speaking for myself, I profited greatly from his influence which reached far beyond the narrow confines of the academic world. When Pelliot spoke the French academic and political world would listen. When in August 1945, we had «won» «our war» and I was tired of administering a small German town, I wrote to Pelliot asking him to intervene - I did not know where - to obtain my demobilisation. He did, but I could thank him only silently when, most anxious concerning my own future, with tears in my eyes, still in uniform, I stood by his coffin on October 31, 1945 and thought of how God could reveal to this exceptional man and scholar all the unimportant secrets he was so fond of exploring.[16]

---

16   Astonishing though it may seem, there exists no Pelliot bibliography. The daunting task to prepare one has now been undertaken by Hartmut Walravens and it is hoped that it will appear in 2000 in the Indiana University Oriental Series.

1901

1. [rev.] Maurice Courant: Bibliothèque nationale, Département des
    manuscrits. Catalogue des livres chinois, coréens, japonais etc. 1e
    fascicule, nos. 1-2496. Paris: Leroux 1900.
    BEFEO 1.1901,145-146
      P. Pelliot

2. [rev.] Claudius Madrolle: Hai-nan et la coté continentale voisine.
    Paris: Challamel 1900. XIV,XVIII,126 pp., 6 pl. 8°
    BEFEO 1.1901,146-147
      P. Pelliot

3. [Un répertoire administratif de l'empire annamite.]
    欽定大南會典事例
    BEFEO 1.1901,159-160

4. [rev.] R. P. Jérôme Tobar: Inscriptions juives de K'ai-fong-fou.
    Chang-hai 1900. VI,112 pp. 8° (Variétés sinologiques.17.)
    BEFEO 1.1901,263-264
      P. Pelliot

5. [rev.] E. H. Parker: China. Her history, diplomacy, and commerce
    from the earliest times to the present day. London: John Murray
    1901. XX,332 pp. 8°
    BEFEO 1.1901,264-265
      P. Pelliot

6. [rev.] R. P. A. Debesse S.J.: Petit dictionnaire chinois-français.
    Chang-hai 1901. 580 pp. 16°
    BEFEO 1.1901,265
      P. Pelliot

7. [rev.] Ed. Chavannes: Le dieu du sol dans l'ancienne religion
    chinoise. Revue de l'histoire des religions 43.1901.
    BEFEO 1.1901,271-273
    [according to index by Pelliot]

8.   [rev.] F. Hirth: Die chinesische Regierung und ihre Organe.
      G. Schlegel: Geographical notes XIV. The old states in the Island of
      Sumatra.
      G. Schlegel: Les termes bouddhiques Yu-lan-pen 盂蘭盆 et Yu-lan-
      p'o 盂蘭婆.
      T'oung Pao 1901.
      BEFEO 1.1901,277-278
      [according to index by Pelliot]

1902
9.   [rev.] Père P. Hoang: Tableau chronologique de la dynastie mand-
      choue-chinoise Ta-ts'ing (Journal of the North China Branch of the
      Royal Asiatic Society. 1899-1900,102-152).
      BEFEO 2.1902,88
         P. P.

10.   [rev.] Père Louis Gaillard: Nankin port ouvert. Chang-hai 1901.
      XXI,483 pp. 8° (Variétés sinologiques.18.)
      BEFEO 2.1902,88-89
         P. Pelliot

11.   [rev.] Edouard Chavannes: De l'expression des vœux dans l'art
      populaire chinois. Journal asiatique, sept.-oct. 1901, pp.193-233.
      BEFEO 2.1902,89-90
         P. P.

12.   [rev.] A. Vissière: Traité des caractères chinois que l'on évite par
      respect. Journal asiatique, sept.-oct. 1901,320-373.
      BEFEO 2.1902,90
         P. P.

13.   [rev.] Maurice Courant: Note sur l'existence, pour certains caractères
      chinois, de deux lectures distinguées par les finales k-n, t-n, p-m.
      Mém. Soc. linguist. de Paris.12, pp.67-72.
      BEFEO 2.1902,90
         P. P.

14. [rev.] G. E. Moule: Notes on the Ting-chi or half-yearly sacrifice to Confucius. Journal of the North China Branch of the Royal Asiatic Society. 1899-1900,37-73.
    BEFEO 2.1902,90-91
    P. P.

15. [rev.] Père Henri Havret: T'ien-tchou, «Seigneur du Ciel», à propos d'une stèle bouddhique de Tch'eng-tou. Chang-hai 1901. 30 pp. 8° (Variétés sinologiques.19.)
    BEFEO 2.1902,91
    P. Pelliot

16. [rev.] E. Bälz: Menschen-Rassen Ost-Asiens mit specieller Rücksicht auf Japan. Verhandlungen der Berliner Gesellschaft für Anthropologie, Ethnologie und Urgeschichte. 1901,166-189,202-220.
    J. Deniker: Les tâches congénitales dans la région sacro-lombaire considérées comme caractère de race. Bulletin et Mém. de la Soc. d'Anthrop. de Paris.1901,274-281.
    BEFEO 2.1902,92
    P. P.

17. [rev.] G. Schlegel: Geographical notes (suite). T'oung Pao 1901, 167-182.
    BEFEO 2.1902,94-96
    P. Pelliot
    Comments by Schlegel: *TP* 3.1902,199-200

18. [rev.] V. Weinstein: Giljaken. Verhandlungen der Berl. Gesellschaft für Anthropologie, Ethnologie und Urgeschichte.1901,36-39
    BEFEO 2.1902,97
    P. P.

19. Mémoires sur les coutumes du Cambodge 真臘風土記, [par Tcheou Ta-Kouan, traduits et annotés.]
    BEFEO 2.1902,123-177
    [not signed.]
    Rev.: E. von Zach: *Lexicographische Beiträge.*1.1902,76.
    [Lalou 1]

20. Avalambana ou vilambin; les ouvrages de mathématiques sous les
     T'ang; les pays des hommes longs.
     BEFEO 2.1902,192-194
       P. Pelliot
     [On Schlegel. *TP* 1901,394.]
     [Lalou 2]

21. [rev.] Geógraphie physique, économique et historique de la
     Cochinchine. IIe fascicule. Monographie de la province d'Hà-tiên.
     Saigon: Ménard 1901. 66 pp., 1 map 8° (Publications de la Société
     des études indochinoises.)
     BEFEO 2.1902,196
       P. P.

22. [rev.] Mémoire de S. G. Mgr. Mossard sur les Ecoles de la Mission
     de Cochinchine. Saigon 1901. 21 pp.
     BEFEO 2.1902,199
       P. Pelliot

23. [rev.] Maurice Courant: Bibliothèque nationale. Catalogue des livres
     chinois, coréens, japonais etc. Deuxième fascicule. Nos. 2497-3469.
     Paris: Leroux 1901. 8°
     BEFEO 2.1902,209
       P. Pelliot

24. [rev.] Donald Ferguson: Letters from Portuguese captives in Canton,
     written in 1534 and 1536 (Indian antiquary. Oct.-Nov. 1901, Jan.
     1902.)
     BEFEO 2.1902,210-211
       P. Pelliot

25. [rev.] Samuel I. Woodbridge: China's only hope. An appeal by her
     greatest vice-roy, Chang Chih-tung, translated from the Chinese
     edition. Edinburgh, London 1901.
     BEFEO 2.1902,213
       P. P.

26. [rev.] Maurice Courant: En Chine: les effets de la crise; intentions de
     réforme. Annales de sciences polit. Nov. 1901.
     BEFEO 2.1902,213-214
     P. P.

27. [rev.] Geo. Edgar Betts: Social life of the Miao tsi (Journal of the
     North China Branch of the Royal Asiatic Society.1899/1900, no. 2,
     pp.1-21)
     BEFEO 2.1902,215
     P. P.

28. [rev.] Takeshi Kitasato: Zur Erklärung der altjapanischen Schrift.
     T'oung Pao 1901.
     BEFEO 2.1902,215-216
     P. Pelliot

29. [rev.] G. Schlegel: Geographical notes. XVI.The old states in the
     island of Sumatra. 2.Po-li 波利 Pulau Puli. 3.The state of Samûdra.
     4.Li-tai 黎代 (Li-de) 5.Nakur那孤兒 Necuran. 6.Lam-put-li
     南淳利 Lâmeri. 7.A-lu 亞魯 Aru. 8.Tam-iang 淡洋 Temiang. 9.A-
     tse 亞齊 Atjeh. 10.Kiu-chow shan. 九州山 11.Lam-pang 覽邦
     Lampong. 12.Pang-ka 彭家 Bangka. 13.Kao-lan 勾欄 Billiton (?).
     BEFEO 2.1902,217
     P. Pelliot

30. [rev.] J. J. M. de Groot: Die antiken Bronzepauken im ostindischen
     Archipel und auf dem Festlande von Südostasien. Mitteilungen des
     Seminars für Orientalische Sprachen. Ostasiatische Studien.1901,76-
     113.
     BEFEO 2.1902,217-218
     P. Pelliot

31. Notes de bibliographie chinoise. Par M. Paul Pelliot, professeur à
     l'Ecole française d'Extrême-Orient.
     BEFEO 2.1902,315-340
     I. Le Kou-yi ts'ong chou 古逸叢書.

32. [rev.] A. Chéon: Thuân-an trúoc chi tù 順安竹枝詞. Poésies
     traduites. Hanoi 1902. 34 pp. autogr. 8°
     BEFEO 2.1902,401
       P. P.

33. [rev.] A. Chéon: Recueil de nouvelles curieuses, publiés sous la di-
     rection de ... Hanoi 1902. 80 pp. 8°
     BEFEO 2.1902,401
       P. P.

34. [rev.] G. Schlegel: Siamese studies. Supplément au T'oung Pao.II,2.
     1902. 128 pp. 8°
     BEFEO 2.1902,401-403
       P. Pelliot

35. [rev.] Père Pierre Hoang: Mélanges sur l'administration. Chang-hai
     1902. 233 pp. 8° (Variétés sinologiques.21.) – Tableaux des titres et
     des appellations de l'empereur, des membres de sa famille et des
     mandarins. Ibid. 55 pp. (Extraits du no. 21 des Variétés sinolo-
     giques.)
     BEFEO 2.1901,405-407
       P. Pelliot

36. [rev.] Père Henri Havret: La stèle chrétienne de Si-ngan-fou, 3e
     partie: Commentaire partiel et pièces justificatives. Chang-hai 1902.
     92 pp. 8° (Variétés sinologiques.20.)
     BEFEO 2.1902,407
       P. P.

37. [rev.] G. Schlegel: On the invention and use of fire-arms and gun-
     powder in China, prior to the arrival of Europeans. T'oung Pao.
     March 1902.
     BEFEO 2.1902,407-409
       P. Pelliot

38. [rev.] E. von Zach: Weitere Beiträge zur richtigen Würdigung Prof.
     Schlegel's. Peking 1902. 15 pp. 8°
     E. von Zach: Einige Worte zu Prof. Gustav Schlegel's La loi du
     parallélisme en style chinois. Peking 1902. 7 pp. 8°

BEFEO 2.1902,409
  P. P.

39. [rev.] Fernand Farjenel: La métaphysique chinoise. Journal asiatique
     IX,20.1901,113-131.
     BEFEO 2.1902,409
       P. P.

40. [rev.] Ed. Chavannes: Le défilé de Long-men dans la province de
     Ho-nan. Journal asiatique IX,20.1901,133-158. 6 pl.
     BEFEO 2.1902,409
       P. P.

1903
41. Le Bhaiṣajyaguru. Par Paul Pelliot.
     BEFEO 3.1903,33-37
     [Lalou 3]

42. [rev.] E. H. Parker: Chinese Buddhism. Asiatic Quarterly Review.
     1902,372-390.
     BEFEO 3.1903,98-99
       P. Pelliot

43. [rev.] E. H. Parker: China, the Avars, and the Franks. *Asiatic
     Quarterly Review.* 1902,346-360 (April).
     E. H. Parker: The Ephthalite Turks. Ibid., July 1902,131-159.
     E. H. Parker: Chinese knowledge of early Persia. Ibid., Oct. 1902,
     144-169.
     BEFEO 3.1903,99-101
       P. Pelliot

44. [rev.] Rev. Ernst Faber: Chronological handbook of the history of
     China. Shanghai: American Presbyterian Mission Press 1902. XVI,
     250,XLV pp. 8° (Œuvre posthume éditée par le Rév. Paul Kranz.)
     BEFEO 3.1903,101
       P. Pelliot

45. [rev.] J. J. M. de Groot: Is there religious liberty in China. Mitteilun-
     gen des Seminars für Orientalische Sprachen zu Berlin. 1.Abt.: Osta-
     siatische Studien. Vol. 5, pp.103-151.
     BEFEO 3.1903,102-108
       P. Pelliot

46. [rev.] Henri Cordier: L'imprimerie sino-européenne en Chine.
     Bibliographie des ouvrages publiés en Chine par les Européens au
     XVIIe et au XVIIIe siècle. Paris. Leroux 1901. IX,75 pp., 1 pl.
     large 8° (Publication de l'Ecole des langues orientales vivantes. V,3.)
     BEFEO 3.1903,108-116
       P. Pelliot

47. [rev.] Ed. Chavannes: Dix inscriptions chinoises de l'Asie centrale
     d'après les estampages de M. Ch. E. Bonin. Mém. présentés par
     divers savants à l'Académie des Inscriptions et Belles-Lettres. 1re
     série, T.11, 2e partie, pp.193-295.
     BEFEO 3.1903,117-120
       P. Pelliot

48. [rev.] E. von Zach: Lexicographische Beiträge. 1. Peking 1902. 98
     pp. 8°
     BEFEO 3.1903,120-121
       P. Pelliot

49. [rev.] Maurice Courant: Supplément à la Bibliographie coréenne (jus-
     qu'en 1899). Paris: Leroux 1901. X,122 pp. large 8° (Publication de
     l'Ecole des langues orientales vivantes.)
     BEFEO 3.1903,133
       P. P.

50. Le Fou-nan. Par M. Paul Pelliot, professeur à l'Ecole française
     d'Extrême-Orient.
     BEFEO 3.1903,248-303
     [Lalou 4]

51.   La secte du Lotus blanc et la secte du Nuage blanc.
      BEFEO 3.1903,304-317
        P. Pelliot
      [Lalou 5]

52.   Les Mo-ni et le Houa-Hou-king [化胡經].
      BEFEO 3.1903,318-327
        P. Pelliot
      [Lalou 6]

52a. [Note sur le récit de Hiuan-tsang relatif à la légende de Sou-la-na.]
      BEFEO 3.1903,334
      [In a review by L. Finot on *Livre de Vesandar.*]
      [Lalou 7]

53.   [rev.] O. Franke, R. Pischel: Kaschgar und die Kharoṣṭhî. Sitzungs-
      berichte der k. preuß. Akademie der Wissenschaften 1903, VII. pp.
      184-196.
      J. Halévy: Le berceau de l'écriture kharoṣthrî. Extrait de la Revue
      sémitique 1903. 15 pp.
      BEFEO 3.1903,339-341
        P. Pelliot

54.   [rev.] Père Stanislas Le Gall: La Chine. Géographie générale à
      l'usage des écoles françaises. Zikawei 1903. 161 pp., maps. 8°
      BEFEO 3.1903,342
        P. P.

55.   [rev.] Edouard Chavannes: Confucius. Revue de Paris, 15 février
      1903, pp.827-844.
      BEFEO 3.1903,342
        P. P.

56.   [rev.] L. Nocentini: Brano di storia cinese e coreana. Rome 1903. 17
      pp. 8° From Rendiconti dell'Academia dei Lincei. Vol.11, pp. 537-
      551.
      BEFEO 3.1903,342
        P. P.

57.   [rev.] Commandant de Marolles: Souvenirs de la révolte des T'ai-
      P'ing (1862-1863). T'oung Pao II,4, pp.1-18.
      BEFEO 3.1903,343
        P. P.

58.   [rev.] Ku Hung-ming: Papers from a viceroy's yamen, published by
      the Shanghai Mercury. Shanghai 1901. XVI,197 pp. 8°
      BEFEO 3.1903,343-344
        P. P.

59.   [rev.] Henri Omont: Missions archéologiques françaises en Orient
      aux XVIIe et XVIIIe siècles. Dans la Collection de documents inédits
      sur l'histoire de France. Paris: Imprimerie nationale 1902. 1237 pp.
      4°
      BEFEO 3.1903,356
        P. P.

60.   [rev.] Franz Heger: Alte Metalltrommeln aus Südostasien. Leipzig:
      Hiersemann 1902. 245 pp., 45 pl., large 4°
      BEFEO 3.1903,356-357
        P. P.

61.   Les Mo-ni et l'inscription de Karabalgassoun.
      BEFEO 3.1903,467-468
        P. Pelliot

62.   [rev.] Docteur Jules Regnault: Médecine et pharmacie chez les Chi-
      nois et chez les Annamites. Paris: Challamel s.d. [1902?]. X,233
      pp., large 8°
      BEFEO 3.1903,469-470
        P. P.

63.   [rev.] Lieut. de vaisseau Nel: Philastre. Sa vie et son œuvre. Bulletin
      de la Société des études indo-chinoises de Saigon 44.1902. Saigon:
      Ménard 1903,7-27.
      BEFEO 3.1903,470-472
        P. Pelliot

64. [rev.] Henri Fontanier: Une mission chinoise en Annam (1840-1841); publié par Henri Cordier. T'oung Pao 1903, 127-145.
BEFEO 3.1903,472-473
P. P.

65. [rev.] Col. Henry Yule, A. C. Burnell: Hobson-Jobson. A glossary of Anglo-Indian terms and phrases. Nouvelle édition par William Crooke 1903. XLVII,1021 pp.
BEFEO 3.1903,477-479
P. Pelliot

66. [rev.] O. Franke, R. Pischel: Kaschgar und die Kharoṣṭhî. II. Sitzungsberichte der k. Pr. Akademie der Wissenschaften zu Berlin 33.1903,735-745.
BEFEO 3.1903,479-480
P. Pelliot

67. [rev.] L. Gaillard: Nankin d'alors et d'aujourd'hui. Aperçu historique et géographique. Chang-hai: Impr. de la mission catholique 1903. VI,350 pp. (Variétés sinologiques.23.)
BEFEO 3.1903,481-486
P. Pelliot

68. [rev.] K. Hemeling: The Nanking kuan-hua. Shanghai: Statistical Department of the Inspectorate General of Customs 1902. 107 pp.
BEFEO 3.1903,486-491
P. Pelliot

69. [rev.] Père L. Wieger: Rudiment de parle chinois. XI. Textes historiques.1. Ho-kien-fou 1903. 770 pp., 9 maps 8°
BEFEO 3.1903,491
P. P.

70. Le sa-pao 薩寶.
BEFEO 3.1903,665-671
P. Pelliot

71. La dernière ambassade du Fou-nan en Chine sous les Leang (539).
     BEFEO 3.1903,671-672
        P. Pelliot   [Lalou 9]

72. [rev.] Henri Cordier: Histoire des relations de la Chine avec les puis-
     sances occidentales, *1860-1900* [le t. III porte 1860-1902]. T.1.
     L'empereur T'oung-tché (1861-1875). Paris: Alcan 1901. 570 pp. 8°
     – T.2. L'empereur Kouang-siu, première partie: 1875-1887. Ibid.
     1902. 650 pp. – T.3. L'empereur Kouang-siu, deuxième partie:
     1888-1902. Ibid. 1902. 598 pp.
     BEFEO 3.1903,689-715
        P. Pelliot

73. [rev.] Dr. O. Franke: Beschreibung des Jehol-Gebietes in der
     Provinz Chihli. Leipzig: Theodor Weicher 1902. XV,103 pp., 1
     map, 16 ill. 8°
     BEFEO 3.1903,715-718
        P. Pelliot

74. [Rez.] Dr. O. Franke: Die wichtigsten chinesischen Reformschriften
     vom Ende des neunzehnten Jahrhunderts. Bulletin de l'Académie im-
     périale des sciences de St.-Pétersbourg. 17.1902,047-059.
     BEFEO 3.1903,718-720
        P. Pelliot

75. [rev.] Maurice Courant: Catalogue des livres chinois etc. de la Biblio-
     thèque nationale. 3me fasc. nos. 3470-4423. Paris: Leroux 1902. – 4^e
     fasc. (nos. 4424-5664). Paris: Leroux 1903. 192 pp.
     BEFEO 3.1903,720-721
        P. Pelliot

76. [rev.] Colonel de Pélacot: Expédition de Chine de 1900 jusqu'à l'arri-
     vée du général Voyron. Paris: Charles Lavauzelle [1903?]. 285 pp. 8°
     Général Henri Frey: Au Pé-tche-li: Français et alliés (1900-1901).
     Revue des deux mondes 1 July 1903,83-117.
     Général Henri Frey: L'armée chinoise. Revue des deux mondes, 1
     Octobre 1903,528-569.
     BEFEO 3.1903,722
        P. Pelliot

77.   [rev.] H. Enselme: A travers la Mandchourie. Paris: J. Ruoff 1903.
      IX,202 pp. 12°
      BEFEO 3.1903,723
        P. P.

78.   [rev.] Ming-hsiang kuo Hsü wen-ting-kung mo-ti
      明相國徐文定公墨蹟. Lithogr. ed. Hung-pao-chai 鴻寶齋.
      Shanghai 1903. 1 pen.
      BEFEO 3.1903,723
        P. P.

79.   Textes chinois sur Pâṇḍuraṅga. Par M. Paul Pelliot.
      BEFEO 3.1903,649-654
      [Lalou 8]

80.   Présentation de manuscrits et de livres chinois anciens. Par M. P.
      Pelliot.
      *Premier Congrès international des études d'Extrême-Orient. Hanoi
      1902. Comptes-rendus analytique des séances.* 1903, 105-107
      [On the *Po-ku-t'u-lu*, a Hsi-hsia work, etc.]

81.   La réforme des examens littéraires en Chine. Par M. P. Pelliot.
      *Premier Congrès international des études d'Extrême-Orient. Hanoi
      1902. Comptes-rendus analytiques des séances.* 1903,107

82.   La réforme des examens littéraires en Chine.
      *Asie française.*III,25.1903,160-165
        P. Pelliot, de l'Ecole française d'Extrême-Orient

83.   *Le mouvement réformiste en Chine.* Conférence faite le 20 avril 1903
      à la section de Hanoi de la Société de géographie commerciale.
      Hanoi: Schneider 1903. 22 pp.
      [not seen.]

1904

84.   Deux itinéraires de Chine en Inde à la fin du VIIIe siècle. Par M. Paul
      Pelliot, professeur à l'Ecole française d'Extrême-Orient.
      BEFEO 4.1904,131-413
      Appendice:

374-376:	Itinéraire du protectorat d'Annam à Yang-tsiu-mei (Ta-li).
376-377:	Itinéraire de Tche-Tong (Yunnansen) à Yang-tsiu-mei.
377-378:	Itinéraires de Ngan-ning (à l'ouest de Yunnansen) vers le Tonkin et le Laos.
379-381:	Le Puṇḍravardhana comme limite orientale de l'Ārya-varta du Bouddhisme indien.
382-385:	Liste provisoire des rois chams nommés par les Chinois jusqu'au milieu du VIIe siècle.
385-412:	Le Fou-nan et les théories de M. Aymonier.
412-413:	Addenda et Errata.

Rev.: *TP* 5.1904,468-473 (Chavannes)
[Lalou 10]

85.   Notes additionnelles sur la secte du Lotus blanc et la secte du Nuage blanc.
BEFEO 4.1904,436-440
  P. Pelliot
[Lalou 11]

86.   [rev.] Ed. Chavannes: Documents sur les Tou-kiue (Turcs) occidentaux. Sanktpeterburg 1903. IV,378 pp., map (Sbornik trudov orxonskoj ėkspedicii.VI.) – Notes additionnelles sur le Tou-kiue (Turcs) occidentaux. TP 5.1904,1-110.
BEFEO 4.1904,479-483

87.   [Remark on Note de M. O. Franke.]
(Ibid. 540-541, on the Gaillard review.)
BEFEO 4.1904,541
  P. Pelliot

88.   Première étude sur les sources annamites de l'histoire d'Annam. Par MM. L. Cadière, missionnaire apostolique, et Paul Pelliot, professeur à l'Ecole française d'Extrême-Orient.
BEFEO 4.1904,617-671
Offprint: Hanoi: Schneider 1904. 55 pp.
622 signed: P. Pelliot

89. [rev.] G. Dumoutier: Le rituel funéraire des Annamites. Hanoi: F. H. Schneider 1904. 299 pp., 9+36 pl. (without 15 and 23), large 8°
BEFEO 4.1904,750-751
P. P.

90. [rev.] A. Ivanovskij: Sur une traduction chinoise du recueil bouddhique Jâtakamâlâ. Traduit du russe par M. Duchesne. Revue de l'histoire des religions 47.1903,298-335.
BEFEO 4.1904,752-755
P. Pelliot
[Lalou 12]

91. [rev.] Dr. F. W. K. Müller: Handschriften-Reste in Estrangelo-Schrift aus Turfan, Chinesisch Turkestan. Sitzungsberichte der Kgl. Preuß. Akademie der Wissenschaften 11.1904,348-352.
BEFEO 4.1904,760
P. P.

92. [rev.] Père J. de Moidrey: Observations anciennes de taches solaires en Chine. Extrait du Bulletin astrononomique 21.1904, no. 2, 11 pp. – Variation diurne de la déclinaison en Chine. Note sur quelques anciennes déclinaisons. Terrestrial magnetism and atmospheric electricity 1904, March, 15-24.
BEFEO 4.1904,760-761
P. P.

93. [rev.] Père S. Couvreur: Dictionnaire classique de la langue chinoise. Ho-kien-fou 1904. XII,1080 pp. 4°
BEFEO 4.1904,761-762
P. Pelliot

94. [rev.] Col. Sir Henry Yule: The book of Ser Marco Polo the Venetian concerning the kingdoms and marvels of the East. 3rd ed., revised by Henri Cordier, with a biography of Sir H. Yule by his daughter Amy Frances Yule. London: Murray 1903. 2 vols. CII,144,462; XXII, 662 pp. 4°
BEFEO 4.1904,768-772
P. Pelliot

95. [rev.] Camille Sainson: Nan tchao ye che 南朝野史. Histoire
     particulière du Nan-tchao, traduction d'une histoire de l'ancien Yun-
     nan. Paris: Leroux 1904. III,294 pp., map (Publications de l'Ecole
     des Langues orientales vivantes.V,4.)
     BEFEO 4.1904,1094-1127
       P. Pelliot

1905
96. Conférence de M. Paul Pelliot. [Les évenements politiques en
     Chine.]
     Bulletin du Comité de l'Asie française. Apr. 1905, 130-136

97. Conférence de M. Paul Pelliot: Sur les civilisations hindoue et
     chinoise anciennes au Turkestan chinois.
     Bulletin du Comité de l'Asie française. Déc. 1905, 458-465, 1 map
     [Lalou 13]

98. [rev.] Stephen W. Bushell: Chinese art. 1. London: Wyman & Sons
     1904. 156 pp. 8°
     BEFEO 5.1905,211-217
       P. Pelliot
     [Lalou 14]

99. [rev.] Prince Esper Uxtomskij: Iz oblasti lamaizma. K poxodu
     angličan na Tibet. Sanktpeterburg: Vostok 1904. 128 pp.
     BEFEO 5.1905,217-218
       P. P.

100. [rev.] A. Vissière: Biographie de Jouàn Yuân, homme d'état, lettré et
     mathématicien (1764-1849). Traduite du chinois et annoté. TP 5,
     561-596.
     BEFEO 5.1905,218
       P. P.

101. [rev.] Robert Kennaway Douglas: Supplementary catalogue of
     Chinese books and manuscripts in the British Museum. London
     1903. 224 pp. 4°
     BEFEO 5.1905,219-224
       P. Pelliot

102. [rev.] Félix Hémon: Sur le Yang-tse. Journal d'un double exploration
     pendant la campagne de Chine (1900-1901). Paris: Delagrave s.d.
     XV,346 pp.
     BEFEO 5.1905,224-225
     P. P.

103. [rev.] Ed. Chavannes: Les prix de vertu en Chine. Paris: Firmin
     Didot 1904. 31 pp. 4°
     BEFEO 5.1905,225
     P. P.

104. [rev.] Lieut. de vaisseau Hourst: Dans les rapides du Fleuve Bleu.
     Voyage de la première cannonière française sur le haut Yang-tse-
     kiang. Préface de Jules Lemaitre. Paris: Plon 1904. III,368,7 pp. 8°
     BEFEO 5.1905,226-228
     P. Pelliot

105. [rev.] H. Kern: Iabadioe. Bijdrag. t. de Taal- Land- en Volkenkunde
     van Ned.-Indië. VII,4. pp.364-367.
     BEFEO 5.1905,232
     P. Pelliot

106. [rev.] H. Kern: Eenige plaatsen uit de Nâgarakretâgama betreffende
     Hayam Wuruk. Ib. 357-363
     BEFEO 5.1905,232
     P. P.

107. [rev.] Thomas Watters: On Yuan Chwang's travels in India, 629-645
     A.D., edited by T. W. Rhys Davids and S. W. Bushell. 1. London:
     RAS 1904. XIII,401 pp. 8° (Oriental Translation Fund. NS 14.)
     BEFEO 5.1905,423-457
     P. Pelliot

108. [Report, beginning: Au moyen âge ...]
     BEFEO 5.1905,497-500

1906

109. Notes sur l'Asie centrale par Paul Pelliot, professeur de chinois à
l'Ecole française d'Extrême-Orient.
BEFEO 6.1906,255-269, 1 Ill., 1 Plan
Offprint: Hanoi: Impr. F. H. Schneider 1906. 15 pp., large 8°
Signed: Kachgar, 10 octobre 1906.
1. Les «trois grottes» et les ruines de Tegurman au nord de Kachgar.
268-269: La légende de la princesse chinoise.
[Lalou 15]

110. [rev.] Ed. Chavannes: Les pays d'Occident d'après le Wei lio.
T'oung Pao. II,6.1905,519-571
BEFEO 6.1906,361-400
   P. Pelliot
[Lalou 16]

111. [rev.] Ed. Chavannes: Fables et contes de l'Inde extraits du Tripiṭaka
chinois. Actes du XIVe Congrès international des Orientalistes. Paris:
Leroux 1905. T.1, pp. 84-145. 8°
BEFEO 6.1906,401-402
   P. Pelliot
[Lalou 17]

112. [rev.] T'ang Tsai-fou: Le mariage chez une tribu aborigène du sud-est
du Yun-nan d'après une relation de Tch'en Ting 陳鼎. T'oung Pao
II,6, pp. 572-622.
BEFEO 6.1906,402-404
   P. Pelliot

113. [rev.] Edward Harper Parker: China and religion. London: John
Murray 1905. XXVIII,317 pp. 8°
BEFEO 6.1906,404-416
   P. Pelliot

114. [rev.] Herbert A. Giles: Adversaria sinica. No 1. Shanghai: Kelly &
Walsh 1905. 25 pp. 8°
BEFEO 6.1906,416-421
   P. Pelliot

115. Nous extrayons d'une lettre de notre collaborateur, M. Paul Pelliot, les renseignements suivant sur la mission qu'il dirige en Asie centrale, assisté du Dr. Louis Vaillant, médecin aide-major de 1re classe de l'armée coloniale, et du M. Charles Nouette, photographe:
     BEFEO 6.1906,482-486

116. La ville de Bakhouân dans la géographie d'Idrîçî. Par Paul Pelliot.
     TP 7.1906,553-556

1907
117. Les Abdal de Païnâp, par M. Pelliot.
     Paris: Impr. nat. 1907. 27 pp. 8°
     From *Journal asiatique* Jan.-Febr. 1907,115-139
     [Lalou 19]

118. La politique intérieure de la Chine de 1898 à 1907.
     *Revue indochinoise.*NS 5,69.1907,1523-1537
        Paul Pelliot, Professeur à l'Ecole française d'Extrême-Orient.

119. [Exploration en Asie centrale.]
     BEFEO 7.1907,204-209
     «Ici je laisse la parole à M. Pelliot:» [Compte-rendu de l'Académie des Inscriptions et Belles-Lettres, 22 mars 1907].

1908
120. Notre mission en Asie centrale.
     La géographie. 17.1908, 425-430
     Offprint: Paris: Masson (1908), pp. 425-430
     M. Pelliot, a adressé à la Société de Géographie la lettre suivante datée de Cha-ts'iuan-tse, le 3 février 1908.
     [Lalou 20]

121. Mission Pelliot.
     La géographie. 17.1908, 410
     Lettre datée de Tourfan, 10 janvier, à M. Senart.

122. La Mission Pelliot.
     Bulletin du Comité de l'Asie française 8.1908, 87-95

Le président du Comité, M. Emile Senart, a reçu la lettre suivante de M. Paul Pelliot datée de Tourfan, le 10 janvier [1908].

123. Une bibliothèque médiévale retrouvée au Kan-sou. Par M. Paul Pelliot, professeur de chinois à l'Ecole française d'Extrême-Orient, chargé de mission en Asie centrale.
BEFEO 1908,501-529
Ts'ien-fo-tong de Touen-houang, le 26 mars 1908.
Extrait d'une lettre à M. Senart, membre de l'Institut.
Offprint: Hanoi: Impr. d'Extrême-Orient 1908. 29 pp. large 8°
[Lalou 21]

1909
124. Une bibliothèque médiévale retrouvée au Kan-sou.
JA X,13. 1909,153-156
«Sous ce titre, le Bulletin de l'Ecole française d'Extrême-Orient, juillet-décembre 1908, p.501 et suiv., publie une lettre de M. Paul Pelliot ...»

125. Notes de bibliographie chinoise. Par M. Paul Pelliot, Professeur de chinois à l'Ecole française d'Extrême Orient.
BEFEO 9.1909,123-152
II.Le droit chinois.

126. Le p'o-lo 婆羅 peut-il être un poids?
BEFEO 9.1909,158-160
  P. Pelliot

127. [rev.] O. Franke: Eine chinesische Tempelinschrift aus Idikuṭṣahri bei Turfan (Turkistan). 92 pp. (Abhandlungen der königl. Preußischen Akademie der Wissenschaften. 1907.)
BEFEO 9.1909,164-166
  P. Pelliot

128. [rev.] Sylvain Lévi: Açvaghoṣa, le Sûtrâlaṃkâra et ses sources. Journal asiatique. July-Aug. 1908,57-184.
BEFEO 9.1909,166-169
  P. Pelliot
[Lalou 22]

129. [rev.] E. Denison Ross: New light on the history of the Chinese
     Oriental College, and a 16th century vocabulary of the Luchuan lan-
     guage. T'oung Pao II,9, pp.689-695.
     BEFEO 9.1909,170-171
       P. Pelliot

130. Notes de bibliographie chinoise. Par M. Paul Pelliot, Professeur de
     chinois à l'Ecole française d'Extrême Orient. III.L'œuvre de Lou
     Sin-yuan 陸心源.
     BEFEO 9.1909,211-249
     1. Che wan kiuan leou ts'ong chou 十萬卷樓叢書.

131. [rev.] Ed. Chavannes: Un faux archéologique chinois. J. A., mai-
     juin 1908, pp.501-510, 4 pl.
     Lettre de M. A. Vissière. Journal asiatique nov.-déc. 1908,455-465.
     BEFEO 9.1909,379-387
       P. Pelliot

132. Notes de bibliographie chinoise. Par M. Paul Pelliot. III.L'œuvre de
     Lou Sin-yuan 陸心源 2. Ts'ien yuan tsong-tsi.
     BEFEO 9.1909,425-469

133. Les nouvelles revues d'art et d'archéologie en Chine.
     BEFEO 9.1909,573-582
       P. Pelliot
     [Especially on *Shen-chou kuo-kuang-chi* 神州國光集]

134. Les populations du Turkestan chinois.
     Revue indochinoise. 11/12.1909,256-273
       Paul Pelliot
     Cette étude est extraite d'une lettre adressée à M. E. Senart par M. P. Pelliot au
     cours de sa mission en Asie centrale. Elle a publié dans le no. 84 du *Bulletin du
     Comité de l'Asie française.*

135. La mission Pelliot en Asie centrale.
     *Annales de la Société de géographie commerciale (section indo-
     chinoise).* Hanoi 1909. 47 pp., 1 folded map: Mission Pelliot. Itiné-
     raire de Andidjan à Pékin.
     Contents:
     III-VII: Historique de la Mission.

     1-18   Les populations du Turkestan chinois (Paul Pelliot)
     19-47   Une bibliothèque médiévale retrouvée au Kan-sou. (Ts'ien-
            fo-tong de Touen-houang, le 26 mars 1908)

135a.M. Paul Pelliot adresse de Koutcha le 23 mars 1907, la lettre suivante
     à M. Henri Cordier:
     TP 8.1909,291-295

1910

135b.M. Pelliot adresse à la Société de Géographie la lettre suivante datée
     de Cha-ts'iuen-tse, le 3 janvier 1908.
     TP 9.1910,627-633

136. [Trois ans dans la Haute-Asie.]
     Conférence de M. Paul Pelliot au grand amphithéâtre de la Sorbonne,
     10 décembre 1909.
     Asie française 1910,11-24
     [Lalou 23]

137. *Trois ans dans la Haute Asie.* - Conférence de M. Paul Pelliot au
     grand amphithéâtre de la Sorbonne le 10 décembre 1909. Extrait du
     «Bulletin du Comité de l'Asie française» (Janvier 1910).
     Paris: Comité de l'Asie française 1910. 16 pp., 1 map. 4°

138. Rapport de M. Paul Pelliot sur sa mission au Turkestan chinois,
     1906-1909.
     *Académie des inscriptions et belles-lettres. Comptes-rendus des
     séances* 1910, 58-68
     Offprint: Paris: Alphonse Picard et fils 1910. 11 pp., 2 pl. 8°
     Also in *BEFEO* 10.1910,655-660
     [Lalou 18]

139. [Exploration en Asie centrale.]
     BEFEO 10.1910,274-281

140. Explorations géographiques et archéologiques dans le Turkestan
     chinois et en Chine.
     *La géographie.*21.1910, 66-70
     Conférence faite à la Sorbonne, 10 déc. 1909.

pp.64-66: Réception de la Mission Pelliot.

140a.Trois ans dans la Haute Asie.
L'illustration 1910,262-266
   Paul Pelliot

141. Charles Nouette.
TP 11.1910,293
   Paul Pelliot

1911

142. [rev.] Emil Smith: Tocharisch. Die neuentdeckte indogermanische
Sprache Mittelasiens. Christiania 1911. 43 pp. 8° (Videnskabs sels-
kabets skrifter. II, Hist.-filos. kl. 1910, no. 5)
Journal asiatique 1911,II,635-636
[On a preceding review by A. Meillet (pp.630-635).]

143. Un traité manichéen retrouvé en Chine, traduit et annoté. Par MM.
Ed. Chavannes et P. Pelliot.
Journal asiatique 1911,II,499-617; 1913,I,99-199, 261-394, 2 pl.
Cf. *Deutsche Wacht* 15.1929:17, p. 24 (E. von Zach)
[Lalou 27, 37]

144. Lettre à M. Chavannes sur le rapport de la mission archéologique
japonaise en Chine.
TP 12.1911,447-450
   Paul Pelliot
[Lalou 24]

145. Deux titres bouddhiques portés par des religieux nestoriens. Par Paul
Pelliot.
TP 12.1911,664-670
On: Havret: *La stèle chrétienne de Si-ngan-fou,* IIIe partie. 1902.
[Lalou 25]

146. Les Kouo-che 國師 ou «Maîtres du Royaume» dans le Bouddhisme
chinois. Par Paul Pelliot.
TP 12.1911,671-676

On: Ivanov: Stranica iz istorii Si-sja. *Izvestija AN* 1911,835; Chavannes in *TP* 12.1911,444.
[Lalou 26]

147. Un bilingue sogdien-chinois.
*Mélanges d'indianisme offerts par ses élèves à M. Sylvain Lévi à
l'occasion des vingt-cinq ans écoulés depuis son entrée à l'Ecole
pratique des hautes études.* Paris: Leroux 1911,329-331
  P. Pelliot
[Lalou 28]

148. En Asie centrale. Conférence faite à la Société normande de
géographie, le 8 novembre 1910, par M. Paul Pelliot.
Rouen: Impr. de E. Cagniard (L. Gy) 1911. 28 pp. 4°
Extrait du *Bulletin de la Société normande de géographie.*1911,1-26:
En Asie centrale. Conférence de M. Paul Pelliot.

149. *Exposé des titres de M. Paul Pelliot, pour la chaire de «Langues,
histoire et archéologie de l'Asie centrale», vacante au Collège de
France.*
Paris: Impr. de Maulde, Doumenc et Cie (1911). 12 pp. 8°
[Biobibliography of Pelliot.]

1912
150. Paul Pelliot: *Les influences iraniennes en Asie centrale et en Extrême-
Orient.* Leçon d'ouverture du cours de langues, histoire et
archéologie de l'Asie centrale au Collège de France. 4 décembre
1911.
Paris: Revue d'histoire et de littérature religieuses [1912]. 25 pp. 8°
Rev.: *Journal of the North China Branch of the Royal Asiatic Society*
44.1913,156-157 (D. MacG.)
[Lalou 29]

151. Les influences iraniennes en Asie centrale et en Extrême-Orient.
Leçon d'ouverture du cours de langues, histoire et archéologie de
l'Asie centrale au Collège de France.
Revue indochinoise. 13.1912,1-15
  Paul Pelliot

152. *La Chine et la révolution.*
1912.
Conférence faite au Foyer le 22 janvier 1912. Cf. *TP* 13.1912,311.
[Not seen.]

153. [rev.] Berthold Laufer: Chinese grave-sculptures of the Han period.
London: E. L. Morice 1911. 45 pp., 10 pl., 14 ill. 8°
Journal asiatique 1912,I, 379
 P. Pelliot

154. Kao-tch'ang, Qočo, Houo-tcheou et Qâra-Khodja, par M. Paul
Pelliot, avec une note additionnelle de M. Robert Gauthiot.
Journal asiatique mai-juin 1912,579-603
Offprint: Paris: Impr. nationale 1913. 26 pp. 8°
597-603: Note additionnelle.
[Lalou 34]

155. [rev.] L. Wieger S.J.: Taoisme. Tome 1. Bibliographie générale:
1.Le Canon (Patrologie). II.Les index officiels et privés. [Ho-kien-
fou] 1911. 337 pp. 8°
Journal asiatique 1912,II,141-156
 Paul Pelliot

156. [rev.] Alfred Forke: Lun-hêng. Part 1. Philosophical essays of Wang
Ch'ung. Translated from the Chinese and annotated. London: Luzac,
Leipzig: Harrassowitz, Shanghai: Kelly & Walsh 1907. IV,577 pp.
8° - Part II. Miscellaneous essays by Wang Ch'ung. Berlin: G. Rei-
mer 1911. VI,536 pp. 8° (Beibände zu den Mitteilungen des Semi-
nars für Orientalische Sprachen.1.)
Journal asiatique. 1912,II,156-171
 Paul Pelliot

157. Les noms tibétains des T'ou-yu-houen 吐谷渾 et des Ouigours.
Journal asiatique 1912,II,520-523
 Paul Pelliot

158. La fille de Mo-tch'o Qaghan et ses rapports avec Kül-tegin. Par Paul
Pelliot.
TP 13.1912,301-306

Occasioned by Chavannes: Epitaphes de deux princesses turques de
l'époque des T'ang. *Festschrift Vilhelm Thomsen*. Leipzig: Harrassowitz 1912,78-87.

159. Autour d'une traduction sanscrite du Tao-tö king. Par Paul Pelliot.
      TP 13.1912,351-430
      1. A propos des missions de Wang Hiuan-ts'ö 王玄策
      2. La traduction sanscrite du Tao tö king 道德經
      [Lalou 30]

160. [rev.] Berthold Laufer: Jade. A study in Chinese archaeology and re-
      ligion. Chicago 1912. XIV,370 pp., 68 pl., 204 ill. (Field Museum
      of Natural History. Publication 154. Anthropological series.10.)
      TP 13.1912,434-446
        P. Pelliot
      [Lalou 31]

161. [rev.] Friedrich Hirth, W. W. Rockhill: Chau Ju-kua: His work on
      the Chinese and Arab trade in the twelfth and thirteenth centuries,
      entitled Chu-fan chi. St. Petersburg: Academy of Sciences 1912. X,
      288 pp., 1 map, large 8°
      TP 13.1912,446-481
        P. Pelliot
      [Lalou 32]

162. [rev.] Trois manuscrits de l'époque des T'ang récemment publiés au
      Japon, par M. Naitô Torajirô.
      TP 13.1912,482-507
        P. Pelliot
      1. Ta T'ang san-tsang Hiuan-tsang fa-che piao-k'i
      大唐三藏玄奘法師表啟
      2. Ming pao ki 冥報記
      3. T'ang Wang P'o tsi ts'an kiuan 唐王勃集殘卷
      [Lalou 33]

163. [Rectification sur la critique de l'ouvrage de T. Naitô.]
      TP 13.1912,674
      Letter from Pelliot, dated Paris, 21 novembre 1912.

164. L'origine du nom de «Chine». Par Paul Pelliot.
     TP 13.1912,727-742
     In connection with: Berthold Laufer: The name China. *TP* 13.
     1912,719-726

165. J. Levacon, avocat à la Cour d'appel: *Chez les Maoris. Tahiti et Nou-
     velle-Zélande. Notes de voyage.* Préface de M. Paul Pelliot, pro-
     fesseur au Collège de France.
     Paris: Emile Larose 1912. III,179 pp. 8°
     Preface I-III, signed: Paul Pelliot
     Paris, 5 novembre 1911

1913
166. Sur quelques mots d'Asie centrale attestés dans les textes chinois. - I.
     Mängü et Möngkä (Monka). - II. Nankiâs. - III. Šaman. Par Paul
     Pelliot.
     Journal asiatique mars-avril 1913,451-469
       Paul Pelliot
     Offprint: Paris: Imprimerie nationale 1913. 23 pp. 8°   [Lalou 40]

167. Le cycle sexagénaire dans la chronologie tibétaine. Par M. Paul Pel-
     liot.
     Journal asiatique 1913,I,633-667
     Offprint: Paris: Impr. nationale 1913. 39 pp.
     [Lalou 41]

168. Les plus anciens monuments de l'écriture arabe en Chine. Par M.
     Paul Pelliot. Avec des notes de MM. Cl. Huart et Denison Ross.
     Journal asiatique, juillet-août, 1913,177-191, 1 pl.
     [Lalou 42]

169. [rev.] Henri Cordier: Bibliotheca japonica. Dictionnaire biblio-
     graphique des ouvrages relatifs à l'empire japonais rangés par ordre
     chronologique jusqu'à 1870, suivi d'un appendice renfermant la liste
     alphabétique des principaux ouvrages parus de 1870 à 1912. Paris:
     Leroux 1912. XII,762 cols. large 8° (Publications de l'Ecole des lan-
     gues orientales vivantes.V,8.)
     Journal asiatique 1913,II,204-206
       P. Pelliot

170. [rev.] A. Ivanov: Materialy po kitajskoj filosofii. Vvedenie. Škola fa.
     Chań Fej-czy. Perevod. St. Petersburg 1912. LXXXVI,354,74 pp.,
     large 8° (Izdanija Fakul'teta Vost. Jazykov Imper. S. Peterb. Univer-
     siteta.39.)
     Journal asiatique 1913,II,401-423
       Paul Pelliot
     [Lalou 38]

171. Le titre mongol du Yuan tch'ao pi che 元朝秘史. [Mongɣol-un
     niɣuča tobčiyan]
     TP 14.1913,131-132
       Paul Pelliot

172. Les pretendus jades de Sou-tcheou (Kan-sou). Par Paul Pelliot.
     TP 14.1913,258-260
     [On Laufer: *Jade.*]

173. Addenda par Paul Pelliot.
     TP 14.1913,365-370
     On: Berthold Laufer: Arabic and Chinese trade in walrus and narwhal
     ivory. *TP* 14.1913,315-364.

174. Encore à propos du nom de «Chine».
     TP 14.1913,427-428
       Paul Pelliot
     [On <164>]

175. Répertoire des «collections Pelliot A» et «B» du fonds chinois de la
     Bibliothèque Nationale. Par Paul Pelliot.
     TP 14.1913,697-781
     [List of 329 + 1743 titles.]
     [Lalou 39]

176. [rev.] Albert Herrmann: Ein alter Seeverkehr zwischen Abessinien
     und Süd-China bis zum Beginn unserer Zeitrechnung. Berlin 1913. 9
     pp. (From Zeitschrift der Gesellschaft für Erdkunde zu Berlin.1913.)
     TP 14.1913,788
       P. Pelliot

177. Un fragment du Suvarṇaprabhâsasûtra en iranien oriental. Texte
transcrit, traduction et commentaire.
Etudes linguistiques sur les documents de la Mission Pelliot, fasc.
IV; extraits des *Memoires de la Société de linguistique de Paris*.18.
1913,89-125
Offprint: Paris: H. Champion 1913. 39 pp.
  P. Pelliot
[Lalou 35]

178. A propos du Keng tche t'ou 耕織圖. Par Paul Pelliot.
Mémoires concernant l'Asie orientale.
Paris: Académie des Inscriptions et Belles-lettres 1913,65-122,
pl.10-61

1914
179. *Les grottes de Touen Houang; peintures et sculptures bouddhiques
des époques des Wei, des T'ang et des Song.* Par Paul Pelliot.
Paris: P. Geuthner 1914-1924. 8 pp.,376 pl. (6 vols.)
(Mission Pelliot en Asie centrale; série in quarto.1.)

    Vol. 1: 8 pp.; Grottes 1 à 30. Mit: Grottes de Touen-houang.
         Elévation et plan.
    Vol. 2: 2 pp. Grottes 31 à 72
    Vol. 3: Grottes 72 à 111
    Vol. 4: Grottes 111 à 120
    Vol. 5: Grottes 120N à 146
    Vol. 6: Grottes 146 à 182

[Note:] Le fascicule 1 des Grottes de Touen-Houang était presque
entièrement imprimé dès la fin de juillet 1914. La guerre en a
suspendu l'apparition jusqu'en 1920. Robert Gauthiot, qui devait être
un des principaux collaborateurs de la Mission Pelliot en Asie
centrale, est mort le 11 Septembre 1916 d'une fracture au crâne reçue
à son poste de combat. Malgré les deuils, nous entendons poursuivre
l'œuvre entreprise et ferons tout pour la mener à bien. P. Pelliot.
[rev.] *Shinagaku* 1:2. 1920, 79 (Kanda Kiichirô 神田喜一郎)
[rev.] 人生と表現10.1921 (Hashikawa Tadashi 橋川正)

180. [rev.] A. Vissière: Etudes sino-mahométanes (deuxième série), avec
     la collaboration de MM. G. Cordier et Cl. Huart et du Révérend A.
     C. Moule. Paris: Leroux 1913. 160 pp., mit Ill. und 12 pl. 8°
     Journal asiatique XI,3.1914,203-208
       P. Pelliot

181. [rev.] Ed. Chavannes: Mission archéologique dans la Chine septen-
     trionale. Planches, 1e partie (nos 1 à 286); 2e partie (nos 287 à 488).
     Paris: Leroux 1909. 2 albums grand in-4°. – T.1, première partie: La
     sculpture à l'époque des Han. Paris: Leroux 1913. 290 pp., pl. 489-
     543 (Publications de l'Ecole française d'Ectrême-Orient.)
     Journal asiatique. XI,3.1914,208-212
       Paul Pelliot
     [Lalou 43]

182. [rev.] Ed. Chavannes: Les documents chinois découverts par Aurel
     Stein dans les sables du Turkestan oriental. Oxford: Imprimerie de
     l'Université 1913. XXIII,232 pp., 37 pl., large 4°
     Journal asiatique XI,3.1914,212-222
       Paul Pelliot
     [Lalou 48bis]

183. Mo-ni et manichéens.
     *Journal asiatique.*XI,3.1914,461-470
       Paul Pelliot
     Re: Nau on the Nestorian tombstones of the Musée Guimet (*Journal
     asiatique* 1913,II,451-453).

184. M. Pelliot fait une communication sur quelques noms d'inscriptions
     nestoriennes du Semireč'e (I) et sur l'origine du nom de Fou-lin (II).
     Journal asiatique. XI,3.1914,498-500
     [Lalou 48ter]

185. Les documents chinois trouvés par la Mission Kozlov à Khara-Kho-
     to, par M. Paul Pelliot.
     *Journal asiatique.*XI,3.1914,503-518
     Offprint: Paris: Impr. nationale 1914. 20 pp. 8°
     [Lalou 44]

186. Notes à propos d'un catalogue du Kanjur, par Paul Pelliot.
     *Journal asiatique.*XI,4.1914,111-150
     On: Hermann Beckh: *Verzeichniss der tibetischen Handschriften,*
     Erste Abteilung. Berlin: Behrend 1914. X,192 pp. 4° (Handschriften-
     verzeichnisse der Königlichen Bibliothek zu Berlin.24.)
     [Lalou 45]

187. [rev.] O. Franke, B. Laufer: *Epigraphische Denkmäler aus China,*
     veröffentlicht mit Unterstützung der Hamburgischen Wissenschaft-
     lichen Stiftung. 1.Teil: Lamaistische Kloster-Inschriften aus Peking,
     Jehol und Si-ngan. Berlin: Dietrich Reimer 1914. 2 portfolios in large
     2°. 7 pp. text and 81 pl.
     *Journal asiatique.*XI,4.1914,177-191
       Paul Pelliot
     [Lalou 46]

188. [rev.] Antoine Cabaton: Brève et véridique relation des événements
     du Cambodge, par Gabriel Quiroga de San Antonio, de l'ordre de
     Saint-Dominique. Nouvelle édition du texte espagnol, avec une
     traduction et des notes. Paris: Leroux 1914. XXVII,261 pp. 8°
     (Documents historiques et géographiques relatifs à l'Indochine.)
     *Journal asiatique.*XI,4.1914,191-204
       P. Pelliot

189. Les noms propres dans les traductions chinoises du Milindapañha.
     Par M. Paul Pelliot.
     Journal asiatique XI,4.1914,379-419
     [Lalou 47]

190. La version ouïgoure de l'histoire des princes Kalyâṇamkara et
     Pâpaṃkara. Par Paul Pelliot.
     TP 15.1914,225-272
     Ms. 3509 from Tun-huang. On the translation by C. Huart. *Journal*
     *asiatique.*1914,I,1-57: Le conte bouddhique des deux frères en lan-
     gue turque et en caractères ouïgours.
     Cf. also: Ed. Chavannes: Une version chinoise du conte bouddhique
     de Kalyâṇamkara et Pâpaṃkara. *TP* 15.1914,469-500
     [Lalou 48]

191. Le nom turc du vin dans Odoric de Pordenone. Par Paul Pelliot.
      TP 15.1914,448-453
      [*bigni*]

192. Chrétiens d'Asie centrale et d'Extrême-Orient. Par Paul Pelliot.
      TP 15.1914,623-644

193. Les Grottes des Mille Bouddhas.
      JRAS 1914,421-426
        Paul Pelliot
      On *JRAS* 1913,696-698 (Legge)
      On Pelliot's article: H. F. Amedroz: Caves of a Thousand Buddhas.
      JRAS 1913,426
      F. Legge: Caves of a Thousand Buddhas. *JRAS* 1913,426-427
      [Lalou 36]

1915

194. Quelques transcriptions chinoises de noms tibétaines. Par Paul Pel-
      liot.
      TP 16.1915,1-26
      On Berthold Laufer: Bird divination among the Tibetans. *TP* 1914,1-
      110.

195. L'origine de T'ou-kiue [突厥], nom chinois des Turcs.
      TP 16.1915,687-689
        P. Pelliot

196. Li-kien, autre nom du Ta-ts'in (Orient méditerranéen).
      TP 16.1915,690-691
        P. Pelliot
      [犁鞬]
      [Lalou 49]

197. «Isol» le pisan.
      *Journal asiatique.*IX,6.1915,495-497
        P. Pelliot
      [On the recipient of a papal letter of 1291 in Central Asia.]

1916

198. Le Chou king en caractères anciens et le Chang chou che wen
      尚書釋文 par Paul Pelliot.
      Mémoires concernant l'Asie orientale (Inde, Asie centrale, Extrême-
      Orient) publiés par l'Académie des Inscriptions et Belles-Lettres sous
      la direction de MM. Senart, Chavannes, Cordier, membres de
      l'Institut. 2. Paris: Leroux 1916,123-177, pl. XX-XXVI
      «J'ai rédigé une grande partie de cet article dans des conditions dé-
      favorables, loin de toute bibliothèque, sur des notes anciennes et
      quelques livres essentiels que mon ami M. Chavannes a eu la com-
      plaisance de m'envoyer. Le même ami a bien voulu vérifier certaines
      références et préciser plusieurs indications. Je m'excuse auprès de
      nos confrères de n'avoir pu toujours donner à mon travail l'ampleur
      ni la précision que j'aurais souhaitée; je reprendrai le problème plus
      en détail quelque jour, s'il se peut.»
      [Re: Fonds Pelliot 3315]

199. Le «Cha tcheou tou tou fou t'ou king» [沙州都督府圖經] et la
      colonie sogdienne de la région du Lob Nor.
      *Journal asiatique.*XI,7.1916,111-123
        Paul Pelliot
      Offprint: Paris: Imprimerie nationale 1916. 15 pp. 8°
      [Lalou 50]

1917

200. Lexicography.
      Samuel Couling: *The Encyclopaedia sinica.* Shanghai: Kelly & Walsh
      1917,298-301
        P. P., translated by Editor

1920

201. «Meou-tseu ou les doutes levés.» [牟子理惑] Traduit et annoté par
      Paul Pelliot.
      TP 19.1920,255-433
      [Lalou 58]

202. A propos des Comans. Par Paul Pelliot.
      Journal asiatique. XI,15.1920,125-185

Re: W. Bang und J. Marquart: *Osttürkische Dialektstudien.* Berlin
1914. 276 pp., 10 pl. 4° (Abhandlungen der K. Gesellschaft der
Wiss. zu Göttingen. Phil.-hist. Kl. NF 13, Nr 1.)
[Lalou 52]

203. [rev.] J. J. M. de Groot: Universismus, die Grundlage der Religion
und Ethik des Staatswesens und der Wissenschaften Chinas. Berlin
1918. VIII,404 pp. 8°
Journal asiatique. XI,16.1920,158-165
  P. Pelliot

204. [rev.] Charles-B. Maybon: La relation sur le Tonkin et la
Cochinchine de M. de la Bissachère, missionnaire français (1807).
Paris: Ed. Champion 1919. 185 pp. 8°
*Journal asiatique.*XI,16.1920,165-167
  P. Pelliot

205. [rev.] Dr. Franz Kuhn: Das Dschong Lun des Tsui Schi, eine konfu-
zianische Rechtfertigung der Diktatur aus der Han-Zeit (2. Jahrh. n.
Chr.). (From: Abhandlungen der k. Preuß. Akademie der Wissen-
schaften). Berlin 1914. 27 pp. 4°
Journal asiatique. XI,16.1920,167-169
  P. Pelliot

206. Monuments de l'écriture tangout. [Traduit du russe et annoté par P.
Pelliot.]
*Journal asiatique.*XI,15.1920,I,107-109
  A. I. Ivanov
[Lalou 51]

207. [M. Pelliot fait une communication sur un manuscrit chinois du
Ts'ien-tseu-wen 千字文 avec transcription tibétaine.]
Journal asiatique XI,15.1920,268
[Lalou 52bis]

208. [M. Pelliot fait une communication sur une version chinoise du Vyâ-
karana de Khotan.]
Journal asiatique 1920, II,354
[Lalou 52ter]

209. *Le sûtra des causes et des effets du bien et du mal.* Edité et traduit
     d'après les textes sogdien, chinois et tibétain par Robert Gauthiot et
     Paul Pelliot. T.1: Fac-simile des textes sogdiens et chinois.
     Paris: Geuthner 1920. 52 pl.
     (Mission Pelliot en Asie centrale, série in-4° II,1.)
     1-44   Sogdian text
     45   Beginning of the Chinese text (Tun-huang ms.)
              [善惡因果經]
     46-52   Chinese text (Ed. Kyôto)
     [Lalou 54]
     (rev.) *Shinagaku* 1:10.1921, 77-78 (Kanda Kiichirô 神田喜一郎)

     T.2,1.Transcription, traduction, commentaire et index. Avec la colla-
     boration d'Emile Benveniste.
     Paris 1926. XI,66 pp.
     Introduction, XI, signed: P. Pelliot

     T.2,2. Paris 1928. pp. 67-101

     Contents:
     Texte sogdien et traduction
     Commentaire de la version sogdienne
     Traduction du texte chinois
     Commentaire du texte chinois
     Glossaire
     Additions et corrections
     Index.

     Cf. *Deutsche Wacht* 13.1927:10, p. 42 (E. von Zach)

1921

210. *T'oung Pao ou Archives concernant l'histoire, les langues, la
     géographie et l'ethnographie de l'Asie orientale.* Revue dirigée par
     Henri Cordier, membre de l'Institut, professeur à l'Ecole spéciale des
     langues orientales vivantes, et Paul Pelliot, membre de l'Institut,
     professeur au Collège de France. 20.1921-37.1944.

211. *Folk-lore et vieux souvenirs d'Argonne (arrondissement de Sainte-
     Menehould).* Par l'abbé Louis Lallement [...]. Ouvrage publié sous

les auspices de la Société d'agriculture, commerce, sciences et arts.
Préface par Paul Pelliot, professeur au collège de France.
Chalons-sur-Marne: A. Robat, Paris: L. Staude 1921. 290 pp.
Préface, 3 pp. unnumbered; signed: Paul Pelliot, professeur au Collège de France

212. Édouard Chavannes (1865-1918). Par Paul Pelliot.
Salle Edouard Chavannes. (Bulletin archéologique de Musée Guimet.
1.1921),11-15
[rev.] *Shinagaku.*2.1922, 78 (Kanda Kiichirô 神田喜一郎)

213. La Mission Pelliot. Par Paul Pelliot.
*Asie centrale et Tibet. Missions Pelliot et Bacot. (Bulletin archéologique de Musée Guimet.*2.1921),5-8

214. Note sur les anciens itinéraires chinois dans l'Orient romain.
Journal asiatique. XI,17.1921,139-145
   Paul Pelliot
J'ai écrit cette note à Pékin en juillet 1917, loin de toute bibliothèque
européenne. Depuis lors, j'en ai communiqué les conclusions à
l'Académie des Inscriptions et Belles-Lettres à la fin de 1919. J'y
apporté quelques modifications de détail en la publiant aujourd'hui.
[On the chapter on foreign countries in the *Wei-lüeh.*]

215. [M. Pelliot fait une communication relative à un catéchisme boud-
dhique ouigour en écriture tibétaine.]
Journal asiatique. XI,18.1921,135-136
[Lalou 58bis]

216. M. Pelliot rend compte de la mission que M. Moret et lui ont remplie
en Amérique, comme délégués de la Société asiatique au Congrès
orientaliste organisé à Boston par l'American Academy of Arts and
Sciences.
Journal asiatique. XI,18.1921,329-330

217. La peinture et la gravure européennes en Chine au temps de Mathieu
Ricci. Par Paul Pelliot.
TP 20.1921,1-18

218. Le juif Ngai 艾, informateur du P. Ricci. Par Paul Pelliot.
     TP 20.1921,32-39

219. [rev.] Albert Chapuis: La montre «chinoise». Neuchatel: Attinger
     frères (1919). XIII,272 pp., 33 pl., 245 ill.
     TP 20.1921,61-68
       Paul Pelliot

220. Quelques transcriptions apparentées à Çambhala dans les textes
     chinois. Par Paul Pelliot.
     TP 20.1921,73-85
     Cette note date de 1914. Je l'ai remaniée tant bien que mal, mais il
     manque, pour la mettre réellement au point, divers travaux parus
     pendant la guerre en Allemagne et en Russie.
     [Lalou 55]

220a.Central-Asian relics of China's ancient silk trade. By Aurel Stein.
     TP 20.1921,130-141
     138-141: Notes additionnelles.
       P. Pelliot

221. [rev.] Lo Tchen-yu 羅振玉 Kou king t'ou lou 古鏡圖錄
     (Album illustré d'anciens miroirs métalliques) 1916. 1 album:
     1,3,17,34,23,1 fol. 2°
     Tomioka Kenzô 富岡謙藏 Kokei no kenkyû 古鏡の研究.
     Kyôto 1920. 2 pl., 8,4,3,416,17 pp., 95 pl., 1 l. Errata
     TP 20.1921,142-156
       P. Pelliot

222. [rev.] Panduranga S. S. Pissurlancar: Recherches sur la découverté
     de l'Amérique par les anciens hommes de l'Inde. Sanquelim, Goa
     1920. 22 pp. 8°
     TP 20.1921,156-157
       P. Pelliot

223. [rev.] Emile Hovelaque: Les peuples d'Extrême-Orient. La Chine.
     Paris: E. Flammarion 1920. 286 pp. 12°
     TP 20.1921,157-163
       P. Pelliot

224. Bibliographie.
      TP 20.1921,164-181
      Bulletin de l'Ecole française d'Extrême-Orient 19-20
      La géographie
      Chinese Maritime Customs
      Journal of the North China Branch of the Royal Asiatic Society 51
      Journal asiatique 1920 [especially: Le Parinirvâṇa et les funérailles du
      Buddha, par Jean Przyluski.]
      Journal of the Royal Asiatic Society 1920
      The geographical journal
      The New China review
      Mémoires de la Société de linguistique 1920
      Burlington magazine 1920
      [Lalou 56]

225. Les «Conquêtes de l'empereur de la Chine». Par Paul Pelliot.
      TP 20.1921,183-274

226. [rev.] Louis Finot: La Marche à la Lumière (Bodhicaryâvatâra). Paris:
      Bossard 1920. 166 pp. 8° (Les classiques de l'Orient.)
      TP 20.1921,294-295
        P. Pelliot
      [Lalou 57]

227. Note sur les T'ou-yu-houen et les Sou-p'i. Par Paul Pelliot.
      TP 20.1921,323-331
      1. Les T'ou-yu-houen [吐谷渾 tribe in the Kukunor region]
      2. Les Sou-p'i [蘇毗 SW of T'u-yü-hun]
      [Lalou 62]
      [rev.] *Shinagaku* 2.1922: 7, p.68-72 (Ishihama Juntarô 石濱純太郎)

228. [rev.] Franz Babinger: Gottlieb Siegfried Bayer (1694-1738), ein
      Beitrag zur Geschichte der morgenländischen Studien im 18. Jahr-
      hundert. Leipzig: O. Harrassowitz 1916. 85 pp. 8°
      TP 20.1921,361-362
        P. Pelliot

229. [rev.] Casimir Schnyder: Eduard Huber, ein schweizerischer Spra-
     chengelehrter, Sinolog und Indochinaforscher. Zürich: Orell Füssli
     1920. VIII,203 pp. 8°
     TP 20.1921,363
       P. Pelliot

1922
230. [rev.] Prof. Dr. Albert Grünwedel: Alt-Kutscha. Archäologische und
     religionsgeschichtliche Forschungen an Tempera-Gemälden aus bud-
     dhistischen Höhlen der ersten acht Jahrhunderte nach Christi Geburt.
     Berlin: Otto Elsner 1920. 49 colour pl. in portfolio, 189,118 pp.,
     84,89 ill. 2°
     Journal asiatique. XI,19.1922,111
       P. Pelliot
     [Lalou 62bis]

231. Lundi 25 Septembre. - Conférence sur l'exploration et la science
     françaises dans l'Asie orientale. Par M. Paul Pelliot, explorateur,
     professeur au Collège de France, membre de l'Institut. Sous la prési-
     dence du Général Marchand.
     Exposition coloniale nationale de Marseille. Semaine internationale
     des géographes, des explorateurs et des ethnologues, 22-28 septem-
     bre 1922... *Compte rendu*, 51-55

232. Les Mongols et la Papauté. Documents nouveaux édités, traduits et
     commentés par M. Paul Pelliot, avec la collaboration de MM. Bor-
     ghezio, Massé et Tisserant.
     *Revue de l'Orient chrétien.*3. série, 3 (23).1922/23,3-30; 4(24).
     1924, 225-335; 8(28).1931/32,3-84
       P. Pelliot
     Offprint: 222 pp.
     Contents:
     I. La lettre du Grand Khan Güyük à Innocent IV (1240)
     II,1. Le Nestorien Siméon Rabban-Ata.
     II,2. Ascelin
     II,3. André de Longjumeau
     [Lalou 63,78]

233. Mongols et papes aux XIIIᵉ et XIVᵉ siècles.
     Bulletin de l'Université l'Aurore.32.1922,1753-1759
     [Not seen.]

234. Mongols et papes au XIIIe et XIVe siècles.
     Asie française.1922,454-456
       Paul Pelliot, de l'Institut

235. *Mongols et papes aux XIIIe et XIVe siècles,* par M. Paul Pelliot.
     Institut de France. Séance publique annuelle des cinq académies du
     mercredi 25 octobre 1922.
     Paris: Firmin-Didot 1922. 15 pp.
     [Not seen.]

236. *Inventaire sommaire des manuscrits et imprimés chinois de la
     Bibliothèque vaticane (13 juin-6 juillet 1922).*
     (Paris 1922.) 126 pp. Ms. [a number of photostats were distributed]
     Revised publication: Edited by Takata Tokio.
     Kyôto 1995. XV,113 pp.
     (Italian School of East Asian Studies. Reference series.1.)

237. Les «Conquêtes de l'empereur de la Chine».
     Byblis.1.1922,107-110, 2 pl.
       P. Pelliot

238. [rev.] G. Bouillard, commandant Vaudescal: Les sépultures impé-
     riales des Ming (Che-san Ling). Hanoi 1920 (i.e. 1921). 128 pp., 44
     pl. 8° (*BEFEO* 20,3.)
     TP 21.1922,57-66
       P. Pelliot

239. [rev.] Histoire littéraire de la France. 35. Paris 1921. XXXV,664 pp.
     4°
     TP 21.1922,67-68
       P. Pelliot

240. Bibliographie.
     TP 21.1922,70-104
     The New China review 1920-1921

Chine, Ceylan, Madagascar 1921
Bulletin of the School of Oriental Studies
Journal of the Royal Asiatic Society 1921
Journal asiatique 1920-1921
Geographical journal 1920-1921
La géographie 1921
[Lalou 59, 79]

241. [rev.] Fir-flower tablets. Poems translated from the Chinese by Florence Ayscough. English versions by Amy Lowell. Boston, New York: Houghton Mifflin 1921. XCV,227 pp.
    TP 21.1922,232-242
      Paul Pelliot
    Rev.: *Deutsche Wacht* 14.1928:7, pp. 47-48 (E. von Zach)

242. [rev.] La légende de Buddhaghoṣa, par Louis Finot. Extrait de Cinquantaire de l'Ecole des hautes études. Mélanges publiés par les directeurs d'études de la section des sciences historiques et philologiques. Paris: Champion 1921, 101-119. 8°
    TP 21.1922,243-244
      Paul Pelliot
    [Lalou 60]

243. [rev.] Société asiatique. Le livre du centenaire (1822-1922). Paris: Paul Geuthner 1922. VIII,294 pp. 8°
    TP 21.1922,319-322
      P. Pelliot

244. [rev.] Arthur Waley: An index of Chinese artists represented in the Sub-Department of Oriental Prints and Drawings in the British Museum. London: British Museum 1922. XII,112 pp. 8°
    TP 21.1922,322-363
      P. Pelliot

245. Le véritable auteur des «Elementa Linguae Tartaricae». Par Paul Pelliot.
    TP 21.1922,367-386

246. [rev.] Voyage du marchand arabe Sulaymân en Inde et en Chine rédigé en 851 suivi de remarques par Abû Zayd Ḥasan (vers 916), traduit par Gabriel Ferrand, bois de Mlle A. Karpelès. Paris: Bossard 1922. 157 pp. 8° (Collection Les classiques de l'Orient.7.)
TP 21.1922,399-413
  P. Pelliot

247. [rev.] The Arabian prophet, a life of Mohammed from Chinese and Arabic sources. A Chinese-Moslem work by Liu Chai-lien, translated by Isaac Mason ... with appendices on Chinese Mohammedanism. Foreword by Rev. Samuel N. Zwemmer. Shanghai 1921. XVII,313 pp. 12°
TP 21.1922,413-425
  P. Pelliot

248. [rev.] A manual of Chinese metaphor, being a selection of typical Chinese metaphors, with explanatory notes and indices, par C. A. S. Williams. Shanghai: Chinese Maritime Customs 1920. XIV,320 pp. 8°
TP 21.1922,426-439
  P. Pelliot

249. Notes bibliographiques.
TP 21.1922,440-441
  P. P.
Especially on: Paul Gendronneau: *De l'influence du Bouddhisme sur la figuration des enfers médiévaux.* Nîmes 1922.
J. Mullie: *Yin-hsüeh ts'o-yao* 音學撮要. Shanghai 1922.
H. Maspero: Etudes sur le taoisme. Le saint et la vie mystique chez Lao-tseu et Tchouang-tseu. *Bulletin de l'Association française des amis de l'Orient* 1922.
[Lalou 61]

1923
250. Les statues en «laque sèche» dans l'ancien art chinois, par Paul Pelliot.
Journal asiatique. 202.1923,182-207
Offprint: Paris: Impr. nat. 1923.
[Lalou 68]

251. [rev.] J. Halphen: Contes chinois traduits du chinois. Paris: Cham-
      pion 1923. 196 pp., small 8°
      Journal asiatique. 202.1923,341
        P. Pelliot

252. [Les noms iraniens dans les mémoires de Hiuan-tsang.]
      Journal asiatique. 1923,I,162
      [Lalou 65]

253. [Sur d'anciennes traductions chinoises perdues d'œuvres bouddhi-
      ques de l'école des Sthavira.]
      Journal asiatique 1923,I,162-163
      [Lalou 67]

254. La gravure sur cuivre en Chine au XVIIIe siècle.
      *Byblis.*2.1923,103-108, 1 pl.
        P. Pelliot

255. Mongols et papes aux XIIIe et XIVe siècles.
      *Revue bleue.*61.1923,110-112
        Paul Pelliot, membre de l'Institut
      [Lalou 66]

256. Notes sur l'histoire de la céramique chinoise. Par Paul Pelliot.
      TP 22.1923,1-54
      Re: *The pottery and porcelain factories of China. Their geographical
      distribution and periods of activity.* By A. L. Hetherington. London:
      Kegan Paul 1921. 15 pp., 1 map. 8° – *The early ceramic wares of
      China.* By A. L. Hetherington, with an introduction by R. L. Hob-
      son. London: Benn 1922. XVIII,180 pp., 45 pl., of which 6 in
      colour. 4°

257. [rev.] Le théâtre chinois. Peintures, sanguines et croquis d'Alexandre
      Jacovleff. Texte de Tchou-Kia-Kien. Paris: de Brunoff 1922. 30 pp.
      4°
      TP 22.1923,55-56
        P. Pelliot

258. [rev.] René Grousset: Histoire de l'Asie. Paris: G. Crès et Cie 1921-
     1922. 8° 1.L'Orient. 1921. III,III,1,308 pp., with maps; 2.L'Inde et
     la Chine. 1922. VIII,2,400 pp. With maps and 4 pp. for replacement
     in vol 1. 3.Le monde mongol, le Japon. 1922. V,II,486 pp. With
     maps.
     TP 22.1923,56-57
       P. Pelliot

259. [rev.] A. von Le Coq: Die buddhistische Spätantike in Mittelasien.
     1.Teil: Die Plastik. Berlin: D. Reimer 1922. 30 pp., 45 pl., 10 of
     which in colour. 2° (Ergebnisse der kgl. preuß. Turfan-Expeditio-
     nen.)
     TP 22.1923,57-59
       P. Pelliot

260. Han Yen-chih's Chü Lu 橘錄 (Monograph on the oranges of Wên-
     chou, Chekiang). Translated by Michael J. Hagerty, with introduct-
     ion by Paul Pelliot.
     TP 22.1923,63-96
     Introduction, pp.63-69
     Note additionnelle, pp.96 [by Pelliot]

261. La théorie des quatre fils du ciel. Par Paul Pelliot.
     TP 22.1923,97-125
     [Based on 十二遊經, translated into Chinese in 392.]

262. Note sur les anciens noms de Kučâ, d'Aqsu et d'Uč-Turfan. Par
     Paul Pelliot.
     TP 22.1923,126-132
     [Lalou 64]
     [On: Heinrich Lüders: Zur Geschichte und Geographie Ostturkestans.
     Sitzungsberichte d. Preuß. Akademie d. Wissensch. 1922,243-261.]

263. [Notes on:] Le père Verbiest, auteur de la première grammaire
     mandchoue. Par le P. Karel de Jaegher, missionnaire de Scheut.
     TP 22.1923,189-192
     [Lalou 70]

264. Les traditions manichéennes au Fou-Kien. Par Paul Pelliot.
     TP 22.1923,193-208

265. [rev.] *Les questions de Milinda, Milindapañha*, traduit du Pâli par
     Louis Finot. Ill. par Andrée Karpelès. Paris: Bossard 1923. 166 pp.
     8° (Les classiques de l'Orient.8.)
     TP 22.1923,209-210
       P. Pelliot
     [Lalou 71]

266. [rev.] Histoire de Nala, conte indien. Episode du Mahâbhârata, tra-
     duit par P. E. Dumont. Bruxelles: M. Lamertin 1923. 169,4 pp. 12°
     TP 22.1923,210
       P. Pelliot

267. Notes bibliographiques.
     TP 22.1923,211-214
     Especially: [Prajñâpâramitâ]. 211-212, signed: P. P.
     Serge Elisséèv: La peinture contemporaine au Japon. Paris: E. de
     Boccard 1923. 212-213, signed: P. P.
     [Lalou 72]

268. Notices sur quelques artistes des Six Dynasties et des T'ang. Par
     Paul Pelliot.
     TP 22.1923,215-291
     Offprint: 77 pp.
     [Lalou 73]

269. [Notes on:] Le tombeau de l'empereur Tao-tsong des Leao, et les
     premières inscriptions connues en écriture K'itan.
     TP 22.1923,292-301
       L. Ker

270. [rev.] *Hai tong kin che yuan* 海東金石苑 8 chap., par Lieou Hi-hai
     劉喜海 avec 2 ch. d'«appendice» (fou-lou), et 6 ch. de «sup-
     plément» (pou-yi); édité par Mr Lieou Tch'eng-kan 劉承幹.
     TP 22.1923,302-308
       P. Pelliot

271. [rev.] The development of the logical method in ancient China by Hu
     Shih (Suh Hu), professor of philosophy at the National University of
     Peking. Shanghai: The Oriental Book Co. 1922. 2,1,1,10,187 pp. 8°
     TP 22.1923,309-315
       P. Pelliot

272. [rev.] Sound and symbol in Chinese. By Bernhard Karlgren. Lon-
     don: Oxford University Press 1923. 112 pp. 12° (Language &
     literature series.)
     TP 22.1923,315-321
       P. Pelliot

273. [rev.] J. B. Chaigneau et sa famille. Par A. Salles. Hanoi-Haiphong
     1923. 200 pp. 8° (Extrait du Bulletin des amis du vieux Hué, janv.-
     mars 1923.)
     TP 22.1923,321-324
       P. Pelliot

274. [Publications of the Museum of Tientsin, T'ien-chin po-wu-yüan
     天津博物院]
     TP 22.1923,326-327
       P. P.

275. [rev.] G. Tucci: Studio comparativo fra tre versioni cinesi e il testo
     sanscrito de l'I° e II° capitolo del Laṅkâvatâra. Memorie, Reale Acca-
     demia dei Lincei V,18.1923,169-200 [and other notes.]
     TP 22.1923,327-329
       P. P.
     [Lalou 74, 75]

276. Un nouveau périodique oriental: Asia major. Par Paul Pelliot.
     TP 22.1923,345-376
     Re: *Hirth Anniversary Volume. Asia major.* Journal devoted to the
     study of the languages, arts and civilisation of the Far East and Cen-
     tral Asia. Introductory volume, edited by Bruno Schindler, Ph. D.
     London: Probsthain 1923. LXXXIII,705 pp. 8°
     [Lalou 76, 77]

277. La date des «céramiques de Kiu-lou» 鉅鹿.
     TP 22.1923,377-382
       P. Pelliot

278. Une «Société d'études orientales» en Chine. 東方學會.
     TP 22.1923,383-384
       P. Pelliot

279. [rev.] Studien zur Kunst des Ostens, Joseph Strzygowski zum sech-
     zigsten Geburtstage von seinen Freunden und Schülern. Wien, Hel-
     lerau: Avalun-Verlag (1923). 258 pp., 30 pl. 4°
     TP 22.1923,385-389

280. [Vostok.3.1923]
     TP 22.1923,391-393
       P. P.

281. [Works by B. Ja. Vladimircov.]
     TP 22.1923,394-395
       P. P.

282. [Japon et Extrême-Orient. No. 1. Dec. 1923]
     TP 22.1923,395-396
       P. P.

283. [East Asian sculpture in the Museum für Ostasiatische Kunst, Köln.
     On works by Salmony and With.]
     TP 22.1923,396
       P. P.

284. [M. Stiassny: Einiges zur «Buddhistischen Madonna». Cicerone
     1923.]
     TP 22.1923,397
       P. P.

1924
285. Chronologie des Khiţâ et des Ouigoures. (Traduction du chapitre
     LXXXVII, § 3, p. 182).

Tagî el-Dîn Aḥmad ibn ʿAlî ibn ʿAbd-el-Qâdir ibn Muḥammad el-Maqrîzî: *El-mawâiz waʾl-iʿtibâr fî dhikr el-khitat waʾl-âthâr*, édité par M. Gaston Wiet. T.4, 2me partie, chap. L-XCIV. Avec un appendice de M. Paul Pelliot, membre de l'Institut, professeur au Collège de France.
Le Caire: Imprimerie de l'Institut français 1924,309-316
(Mémoires publ. par les membres de l'Institut français d'archéologie orientale du Caire. 49.)
   P. Pelliot

286. *Bronzes antiques de la Chine appartenant à C. T. Loo et Cie.*, par M. Tchʿou Tö-yi. Avec une préface et des notes de M. Paul Pelliot, membre de l'Institut.
Paris, Bruxelles: Librairie nationale d'art et d'histoire G. van Oest 1924. 68 pp., 40 pl. 4° 1 p. [unpag.] preface by Pelliot.

287. Les classiques gravés sur pierre sous les Wei en 240-248. Par Paul Pelliot.
TP 23.1924,1-4

288. Kouo hio ki kʿan 國學季刊. The journal of sinological studies. 1.1923. Par Paul Pelliot.
TP 23.1924,5-14

289. Manuscrits chinois au Japon.
Kyôto teikoku daigaku bungaku-bu eiin Tô-shôhon dai-ichi-shû 京都帝國大學文學部景印唐鈔本第一集. Kyôto 1922. 3 pen, 1 tʿao. Par Paul Pelliot.
TP 23.1924,15-30

290. [rev.] Vocabulaire des sciences mathématiques, physiques et naturelles. II.Vocabulaire chinois-français. Par le P. Charles Taranzano, S.J. Sien-hsien 1921. 964 pp., 1 l. Errata. 8°
TP 23.1924,40-41
   P. Pelliot

291. [rev.] Chine moderne. T.1: Moralisme officiel. Par le P. L. Wieger, S.J. Hien-hien 1921. 529 pp. 8° T.2: Le flot montant. Ibid. 423 pp.

TP 23.1924,41-53
P. Pelliot

292. [rev.] Guide-catalogue du Musée Guimet. Les collections bouddhi-
ques (Exposé historique et iconographique.) Inde centrale et Gandhâ-
ra, Turkestan, Chine septentrionale, Tibet. Par M. J. Hackin. Paris,
Bruxelles: Van Oest 1923. 175 pp. 8°
TP 23.1924,43-46
P. Pelliot

293. [rev.] Baukunst und Landschaft in China. Eine Reise durch zwölf
Provinzen. Von Ernst Boerschmann. Berlin: E. Wasmuth (1923).
XXV pp., 288 pl. 4°
TP 23.1924,46-48
P. Pelliot

294. [rev.] Esquisse d'une histoire de la philosophie indienne. Par Paul
Masson-Oursel. Paris: Geuthner 1923. 314 pp. 8°
La philosophie comparée. Par Paul Masson-Oursel. Paris: F. Alcan
1923. 201 pp. 8° (Bibliothèque de philosophie contemporaine.)
TP 23.1924,48-50
P. Pelliot

295. [rev.] L'origine de la rose des vents et l'invention de la boussole. Par
M. L. de Saussure. Genève 1923. 69 pp. 8° (Extrait des Archives des
sciences phys. et natur. 128ᵉ année, no. 3 et 4.)
TP 23.1924,51-54
P. Pelliot

296. [rev.] Ju-Tao-Fo 儒道佛 Die religiösen und philosophischen Systeme Ostasiens. Von Dr. F. E. A. Krause. München: E. Reinhardt
1924. 588 pp. 8° – Terminologie und Namensverzeichnis zu Religion
und Philosophie Ostasiens. Beiheft zu Jao-Tao-Fo. Autogr. 226 pp.
TP 23.1924,54-62
P. Pelliot

297. Quelques remarques sur le Chouo Fou 說郛. Par Paul Pelliot.
TP 23.1924,163-220

298. A propos des bronzes de Sin-Tcheng 新鄭.
      TP 23.1924,255-259
        P. Pelliot

299. Deux termes techniques de l'art chinois 脱沙 t'o-cha et yin-k'i 隱起.
      TP 23.1924,260-266
        P. Pelliot
        [Lalou 80]

300. [75th anniversary of Henri Cordier.]
      TP 23.1924,272
        P. P.

301. [Champollion: Lettre à M. Dacier. 1822.]
      TP 23.1924,273
        P. P.

302. [Works by Henri Imbert.]
      TP 23.1924,273-278
        P. P.

303. [Tch'ou Tö-yi: Bronzes antiques de la Chine appartenant à C. T. Loo
      et Cie. Paris, Bruxelles: G. van Oest 1924.]
      TP 23.1924,278-279
        P. P.

304. [H. Bosmans prepares an edition of F. Verbiest's correspondence.]
      TP 23.1924,284
        P. P.

305. [Note on the Mongol and Manchu Kanjur and Tanjur.]
      TP 23.1924,284-285
        P. P.
        [Lalou 81]

306. [Collapse of the Lei-feng-t'a 雷峰塔, Hang-chou, Sept. 25, 1924.]
      TP 23.1924,285
        P. P.

307. Un recueil de pièces imprimées concernant la «Question des rites».
     TP 23.1924,347-355
       P. Pelliot
     [24 titles.]

308. La Brevis Relatio.
     TP 23.1924,355-372
       P. Pelliot

309. [The Mongolian Learned Committee.]
     TP 23.1924,394
       P. P.

310. [P. Perny: Vocabularium Latino-Sinicum. 1862: Les éditions xylo-
     gra–phiques.]
     TP 23.1924,394
       P. P.

311. Maurice Abadie, Lieutenant-colonel d'infanterie coloniale: *Les races
     du Haut-Tonkin de Phong-Tho à Lang-Son*. Préface de M. Paul
     Pelliot, de l'Institut.
     Paris: Société d'éditions géographiques, maritimes et coloniales
     1924. VI,194 pp. large 8°
     Lettre-préface, VI, signed: Paul Pelliot
     Paris, 23 décembre 1923
     Rev.: *TP* 23.1924,156-157 (Henri Cordier)
     OLZ 1926,452-453 (H. Stönner)

1925
312. Two new Manichean manuscripts from Tun-huang.
     Journal of the Royal Asiatic Society 1925,113
       Paul Pelliot
     [Lalou 85]

313. Les mots à h initiale, aujourd'hui amuie, dans le mongol des XIIIe et
     XIVe siècles. Par Paul Pelliot.
     Journal asiatique 206.1925,193-263
     Offprint 1925.

Re:
G. J. Ramstedt: Ein anlautender stimmloser Labial in der mongolisch-türkischen Ursprache. *Journal de la Société finno-ougrienne.* 32. 1916/20. 10 pp.
P. Schmidt: The language of the Negidals. *Acta Universitatis Latviensis.*5.1923,3-38
P. Schmidt: The language of the Olchas. *Acta Universitatis Latviensis.*8.1923,229-288
S. Shirokogoroff: Study on Tungus languages. *Journal of the North China Branch of the Royal Asiatic Society* 55.1924,261-269

314. Note sur Karakorum.
Journal asiatique 206.1925,372-375
    Paul Pelliot

315. Les anciens rapports entre l'Egypte et l'Extrême-Orient.
Compte-rendu du Congrès international de géographie. Le Caire 1925. T. 5, p.21-22
[Lalou 82] [Not seen.]

316. Les systèmes d'écriture en usage chez les anciens Mongols. Par Paul Pelliot.
Asia major. 2.1925,284-289
[Lalou 83]

317. Quelques textes chinois concernant l'Indochine hindouisée. Par Paul Pelliot, membre de l'Institut.
Etudes asiatiques, publiées à l'occasion du 25e anniversaire de l'Ecole française d'Extrême-Orient 2.[Paris, Bruxelles: G. Van Oest] 1925 (Publications de l'Ecole française d'Extrême-Orient.20),243-263
[Lalou 84]

318. Pelliot & Salmony: Errata.
AA 1.1925/26,55-63
On: Salmony: *Chinesische Steinplastik.* Berlin 1922.
p.57 signed: Paul Pelliot
p.63 signed: Alfred Salmony
[Lalou 69]

319. [rev.] Bildwerke Ost und Südasiens aus der Sammlung Yi Yuan, mit
     Einleitung und beschreibendem Text von Karl With. Basel: Benno
     Schwabe 1924. 74 pp., 112 pl.
     Artibus Asiae 1.1925/26,152-155
       P. Pelliot

320. *Jades archaiques de Chine, appartenant à C. T. Loo*, publiés par M.
     Paul Pelliot, membre de l'Institut.
     Paris, Bruxelles: Librairie nationale d'art et d'histoire G. van Oest
     1925. 35 pp., 46 pl. with explan. 4°

321. Lingots d'argent à inscriptions chinoises. Par M. Bauer, du Musée de
     l'Ermitage, avec un post-scriptum de M. P. Pelliot, membre de
     l'Institut.
     Revue des arts asiatiques.1925,no. 4, pp. 10-13, 2 pl.

1926

322. Indian influences in the early Chinese art in Tun-huang.
     Indian art and letters.2.1926,20-34
     pp. 21-28 contain Pelliot's lecture.
     Report of a lecture on «Indian influences in the early Chinese art in Tun-huang»,
     delivered by M. Paul Pelliot at 21, Cromwell Road, S.W.7, on Wednesday,
     November 18,1925. Chairman: Lieut.-Colonel Sir Francis Younghusband,
     K.C.S.I., K.C.I.E.

323. Henri Cordier (1849-1925). Par Paul Pelliot.
     TP 24.1926,1-15
     Offprint: Leiden. 15 pp.

324. Le Kin kou k'i kouan 今古奇觀. Par Paul Pelliot.
     TP 24.1926,54-60
     On: *Chin ku ch'i kuan. The inconstancy of Madam Chuang and other
     stories from the Chinese*, translated by E. B. Howell, with twelve il-
     lustrations by a native artist. London: T. Werner Laurie [1925]. VII,
     259 pp. 8°

325. Le mot bigni (ou begni?) «vin» en turc.
     TP 24.1926,61-64
       P. Pelliot

326. Encore à propos des «Elementa linguae tartaricae».
     TP 24.1926,64-66
       P. Pelliot

327. [rev.] Mille et un contes, récits & légendes arabes. Par R. Basset.
     T.1. Contes merveilleux, contes plaisants. Paris: Maisonneuve frères
     1924. 552 pp. 8°
     TP 24.1926,70-72
       P. Pelliot

328. [rev.] Formulaire sanscrit-tibétain du Xe siècle, édité et traduit par Jo-
     seph Hackin. Paris: Geuthner 1924. IX,27,130 pp. (Mission Pelliot
     en Asie centrale. Série petit in-octavo.2.)
     TP 24.1926,72-74
       Paul Pelliot

329. [rev.] Otto Pelka: Ostasiatische Reisebilder im Kunstgewerbe des 18.
     Jahrhunderts. Mit 224 ill. auf 87 pl. Leipzig: K. W. Hiersemann
     1924. 58 pp. 4°
     TP 24.1926,74-76
       P. Pelliot

330. [rev.] The walls and gates of Peking, by Osvald Sirén. London: John
     Lane, The Bodley Head 1924. XIX,239 pp., 53 text ill., 1 plan of
     Peking, 128 pl. Edition of 800 copies. 4°
     TP 24.1926,76-79
       P. Pelliot

331. [rev.] Wei chou tsong che tchouan tchou 魏書宗室傳注 («Com-
     mentaire sur les biographies des agnats impériaux dans l'Histoire des
     Wei») [Wei-shu tsung-shih chuan-shu by Lo Chen-yü 羅振玉]
     1924. 4 pen. 8°
     TP 24.1926,79-86
       P. Pelliot

332. Notes bibliographiques.
     TP 24.1926,87-90
       P. P.
     [Publications de l'Ecole française d'Extrême-Orient]

La Vallée-Poussin: *Indo-européens et Indo-iraniens.* Paris 1924.
Laurence Binyon: *L'art asiatique au British Museum* (sculpture et peinture). 1925.
Le journal d'André Ly, prêtre chinois, missionnaire et notaire apostolique, 1746-1763.
[Collections of Baron Iwasaki.]

333. Revue des périodiques.
    TP 24.1926,91-120
    91-95: Mitteilungen des Seminars für Orientalische Sprachen. Ostasiatische Studien. 26 and 27. Berlin 1924. 213 pp.
    95-113: Jahrbuch der asiatischen Kunst, hrsg. von Georg Biermann unter Mitarbeit von Ernst Grosse, Fr. Sarre, William Cohn und Heinrich Glück. Berlin: Klinkhardt & Biermann 1924. 274 pp. 4°
    113-119: Ostasiatische Zeitschrift NF 2.1925.
    119-120: The Young East.

334. [Exhibition of documents and objects from Afghanistan.]
    TP 24.1926,129
    [Lalou 86]

335. [Gaston Wiet: Mémoires publiés par les membres de l'Institut français d'Archéologie orientale.]
    TP 24.1926,129
    P. P.

336. Nécrologie: Auguste Conrady.
    TP 24.1926,130-132
    P. Pelliot

337. Le voyage de MM. Gabet et Huc à Lhasa. Par Paul Pelliot.
    TP 24.1926,133-178
    On: *Souvenirs d'un voyage dans la Tartarie et le Thibet pendant les années 1844, 1845 et 1846,* par E. Huc, prêtre-missionnaire de la congrégation de Saint-Lazare. Nouvelle édition. Annotée et illustrée par J.-M. Planchet, missionnaire lazariste. Pékin: Imprimerie des Lazaristes 1924. 426,493 pp. 8°
    [Lalou 87]

338. Le Ts'ien tseu wen ou «Livre des mille mots». Par Paul Pelliot.
     TP 24.1926,179-214,293 (notes additionnelles)
     On: Das 千字文 Ts'ien[1]-tze[4]-wen[2] in vier chinesischen Schriftformen
     mit einer Übersetzung. Herausgegeben und erklärt von Erich Hauer.
     Berlin 1925. 47 pp., 14 fol. Chin. text. 8° Sonderdruck aus *Mittei-
     lungen des Seminars für Orientalische Sprachen*. 1.Abt. Bd 28.

339. L'inscription chinoise d'Idïqut-šahri.
     TP 24.1926,247-251
       P. Pelliot

340. Le San tseu king [三字經] ou Livre des trois mots.
     TP 24.1926,251-253
       P. Pelliot

341. Le nom persan du cinabre dans les langues «altaïques».
     TP 24.1925,253-255
       P. Pelliot
     [Re: Laufer: *Sino-Iranica*, 572-576.]

342. [rev.] Comm. Lefebvre des Noëttes: La force motrice animale à
     travers les âges. With 217 ill. on 80 pl. Paris: Berger-Levrault 1924.
     VIII,132 pp. 8°
     TP 24.1926,256-268
       P. Pelliot

343. [rev.] The George Eumorfopoulos Collection. Catalogue of the
     Chinese, Corean and Persian pottery and porcelain. By R. L.
     Hobson. Vol.1. Chou - end of T'ang. London: E. Benn 1925.
     XXVII,66 pp., 75 pl., 25 of which in colour. 2°
     TP 24.1926,268-270
       P. Pelliot

344. [rev.] 華德辭典 Chinesisch-deutsches Wörterbuch. 6400 Schrift-
     zeichen mit ihren Einzelbedeutungen und den gebräuchlichen Zusam-
     mensetzungen, von Werner Rüdenberg. Hamburg: L. Friederichsen
     & Co. 1924. IX,687 pp.
     TP 24.1926,271-282
       P. Pelliot

345. [rev.] 大理院判例要旨匯覽　Recueil des sommaires de la juris-
prudence de la Cour Suprême de la République de Chine en matière et
commerciale (1912-1918). 1er fasc., par J. Escarra ... et MM. Liou
Tcheng-tchong, Houx Koung-ou, Liang J'en-kié et Hou Wen-Ping.
Changhai: Impr. de T'ou-sè-wè 1924. XXII,258,6 pp., 3 tab. Fasc.
2. 1925. pp.259-528.
TP 24.1926,282-285
P. Pelliot

346. [rev.] A thousand years of the Tartars. By E. H. Parker. London:
Kegan Paul, Trench, Trübner & Co. 1924. XIII,288 pp., 3 maps, 2
pl. 8°
TP 24.1926,285-287
P. Pelliot

347. [Misprints in *Jades archaïques* ...]
TP 24.1926,293
P. P.

348. Claude Eugène Maître (Nécrologie.)[† Aug. 3, 1925.]
TP 24.1926,294-295
P. Pelliot

349. Léopold de Saussure. (Nécrologie.) [† July 30, 1925.]
TP 24.1926,296-300
P. Pelliot

350. Charles Maybon. (Nécrologie.) [† April 29, 1926.]
TP 24.1926,300-302
P. Pelliot

351. Edward Harper Parker. (Nécrologie.) [† end of Jan. 1926.]
TP 24.1926,302-303
P. Pelliot

352. Thomas Francis Carter. (Nécrologie.) [† Aug. 6, 1925.]
TP 24.1926,303-304
P. Pelliot

353. Charles Vapereau. (Nécrologie.) [† Dec. 15, 1925.]
     TP 24.1926,304
       P. Pelliot

354. Un bronze bouddhique de 518 au Musée du Louvre.
     TP 24.1926,381-382
       P. Pelliot
     [Lalou 88]

355. [rev.] Early Jesuit travellers in Central Asia, 1603-1721, by C. Wes-
     sels. The Hague: Nijhoff 1924. XVI,344 pp., 1 map, 4 pl.
     TP 24.1926,387-395
       P. Pelliot

356. [rev.] The chronicles of the East India Company trading to China
     1635-1834, by Hosea Ballou Morse. Oxford: Clarendon Press 1926.
     4 vols. XXII,313; VII,451; VIII,398; VIII,427 pp. 8°
     TP 24.1926,395-398
       P. Pelliot

357. [rev.] A brief manual of the Si-hia characters with Tibetan tran-
     scriptions, by Nicolas Nevsky. Osaka: The Osaka Asiatic Society
     1926. 84 pp., 1 p. Errata. Autogr. (Research review of the Osaka
     Asiatic Society. No 4.)
     TP 24.1926,399-403
       P. Pelliot
     [Lalou 89]

358. [rev.] Won Kenn (Houang Kiuan-cheng 黃涓生): Origine et
     évolution de l'écriture hiéroglyphique et de l'écriture chinoise. Lyon:
     Bosc et Riou; Paris: Geuthner 1926. 95 pp. 8° (Bibliotheca Franco-
     Sinica Lugdunensis. Etudes et documents publiés par l'Institut Fran-
     co-Chinois de Lyon.1.)
     TP 24.1926,403
       P. P.

359. Nécrologie: Joseph Brucker. [† April 26, 1926.]
     TP 24.1926,407
       P. Pelliot

360. Le k'ong-heou et le qobuz. Par Paul Pelliot.
     Naitô hakushi kanreki shukuga Shinagaku ronsô.
     內藤博士還歷祝賀支那學論叢
     Kyôto: Kôbundô shobô 1926,207-210
     空侯 [with bamboo radical]
     [Lalou 90]

361. *Tonkô isho* 敦煌遺書 [Manuscrits de Touen-houang, conservés à la
     Bibliothèque nationale de Paris et publiées par le Tôa-Kôkyûkwai de
     Changhai, sous la direction du P. Pelliot et T. Haneda 羽田亨. Série
     in-folio. 1-4; sér. in-octavo. 1-9.]
     Kyôto 1926. 2 vols. [all published] (14,55,1; 3,2,18,2,4,2,14,1,12,
     2,1 pp.)
       [rev.] *Ryutani daigaku ronshû.* 273.1927,115 (Kô 功)
       [rev.] *Shirin* 12:1. 1927,148-149 (Naba Toshisada 那波利貞)
       [rev.] *Shinagaku* 4.1927:2, 158-160 (Ishihama Juntarô 石濱純
       太郎)

361a.Les dessins et peintures d'Extrême-Orient d'Alexandre Iacovleff.
     L'illustration 84.1926,719-722
     Paul Pelliot

1927
362. [rev.] Alfred Salmony: Chinesische Plastik. Ein Handbuch für
     Sammler. Berlin: Richard Carl Schmidt 1925. XI,172 pp., 129 ill. 8°
     Artibus Asiae 2.1927,69-75
       P. Pelliot

363. Paul Pelliot: Sur l'interprétation des marques des porcelaines chi-
     noises.
     Artibus Asiae 2.1927,179-187

364. [rev.] The year-book of Oriental art and culture, 1924-1925. Edited
     by Arthur Waley. London: Ernest Benn 1925. XI,142 pp., 1 port-
     folio with 60 pl. 4°
     Artibus Asiae 2.1927,225-230
       Paul Pelliot
     [Lalou 101]

365. Paul Pelliot: Un bronze bouddhique de 502 A.D.
     Artibus Asiae 2.1927,244-246
     [Collection Alexander von Frey, Paris.]

366. Le prétendu vocabulaire mongol des Ķaitaķ du Daghestan. Par Paul
     Pelliot.
     Journal asiatique 210.1927,279-294

367. A propos du Chinese biographical dictionary de M. H. Giles. Par
     Paul Pelliot.
     Asia major 4.1927,377-389
     [Lalou 100]

368. M. Pelliot fait une communication sur l'origine de l'alphabet dit
     'phags-pa.
     Journal asiatique 210.1927,372
     [Lalou 102]

369. «Šûl» ou sarag?
     Journal asiatique 211.1927,138-141
       Paul Pelliot
     [Lalou 103]

370. Une ville musulmane dans la Chine du nord sous les Mongols. Par
     Paul Pelliot.
     Journal asiatique.211.1927,261-279
     Rev.: *Deutsche Wacht* 15.1929:4, p. 46 (E. von Zach)

371. Pelliot: Chinesisches Drama.
     Veranstaltungen des China-Instuts.
     Sinica 2.1927,7

372. *Guide-posts to Chinese painting*, by Louise Wallace Hackney. Edited
     [!] by Dr. Paul Pelliot, Collège de France. With illustrations.
     Boston, New York: Houghton Mifflin 1927. XII,221 pp.
     Cf. Rectification. *Revue des arts asiatiques*.5.1928,51 (Pelliot)

373. Écriture chinoise.
      Notices sur les caractères étrangers anciens et modernes, rédigées par
      un groupe de savants, réunis par M. Charles Fossey, professeur au
      Collège de France, Inspecteur de la typographie orientale à l'Im-
      primerie nationale. Paris: Imprimerie nationale 1927,297-305
        P. Pelliot
      New edition: Paris 1948,381-389 (P. Pelliot, 1927. – Mestre, 1948)

1928
374. [Evariste Régis] Huc and Gabet: *Travels in Tartary, Thibet and
      China, 1844-1846,* translated by William Hazlitt; now edited with an
      introduction by Professor Paul Pelliot.
      London: George Routledge & Sons (1928). XLIV,387 pp.; VIII,406
      pp. (The Broadway traveller, edited by Sir E. Denison Ross and
      Eileen Power.)
      V-XXXV: Introduction by Paul Pelliot.
      Rev.: *OLZ* 1929,579-581 (J. C. Tavadia)

375. L'origine des relations de la France avec la Chine. Le premier voyage
      de *l'Amphitrite* en Chine.
      François Froger: Relation du premier voyage des François à la Chine
      fait en 1698,1699 et 1700 sur le vaisseau *l'Amphitrite*, edited by E.
      A. Voretzsch. Leipzig: Verlag der Asia Major 1926. XVI,187 pp.
      *Journal des savants.*1928, 433-451; 1929, 110-125,252-267,289-
      298
      Offprint: Paris 1930. 79 pp.

376. The international aspect of China's educational problem. / M. Paul
      Pelliot, Professor of Languages, History and Civilizations of Central
      Asia, of the Collège de France, Paris.
      *Proceedings of the Academy of Political Science in the City of New
      York.* 12.1926/28,251-252

377. Les fresques de Touen-houang et les fresques de M. Eumorfopoulos.
      Par Paul Pelliot.
      Revue des arts asiatiques 5.1928,142-163,193-214
      Re: *The George Eumorfopoulos Collection. Catalogue of the Chinese
      frescoes,* by Laurence Binyon. London: Ernest Benn. 22 pp., 50
      colour pl. 2°

377a.Nécrologie: Émile Senart, 1847-1928.
      *Revue des arts asiatiques.*5.1928,6-8
      [From: *Journal des débats.*]

378. *Les antiquités bouddhiques de Bâmiyân*, par A. Godard, architecte
      diplômé par le gouvernement, membre de la Délégation archéologique
      française en Afghanistan, Y. Godard, J. Hackin, Conservateur du
      Musée Guimet, membre de la Délégation archéologique française en
      Afghanistan; avec des notes additionnelles de M. Paul Pelliot, mem-
      bre de l'Institut.
      Paris, Bruxelles: Les éditions G. van Oest 1928. 113 pp., 48 pl.,of
      which 4 in colour. 2° (Délégation archéologique française en Afgha-
      nistan. Mémoires.2.)
      [Dedication:] A Monsieur Émile Senart, membre de l'Institut, hom-
      mage d'affectueuse gratitude.
      Contains:
      63   La statue du Buddha couché et le dragon (ajdaha). Par Paul
                Pelliot.
      75-83   Bâmiyân dans les textes chinois autres que Mémoires et la
                Vie de Hiuan-tsang et le récit de Houei-tch'ao, par Paul
                Pelliot.
      Rev.: *OLZ* 1930,686-669 (E. Waldschmidt)

379. Les Yi nien lou 疑年錄. Par Paul Pelliot.
      TP 25.1928,65-81
      On: *I-nien-lu hui-pien* 彙編 by Chang Wei-hsiang 張惟驤 1925.

380. L'évêche nestorien de Khumdan et Sarag.
      TP 25.1928,91-92
        Paul Pelliot

381. Le terme de siang-kiao 象教 comme désignation du bouddhisme.
      TP 25.1928,92-94
        Paul Pelliot
      Rev.: *Deutsche Wacht* 13.1927:8, p. 39 (E. von Zach)
      [Lalou 91]

382. Note sur la carte des pays du Nord-Ouest dans le King che ta tien
      經世大典.

TP 25.1928,98-100
P. Pelliot

383. [rev.] The George Eumorfopoulos Collection. Catalogue of the Chinese, Corean and Persian pottery and porcelain. By R. L. Hobson. London: Ernest Benn 1926. Vol. 2: XVII,54 pp., 75 pl., 25 of which in colour; Vol. 3: XIII,66 pp., 75 pl., of which 25 in colour.
TP 25.1928,110-116
P. Pelliot

384. [rev.] Chinese art. An introductory review of painting, ceramics, textiles, bronzes, sculture, jade, etc. By Roger Fry, Bernard Rackham, Laurence Binyon, W. Perceval Yetts, A. F. Kendrick, Osvald Sirén, W. W. Winkworth. London: B. E. Batsford (1925). XVIII,62 pp. 4°
TP 25.1928,110-116
P. Pelliot

385. [rev.] Chinese lacquer. By Edward F. Strange. London: Ernest Benn 1926. XII,72 pp., 55 pl., of which 17 in colour. 4°
TP 25.1928,116-134
P. Pelliot

386. [rev.] The Ocean of Story, being C. H. Tawney's translation of Somadeva's Kathâ Sarit Sagara (or Ocean of Streams of Story), now edited with introduction, fresh explanatory notes and terminal essay by N. M. Penzer ... in ten volumes. Vol. 4 with preface by F. W. Thomas. London: Chas. J. Sawyer 1925. XX,315 pp. 8° Vol. 6 with introductory note by E. Denison Ross. 1926. XXXI,324 pp.
TP 25.1928,134-139
  P. Pelliot
  [Lalou 92]

387. [rev.] Tibet, past and present. By Sir Charles Bell. Oxford: Clarendon Press 1924. XIV,326 pp. 8°
TP 25.1928,139-148
  P. Pelliot
  [Lalou 93]

388. [rev.] Dr. F. E. A. Krause: Geschichte Ostasiens. Göttingen: Van-
     denhoeck & Ruprecht 1925. 400,488 pp. 2 maps, 80 pp., 3 tables.
     TP 25.1928,149-155
       P. Pelliot

389. [rev.] Le livre de Marco Polo, citoyen de Venise, haut fonctionnaire à
     la cour de Koubilai-Khan, géneralissime des armées mongoles,
     gouverneur de province, ambassadeur du grand Khan vers l'Indo-
     Chine, les Indes, la Perse et les royaumes chrétiens d'Occident,
     rédigé en français sous la dictée de l'auteur en 1295 par Rusticien de
     Pise, revue et corrigé, par Marco Polo lui-même, en 1307, publié par
     G. Pauthier en 1867, traduit en français moderne et annoté d'après
     les sources chinoises par A. J. H. Charignon. Pékin: A. Nachbaur.
     8° T.1.1924: V,1,268 pp., 1 p. Errata; T.2.1926. 275 pp.
     TP 25.1928,156-169
       Paul Pelliot

390. [rev.] Harsha. By Radhakumud Mookerji. Oxford University Press
     1926. 203 pp., 2 pl., 1 map, small 8°
     TP 25.1928,169-174
       P. Pelliot
     [Lalou 94]

391. [rev.] Karman. Ein buddhistischer Legendenkranz. Übers. von Hein-
     rich Zimmer. München: Bruckmann 1925. 224 pp. 12°
     TP 25.1928,175
       P. Pelliot
     [Lalou 95]

392. Revue des périodiques.
     TP 25.1928,176-192
       P. Pelliot
     On: Ostasiatische Zeitschrift NF 2.1925-3.1926
     Jahrbuch der asiatischen Kunst 2.1925
     [rev.:] *Deutsche Wacht* 13.1927:8, p. 39 (E. von Zach)
     [Lalou 96, 97]

393. Notes bibliographiques.
     TP 25.1928,193-195

P. P.
On: *L'Indochine du sud*. Paris: Hachette 1926.
Goblet d'Alviella: *Ce que l'Inde doit à la Grèce. Des influences classiques dans la civilisation de l'Inde*. Paris: Geuthner [Reprint].
Lewis Einstein: A Chinese design in Saint-Mark's at Venice. (*Revue archéologique*, juillet-sept. 1926,28-29).

394. [On the appointment of six Chinese priests as bishops, in historical perspective.]
TP 25.1928,216
P. P.

395. Nécrologie: Théodore Duret [1838-1927].
TP 25.1928,218
P. Pelliot

396. [Notes on:] Einige Bemerkungen zu Pelliot's Sûtra des Causes et des Effets.
TP 25.1928,403-413
E. von Zach
[The introductory note is signed «Paul Pelliot», the concluding remark «P. P.». Pelliot's additions are added in square brackets.]

397. [rev.] Les peintures chinoises dans les collections d'Angleterre, par Laurence Binyon. Paris, Bruxelles: Vanoest 1927. 69 pp., 64 pl. 4° (Ars asiatica.9.)
TP 25.1928,414-426
Paul Pelliot
[Lalou 98]

398. [rev.] Ernst Waldschmidt und Wolfgang Lentz: Die Stellung Jesu im Manichäismus. Berlin 1926. 131 pp., 4 pl. 4° (Abhandlungen d. preuß. Akademie der Wissenschaften, phil.-hist. Klasse.1926:4.)
TP 25.1928,426-435
Paul Pelliot
[Lalou 99]

399. [rev.] Huang-Ts'ing k'ai-kuo fang-lüeh. Die Gründung des mandschurischen Kaiserreiches. Übersetzt und erklärt von Dr. jur. et

phil. Erich Hauer. Berlin, Leipzig: de Gruyter 1926. XXV,710 pp.,
1 map. 8°
TP 25.1928,435-444
P. Pelliot

400. [rev.] The Hung Society or The Society of Heaven and Earth. By J.
S. M. Ward and W. G. Stirling. London: Baskerville Press 1925-26.
Vol. 1.1925: XV,180 pp., 26 pl.; Vol. 2.1926: VIII,196 pp., 44 pl.;
Vol. 3.1926: VI,148 pp., 17 pl. 8°
TP 25.1928,444-448
P. Pelliot

401. [rev.] Erich Schmitt: Die Grundlagen der chinesischen Ehe. Deutsche
Morgenländische Gesellschaft 1927. 223 pp. 8°
TP 25.1928,448-450
P. Pelliot

402. [rev.] Annuaire du monde musulman statistique, historique, social et
économique, rédigé par L. Massignon. 2ᵉ édition. Paris: Leroux
(1925). VI,396 pp. 8°
TP 25.1928,450-452
P. Pelliot

403. [rev.] 10,000 Chinese-Japanese characters, by J. L. Pierson, Jr.
Leiden: E. J. Brill 1926. XII,VIII,746 pp. 4°
TP 25.1928,452-457
P. Pelliot

404. Nécrologie: Bunyiu Nanjio. [†1927]
TP 25.1928,466
P. Pelliot

1929
405. Paul Pelliot: *Quelques réflexions sur l'art sibérien et l'art chinois à
propos de bronzes de la Collection David-Weill.*
Paris: Éditions Documents 1929. 7 unnumbered leaves 4°
Paul Pelliot, de l'Institut
Also published as: *Documents* 1,1.1929, pp.9-21

406. *Asiatische Kunst. Ausstellung Köln 1926.* Bearbeitet von Alfred Sal-
mony. Mit Anmerkungen von Paul Pelliot.
München: F. Bruckmann (1929). 80 pp., 100 pl. 4°
[Dedication:] In Dankbarkeit und Verehrung Herrn Baron Eduard von
der Heydt gewidmet.
Rev.: *Sinica* 4.1929,186 (H. Wilhelm)

407. Notes sur quelques livres ou documents conservés en Espagne.
TP 26.1929,43-50
	Paul Pelliot
[German extracts in: Die chinesischen Bücher der Kgl. Bibliothek des
Escorial. *Oriens extremus* 40.1997,263-274]

408. Encore à propos du Sûtra des causes et des effets et de l'expression
siang-kiao 象教
TP 26.1929,51-52
	Paul Pelliot
[On E. von Zach's Bemerkungen.]
Rev.: *Deutsche Wacht* 15.1929:1, p. 44 (E. von Zach)

409. [rev.] Sseu yi kouan tsö 四譯館則 («Règlements du Bureau des tra-
ducteurs») par Lu Wei-k'i 呂維棋, édité par la Faculté des Lettres de
l'Université de Kyôto. 1928. 2 pen, 20 ch. 8°
TP 26.1929,53-61
	Paul Pelliot

410. [rev.] Osvald Sirén: Les peintures chinoises dans les collections amé-
ricaines. 1re, 2e et 3e séries. Paris, Bruxelles: Vanoest 1927-1928. 70
pp., 120 pl. 2° (Annales du Musée Guimet. Bibliothèque d'art. N.S.
2.)
TP 26.1929,61-67
	P. Pelliot

411. [rev.] Louis Wallace Hackney: Guide-posts to Chinese painting.
Edited by Dr. Paul Pelliot, Collège de France. Boston, New York:
Houghton Mifflin 1927. XII,221 pp. 8°
TP 26.1929,67
	Paul Pelliot

«j'ai déjà protesté ... contre l'abus scandaleux qui est fait ici de mon nom.»

412. Nécrologie: Emile Senart [1847-1928].
TP 26.1929,68-70
(*Journal des débats*, 23 février 1928)
   Paul Pelliot

413. Wang Kuo-wei 王國維 [1877-1927].
TP 26.1929,70-72
   Paul Pelliot

414. Des artisans chinois à la capitale abbaside en 751-762. Par Paul Pelliot.
TP 26.1929,110-112

415. L'édition collective des œuvres de Wang Kouo-wei. Par Paul Pelliot.
TP 26.1929,113-182
海甯王忠愨公遺書

416. [rev.] Les antiquités bouddhiques de Bâmiyân, par A. Godard, Y. Godard et J. Hackin. Avec des notes additionelles de M. Paul Pelliot. Paris, Bruxelles: G. Van Oest 1928. 115 pp., 48 pl., of which 4 in colour. 2° (Mémoires de la délégation archéologique française en Afghanistan.2.)
TP 26.1929,183-187
   Paul Pelliot

417. Notes bibliographiques.
TP 26.1929,188-189
   P. P.
[Re: E. von Zach in *Deutsche Wacht*. July 1928.]

418. Nécrologie: Henri Bosmans, S.J. [1852-1928].
TP 26.1929,190-199
   Paul Pelliot

419. Neuf notes sur des questions d'Asie centrale. Par Paul Pelliot.
TP 26.1929,201-265

1. La transcription chinoise du nom de Vema-kadphises.
2. Le plus ancien exemple du cycle des douze animaux chez les Turcs.
3. Le mont Yu-tou-kin (Ütükän) des anciens Turcs.
4. Deux mots turcs chez Hiuan-tsang.
5. Une particularité des transcriptions sino-turques.
   Appendice: La valeur de k'i 俟 dans les transcriptions des Wei et des T'ang.
6. L'inscription chinoise de Bilgä qaɣan.
   Appendice: Les funérailles de Kül-tegin.
7. Un exemple méconnu du rite manichéen de maɣistag.
8. Un mot mongol sous les T'ang.
9. Sur quelques documents de Tourfan.

420. Les publications du Tôyô Bunko 東洋文庫. Par Paul Pelliot.
TP 26.1929,357-366
[Especially 東洋文庫論叢 and *Memoirs of the Research Department of the Tôyô Bunko.*]

421. Monsieur E. von Zach.
TP 26.1929,367-378
   Paul Pelliot
«Il ne sera plus question de M. E. von Zach dans le T'oung Pao.»
Rev.: *Deutsche Wacht* 16.1930:2, p. 28 (E. von Zach)

422. [rev.] Ananda K. Coomaraswamy: History of Indian and Indonesian art. London: E. Goldston 1927. 295 pp., 128 pl. 4°
Ananda K. Coomaraswamy: Geschichte der indischen und indonesischen Kunst. Aus dem Englischen übersetzt von Hermann Götz. Leipzig: Hiersemann 1927. XI,324 pp., 128 pl. 4°
TP 26.1929,379-388
   P. Pelliot

423. [rev.] Oskar Nachod: Bibliographie von Japan, 1906-1926. Leipzig: Hiersemann 1928. XVI,832 pp. in 2 vols. 8°
TP 26.1929,389-391
   P. Pelliot

424. P. Pelliot: Termez 呾蜜] dans les textes chinois et tibétains. (Présenté par S. de Oldenbourg, membre de l'Académie, le 28 octobre 1929.)
Doklady Akademii Nauk Sojuza Sovetskix Socialističeskix Respublik. B,1929,297-298

1930
425. Nécrologie: Albert von Le Coq.
Revue des arts asiatiques 6.1929/30,187-188
Paul Pelliot

426. Lettre ouverte à M. Carl Hentze, codirecteur d'«Artibus Asiae».
Revue des arts asiatiques 6.1929/30,103-122
Paul Pelliot
Also: Paris: Van Oest 1930.
Cf. W. Perceval Yetts: A propos de la «Lettre ouverte à M. Carl Hentze».
Revue des arts asiatiques 6.1929/30,191-192
Carl Hentze: *Lettre ouverte à M. Paul Pelliot.*
Anvers: De Sikkel 1930. 32 pp.
Again: P. Pelliot in *Revue des arts asiatiques* 6.1929/30,196
Rev.: *Deutsche Wacht* 16.1930:22, p. 26 (E. von Zach)

427. Les mots mongols dans le Korye Să 高麗史. Par Paul Pelliot.
Journal asiatique 217.1930,253-266

428. Les stances d'introduction de l'Abhidharmahṛdayaśâstra de Dharmatrâta.
Journal asiatique 217.1930,267-273
P. Pelliot

429. *L'origine des relations de France avec la Chine: Le premier voyage de «l'Amphitrite» en Chine.* Par Paul Pelliot (Extrait du Journal des savants.)
Paris: Paul Geuthner 1930. 78 pp.
Corrected reprint with addenda and index.
On: François Froger: *Relation du premier voyage des François à la Chine fait en 1698, 1699 et 1700 sur le vaisseau «L'Amphitrite»*, edited by E. A. Voretzsch.

Leipzig: Asia Major 1926. XVI,187 pp. 8°
Rev.: *OLZ* 1932,499 (W. Vogel)

430. Christianity in Central Asia in the Middle Ages. By Professor Paul
Pelliot.
Journal of the Royal Central Asian Society 17.1930,301-312

431. Notes sur le «Turkestan» de M. W. Barthold. Par Paul Pelliot.
TP 27.1930,12-56
On: W. Barthold: *Turkestan down to the Mongol invasion.* 2d ed.,
translated from the Russian original and revised by the author, in
coop. with H. A. R. Gibb. London: Luzac & Co. 1928. XX,514
pp., 1 map 8°

432. [rev.] Hosea Ballou Morse: The chronicles of the East India Company trading to China 1635-1834. Vol.5: Supplementary, 1742-
1774. Oxford: Clarendon Press 1929. X,212 pp., 2 pl. 8°
TP 27.1930, 62-67
Paul Pelliot

433. [rev.] Frühling und Herbst des Lü Bu We. Aus dem Chinesischen
verdeutscht und erläutert von Richard Wilhelm. Jena: E. Diederichs
1928. XIII,542 pp. 8°
TP 27.1930,68-91
P. Pelliot

434. [rev.] Alfred Forke: Geschichte der alten chinesischen Philosophie.
Hamburg: Friederichsen 1927. XVI,594 pp., large 8° (Abhandlungen
aus dem Gebiet der Auslandskunde, Hamburg. Universität. Bd 25,
Reihe B: Völkerkunde, Kulturgeschichte und Sprachen.Bd 14.)
TP 27.1930,91-106
Paul Pelliot

435. [rev.] René Grousset: Sur les traces du Bouddha. Paris: Plon 1929.
IV,329 pp., 1 map, 8 pl. 8°
TP 27.1930,106-108
P. Pelliot

436. Livres reçus.
     TP 27.1930,109-118
     [Not signed.]

437. Le nom turc des «Mille sources» chez Hiuan-tsang.
     TP 27.1930,189-190
       P. Pelliot

438. Le prétendu mot «iascot» chez Guillaume de Rubrouck.
     TP 27.1930,190-192
       Paul Pelliot

439. Sur yam ou ǰam, «relais postal».
     TP 27.1930,192-195
       P. Pelliot
     [Re Vladimircov in *Doklady Akademii nauk.* 1929,289-296.]

440. Les kökö-däbtär et les hou-k'eou ts'ing-ts'eu 戶口青冊.
     TP 27.1930,195-198
       P. Pelliot
     Rev.: *Deutsche Wacht.*16.1930:22, p. 26 (E. v. Zach)

441. Un passage altéré dans le texte mongol ancien de l'Histoire secrète
     des Mongols.
     TP 27.1930,199-202
       P. Pelliot

442. [rev.] G. I. Bratianu: Recherches sur le commerce génois dans la Mer
     noire au XIIIe siècle. Paris: Geuthner 1929. XII,359 pp., 5 pl., 1
     map. 8°
     TP 27.1930,203-211
       P. Pelliot

443. [rev.] C. Hentze: Les figurines de la céramique funéraire. Matériaux
     pour l'étude des croyances et du folklore de la Chine ancienne. Hel-
     lerau: Avalun s.d. VII,105 pp., 114 pl. large 4°
     TP 27.1930,211-212
       P. Pelliot

444. [M. R. Cagnat: Notice sur la vie et les travaux de M. Henri Cordier.]
     TP 27.1930,216
       P. P.

445. Livres reçus.
     TP 27.1930,217-231
     [Not signed.]

446. Charles Eudes Bonin. (Nécrologie.)[† Sept. 29, 1929.]
     TP 27.1930,235-236
       P. Pelliot

447. Arnold Vissière. (Nécrologie.)[† March 28, 1930.]
     TP 27.1930,236
       P. Pelliot

448. Josef Markwart (Marquart). (Nécrologie.)[1864-1930.]
     TP 27.1930,236-237
       P. Pelliot

449. Richard Wilhelm. (Nécrologie.)[† March 1, 1930.]
     TP 27.1930,237-239
       Paul Pelliot

450. Friedrich Wilhelm Karl Müller. (Nécrologie.)[† April 18, 1930.]
     TP 27.1930,239-241
       Paul Pelliot

451. Albert von Le Coq. (Nécrologie.)[† April 21, 1930.]
     TP 27.1930,241-243
       P. Pelliot

452. A. H. Francke. (Nécrologie.)[† Febr. 16, 1930.]
     TP 27.1930,243-244
       P. Pelliot

453. Jörg Trübner. (Nécrologie.)[† Febr. 7, 1930.]
     TP 27.1930,244
       P. Pelliot

454. Heinrich Glück. (Nécrologie.)[† June 24, 1930.]
      TP 27.1930,244-245
        Paul Pelliot

455. Alfred Dirr. (Nécrologie.)
      TP 27.1930,245
        Paul Pelliot

456. Frédéric Courtois, S. J. (Nécrologie.)[† Sept. 21, 1929.]
      TP 27.1930,245-246
        P. Pelliot

457. Mathias Tchang, S. J. (Nécrologie.)[† May 3, 1929.]
      TP 27.1930,246
        P. Pelliot

458. Sur la légende d'Uγuz-khan en écriture ouigoure. Par Paul Pelliot.
      TP 27.1930,247-358
      Re: Riza Nour: *Oughouz-namé, épopée turque.* Transcription en
      lettres phonétiques, notes, traduction française, texte en turc de Tur-
      quie, facsimilé. Alexandrie: Soc. de public. égyptiennes 1928. 64
      pp., 4 pl. 8°
      Rejoinder:
      Prof. Dr. Riza Nour [Riẓâ Nûr]: *Réponse à un article de M. Paul
      Pelliot sur l'Oughouz-namé.* Alexandrie: Société de publications
      égyptiennes 1931. 41 pp. 4°
      [«Il a cherché, avec beaucoup de soin, de fautes dans mon travail. Il a
      mis même en cause des choses insignificantes qui ne prêtent pas à la
      discussion. Il a voulu leur donner de l'importance; de là une partie de
      ses erreurs ...»]
      Rev.: *Deutsche Wacht* 17.1931:13, p. 31 (E. von Zach)

459. Les bronzes de la collection Eumorfopoulos publiés par M. W. P.
      Yetts (I et II). Par Paul Pelliot.
      TP 27.1930,359-406
      On: W. Perceval Yetts: *The George Eumorfopoulos Collection.
      Catalogue of the Chinese & Corean bronzes, sculpture, jades,
      jewellery and miscellaneous objects.* Vol.1: Ritual and other vessels,
      weapons etc. London: Ernest Benn 1929. XII,89 pp., 75 pl., 25 of

which in colour. 2° Vol.2: Bronzes: Bells, drums, mirrors etc. Ibid. 1930. VIII,99 pp., 75 pl., 25 of which in colour. 2°

460. Arnold Vissière. Par Paul Pelliot.
     TP 27.1930,407-420
     [With list of publications (150 entries).]

461. L'ambassade de Manoel de Saldanha à Pékin. [1670.]
     TP 27.1930,421-424
     Paul Pelliot

462. «Tchin-mao» ou Tch'en Ngang 陳昂? [*tsung-ping* 總兵 in Kuang-tung, 1717.]
     TP 27.1930,424-426
     Paul Pelliot

463. [rev.] Annemarie von Gabain: Ein Fürstenspiegel: Das Sin-yü des Lu Kia. Inaugural-Dissertation zur Erlangung der Doktorwürde der Hohen Philosophischen Fakultät der Friedrich-Wilhelm-Universität zu Berlin. Berlin 1930. 82 pp. 8° (From: Mitt. des Seminars für Orientalische Sprachen, 1.Abt. Vol. 33.1930.)
     TP 27.1930,429-434
     Paul Pelliot
     Rev.: *Deutsche Wacht* 17.1931:13, pp. 29-31 (E. von Zach)

464. Livres reçus.
     TP 27.1930,435-449

465. Les nouvelles provinces chinoises.
     TP 27.1930,450
     P. P.

466. Georges Bouillard. (Nécrologie.) [† Sept. 5, 1930.]
     TP 27.1930,454-457
     P. Pelliot

467. Antoine Charignon. (Nécrologie.) [† Aug. 17, 1930.]
     TP 27.1930,457-458
     P. Pelliot

468. W. Barthold. (Nécrologie.) [† Aug. 20, 1930.]
     TP 27.1930,458-459
       P. Pelliot

1931
469. Les formes turques et mongoles dans la nomenclature zoologique du
     «Nuzhatu-'l-ḳulûb». Par Paul Pelliot.
     *Bulletin of the School of Oriental Studies.*6.1931,555-580
     Re: Lieut.-Colonel J. Stephenson: *The zoological section of the
     Nuzhatu-l-Qulûb of Ḥamdullâh al-Mustaufî al-Qazwînî*, edited, trans-
     lated and annotated. London 1928. XIX,100,127 pp. 8° (Oriental
     Translation Fund. NS 30.)

470. Un témoignage éventuel sur le christianisme à Canton au XIe siècle.
     Par Paul Pelliot.
     Mélanges chinois et bouddhiques 1.1931/32 (1932),217-219

471. Le prof. P. Pelliot (Paris): Le tâches urgentes de la sinologie.
     Congrès international des Orientalistes. Actes. 18. Leiden 1931
     (1932),134-135

472. *Les explorations et les fouilles en Asie centrale depuis 1900.* Allo-
     cution de M. Henri Berr. Conférence de M. Paul Pelliot.
     Paris: La Renaissance du livre 1931,291-307
     From *Revue de synthèse.* 51.1931,291-307

473. Paul Pelliot: *La Haute Asie.*
     (Paris:) L'édition artistique J. Goudard (1931). 37 pp., 1 pl. With
     annex: Explorations et voyages dans la Haute Asie. 3 pp., 1 map
     Rev.: *Monumenta serica* 1.1935/36,203 (H. Bernard)

474. Addenda à la bibliographie des publications de G. Bouillard.
     TP 28.1931,87-88
       P. Pelliot

475. Singing sands. To the editor of *The Times.*
     TP 28.1931,86-87
       Trumpington, 3 march 1931. A. C. Moule
     [With notes by P. Pelliot.]

476. [rev.] Mario Longhena: *Viaggi in Persia, India e Giava di Nicolò de'
     Conti, Girolamo Adorno e Girolamo da Santo Stefano*. Milano:
     «Alpes» 1929. 259 pp. 8°
     TP 28.1931,89-92
     P. Pelliot

477. [rev.] Lim Boon Keng 林文慶 (Lin Wen-ch'ing): *The Li Sao, an
     elegy on encountering sorrows, by Ch'ü Yüan*. Introd. by Sir Hugh
     Clifford, prefaces by H. Giles, Rabindranath Tagore and Chen
     Huan-chang. Shanghai: Commercial Press 1929. XXVIII,200 pp., 3
     pl. 8°
     TP 28.1931,92-95
     P. Pelliot

478. [rev.] *Hôbôgirin. Dictionnaire encyclopédique du bouddhisme
     d'après les sources chinoises et japonaises*. Deuxième fascicle:
     Bombai – Busso-kuseki. Tokyo: Maison française 1930. pp.97-188,
     pl. 9-17, 1 folded tab. with fig. 42-43, 4 pp. Supplement. 8°
     TP 28.1931,95-104
     P. Pelliot

479. [rev.] (Ôtani Daigaku Library 大谷大學圖書館:) A *comparative
     analytical catalogue of the Kanjur division of the Tibetan Tripiṭaka
     edited in Peking during the K'ang-hsi era*, and at present kept in the
     Library of the Ôtani Daigaku Kyôto in which the contents of each
     sutra are collated with their corresponding parts in the existing
     Sanskrit, Pali and Chinese texts, and in which page-references to the
     Narthang and the Derge edition of the Tripitaka are also entered. 1-2.
     Kyôto: Ôtani Daigaku Library 1930-1931. 4,360 pp. large 8°
     TP 28.1931,104-108
     P. Pelliot

480. [rev.] S. M. Shirokogoroff: *Social organization of the Northern
     Tungus*, with introductory chapters concerning geographical distrib-
     ution and history of these groups. Shanghai: Commercial Press
     1929. XV,427 pp., 7 maps, 2 colour pl. 4°
     TP 28.1931,108-110
     P. Pelliot

481. [rev.] N. N. Poppe: *Dagurskoe narečie* («Le dialecte dahur»). Le-
ningrad: Ac. des sciences 1930. 176 pp. 8°
TP 28.1931,111-113
  P. Pelliot

482. [rev.] G. D. Sanžeev: *Mańčžuro-mongol'skie jazykovye paralleli.*
Leningrad 1930. 8° (From: Izvestija Ak. Nauk 1930,601-708).
TP 28.1931,113-118
  P. Pelliot

483. [rev.] André Wedemeyer: *Japanische Frühgeschichte.* Untersu-
chungen zur Chronologie und Territorialfassung von Altjapan bis
zum 5. Jahrhund. n. Chr. Tokyo 1930. XVI,346 pp., 3 maps. 8°
(Mitteilungen der Deutschen Gesellschaft für Natur- u. Völkerkunde
Ostasiens. Supplementband 11.)
TP 28.1931,118-125
  P. Pelliot

Livres reçus.
TP 28.1931,129-240
Not signed.

484. [rev.] Maurice Adam: Us et coutumes de la région de Peking d'après
le Je sia kieou wen k'ao 日下舊文考   ch.146-147-148. Pékin:
Nachbaur 1930. VIII,48 pp. 4°
TP 28.1931,129

485. [rev.] Maurice Adam: A propos de Ha-ta-men 哈達悶. [1927.] 4 pp.
4° (From: Journal de Pékin. May 21, 1927)
TP 28.1931,129

486. [rev.] Maurice Adam: Chen Mou Tch'ang 神木廠, le Hangar du
Bois-génie. Pékin: Polit. de Pékin 1927. 36 pp. 8° (Collection
«Politique de Pékin».)
TP 28.1931,130

487. [rev.] Maurice Adam: Description sommaire de 25 districts des environs de Pékin d'après le Je sia kieou wen k'ao ch.118 à 144. Pékin: Impr. des Lazaristes 1928. VII, 134 pp., 5 pl. 8°
V. M. Alekseev: Les problèmes de la littérature chinoise contemporaine (From: Revue de Paris. 1929, pp. 907-920)
TP 28.1931,130

488. [rev.] B. M. Alexéiev: Die chinesische Dichtung. (Sinica. 5.1930 117-133)
Angelico: Mélanges chronologiques chinois. 1ʳᵉ série. Pékin 1929. 119 pp. 8°, 2ᵉ serie. 1930. 155 pp. 8°
TP 28.1931,130

489. [rev.] Annual report of the Imperial Household Museums Tokyo and Nara for the year 1929. Tôkyô 1930. 8,103,3 pp. 8°
TP 28.1931,131

490. [rev.] J. Bacot: Dictionnaire tibétain-sanscrit par Tse-ring-ouang-gyal (Che riṅ dbaṅ rgyal). Reproduction phototypique. Paris: Geuthner 1930. 101 pp. (Buddhica.II,2.)
TP 28.1931,131

491. [rev.] W. Bang und A. von Gabain: Türkische Turfan-Texte.3. Berlin 1930. 8° (Sitzungsberichte d. preuß. Akad. d.Wiss. Phil.-hist. Kl. 1930,183-211, 2 pl.)
TP 28.1931,131

492. [rev.] W. Bang und A. von Gabain: Türkische Turfan-Texte.4. Berlin 1930. 20 pp. 8° (Sitzungsber. d. preuß. Akad. d. Wiss. Phil.-hist. Kl. 1930,434-450.)
TP 28.1931,131-132

493. [rev.] W. Bang und A. von Gabain: Uigurische Studien.1. From: Ungar. Jahrbücher.10.1930,193-210.
TP 28.1931,132

494. [rev.] (W. Barthold:) Ḥudûd al-'alem. Rukopiś Tumanskogo, s vvedeniem i ukazatelem V. Bartol'da. Leningrad: Akad. nauk 1930. 45,78 pp. 8°

TP 28.1931,132-134

495. [rev.] Georges Bataille: Les monnaies des Grands Mongols. Paris: Florange. 32 pp. 4° From: Aréthuse.13/14.1926/27.
TP 28.1931,134

496. [rev.] Festbundel uitgegeven door het Koninklijk Bataviaasch Genootschap van Kunsten en Wetenschappen bij gelegenheid van zijn 150-jarig bestaan 1778-1928. 2.pt. Weltevreden: G. Kolff 1929. II,437 pp. 8°
TP 28.1931,134

497. [rev.] Luigi Foscolo Benedetto: Di una pretesa redazione latina che Marco Polo avrebbe fatta del suo libro. Firenze: Olschki 1930. 12 pp. 8° From: Arch. Stor. Ital. VII,13.1930, 207-216.
TP 28.1931,134

498. [rev.] Luigi Foscolo Benedetto: Perché fu chiamato «Milione» il libro di Marco Polo. From: Marzocco. Firenze Sept. 14, 1930.
TP 28.1931,135

499. [rev.] Emile Benveniste: The Persian religion according to the chief Greek texts. Paris: Geuthner 1929. 121 pp. 12°
TP 28.1931,135

500. [rev.] Bibliographie bouddhique.1.1928/1929. Paris: Geuthner 1930. XII,64 pp. 4° (Buddhica.II,3.)
TP 28.1931,135-136

501. [rev.] Carl W. Bishop: The find at Hsin Chêng Hsien. From: Artibus Asiae.1928/29,110.
TP 28.1931,136

502. [rev.] Davidson Black: Preliminary notice of the discovery of an adult Sinanthropus skull at Chou Kou Tien. Peking 1929. 8° From: Bull. Geol. Soc. of China. 8, pp. 207-211, 9 pl.
TP 28.1931,136

503. [rev.] Davidson Black: Interim report on the skull of Sinanthropus. Peiping 1930. 8° From: Bull. Geol. Soc. of China.9, pp.7-10, 6 pl.
TP 28.1931,136

504. [rev.] Davidson Black: Notice of the recovery of a second adult Sinanthropus skull specimen. Peiping 1930. 8° From: Bull. Geol. Soc. of China.9, no. 2, pp.97-98,1 pl.
TP 28.1931,136

505. [rev.] A. K. Bogdanov: K značeniju slov jigür-ê aγulγan v pišme il'-chana Arguna k Filippu Krasivomu. Dokl. Ak. Nauk. 1928,237-240.
TP 28.1931,136-137

506. [rev.] C. R. Boxer: Dom Francisco da Gama, Conde da Vidigueira e sua viagem para a India no ano de 1622, Combate naval de Moçambique em 23-25 de Julho de 1622. Lisboa: Imprensa de Armada 1930. 24 pp., 1 pl. 8° From: Anais do Club Militar Naval. No. 5/6.1930.
TP 28.1931,137

507. [rev.] C. R. Boxer: Uma desconhecida vitória naval portuguesa no século XVII. Lisboa 1929. 14 pp. 8° From: Bol. da Ag. Geral das Col. Nʳᵒ. 52.
TP 28.1931,137

508. [rev.] C. R. Boxer: Nuno Alvares Botelho e a sua armada de alto bordo (1624-1625). Porto 1928. 30 pp. 8°
TP 28.1931,138

509. [rev.] C. R. Boxer: A situação dos Portugueses no Japão em 1635 From: Bol. da Ag. Geral das Col. No. 64.1930,47-55.
TP 28.1931,138

510. [rev.] C. R. Boxer: A Portuguese embassy to Japan (1644-1647). London: Kegan Paul 1928. VIII,64 pp., 3 pl. From: Transact. of the Japan Soc. 25.1927/28.
TP 28.1931,138

511. [rev.] Juliet Bredon: Le roman d'une ville interdite. Pékin: Polit. de
Pékin 1930. 61 pp. 8°
TP 28.1931,138-139

512. [rev.] C. Brockelmann: Mitteltürkischer Wortschatz nach Maḥmûd al-
Kâšγarîs Dîvân luγât at-Turk. Budapest, Leipzig 1928. VI,252 pp. 8°
(Bibl. Orient. Hungarica.1.)
TP 28.1931,139

513. [rev.] René Cagnat: Notice sur la vie et les travaux de M. Henri
Cordier. Paris: Firmin-Didot 1929. 20 pp., 1 portr. (Publ. de
l'Institut.1929, 29ter.)
TP 28.1931,139

514. [rev.] N. P. Chakravarti: L'Udânavarga sanskrit. T.1.(ch. I à XXI).
Paris: Geuthner 1930. 272 pp. 8° (Mission Pelliot en Asie Centrale.
Série petit in-octavo.4.)
TP 28.1931,139

515. [rev.] G. L. M. Clauson: The geographical names in the Staël-Holstein scroll. From: JRAS.1931,297-309.
TP 28.1931,139-141

516. [rev.] Georges Cœdès: Etudes cambodgiennes.23/24. From: BEFEO
29.1929,289-330.
Georges Cœdès: Les inscriptions malaises de Srîvijaya. 52 pp.,7 pl.
From: BEFEO 30.1930, 29-80.
TP 28.1931,141

517. [rev.] William Cohn: Chinese art. London: The Studio 1930. XVI,75
pp., 1 frontisp., 56 pl. 8°
TP 28.1931,141-142

518. [rev.] Eudore de Colomban (= Mr Gervaix): Histoire abrégé de
Macao. Pékin: Impr. de la «Polit. de Pékin» 1928. 143, 136 pp. 8°
TP 28.1931,142

519. [rev.] August Conrady: Das älteste Dokument zur chinesischen
     Kunstgeschichte, T'ien-wen Die «Himmelsfragen» 天問 des K'üh
     Yüan, beendet von Ed. Erkes. Leipzig: Asia Major 1931.VIII,267
     pp. 8°
     TP 28.1931,142

520. [rev.] Ananda K. Coomaraswamy, Francis Stewart Kershaw: A
     Chinese buddhist water vessel and its Indian prototype. From: Arti-
     bus Asiae.1928/29,122-141.
     TP 28.1931,142-143

521. [rev.] Ananda K. Coomaraswamy: Pali kaṇṇikâ = circular roof-plate.
     The parts of a viṇâ. From: JAOS 50, pp.238-253, 1 pl.
     TP 28.1931,143

522. [rev.] J. Daridan, S. Stelling-Michaud: La peinture séfévide d'Ispa-
     han: Le palais d'Alâ Qapy. Paris: Les Beaux-Arts 1930. 24 pp., 21
     pl. 4°
     TP 28.1931,143

523. [rev.] Henri Dehérain: Orientalistes et antiquaires. La vie de Pierre
     Ruffin, orientaliste et diplomate 1742-1824. T.1. Paris: Geuthner
     1929. VIII,292 pp.,1 map, 8 pl. 8°
     TP 28.1931,143-144

524. [rev.] H.-R. Diwekar: Les fleurs de rhétorique dans l'Inde. Paris:
     Maisonneuve 1930. 133 pp. 8°
     TP 28.1931,144

525. [rev.] Dragages de Cochinchine, Canal Rachgia-Hatien. Saigon
     1930. 81 pp.,15 pl, 4 maps. 8°
     TP 28.1931,144

526. [rev.] André Duboscq: La Chine et le Pacifique. Paris: Fayard 1931.
     204 pp. 12°
     TP 28.1931,144

527. [rev.] J. J. L. Duyvendak: Het sinologisch Instituut. Leiden: Brill
1930. 15 pp. 8°
TP 28.1931,144

528. [rev.] J. J. L. Duyvendak: Historie en confucianisme. Leiden: Brill
1930. 32 pp. 8°
TP 28.1931,144-145

529. [rev.] P. Dr. Andreas Eckardt: Koreanische Musik. Tôkyô 1930. 63
pp.,24 pl. 8° (Mitt. d. Dt. Gesellschaft f. Natur- u.Völkerkunde Ost-
asiens.24 B.)
TP 28.1931,145

530. [rev.] Robert Eisler: Das Geld, seine geschichtliche Entstehung und
gesellschaftliche Bedeutung. München: Verlag der Diatypie 1924.
383 pp. 8°
TP 28.1931,145-146

531. [rev.] Pasquale M. d'Elia, S.J.: Le triple démisme de Suen Wen. 2e
éd. Shanghai 1930. XXV,45,637 pp. 8°
TP 28.1931,146

532. [rev.] Eduard Erkes: A neolithic Chinese idol? From: Artibus Asiae.
1928/29,141-143.
TP 28.1931,146

533. [rev.] Ed. Erkes: Aus den Beständen des Rautenstrauch-Joest-Muse-
ums. Eine merkwürdige chinesische Bronze. Leipzig: Wiegandt
1930. 4 pp. 4° From: Ethnologica.4.
TP 28.1931,146-147

534. [rev.] J. Escarra: Le régime des concessions étrangères en Chine.
Paris: Hachette 1929. 140 pp. 8°
TP 28.1931,147

535. [rev.] Jean Escarra: La loi chinoise sur les effets de commerce du 30
octobre 1929. Paris: Rousseau 1930. 28 pp. 8° From: Ann. de droit
commercial français.1930, no. 1.
TP 28.1931,147

536. [rev.] Jean Escarra: La loi chinoise sur les assurances du 30 décembre 1929. Paris 1930. 18 pp. 8° From: Rev. gén. des assurances terrestres. Mai-juin 1930.
TP 28.1931,147

537. [rev.] Jean Escarra: La codification contemporaine du droit privé chinois. Agen 1930. 43 pp. 8° From: Bull. de la Soc. de legisl. comparée.
TP 28.1931,147

538. [rev.] Les études chinoises. (Bruxelles) 1930. 1,24 pp. 8°
TP 28.1931,147

539. [rev.] N. Fettich: Bronzeguß und Nomadenkunst auf Grund der ungarländischen Denkmäler. Prag: Seminarium Kondakovianum 1929. 96 pp., 17 pl. 4° (Σκυθικα.2.)
TP 28.1931,148-149

540. [rev.] Spedizione italiana de Filippi nell' Himalaya, Caracorúm e Turchistàn Cinese (1913-1914). I,3. Bologna: N. Zanichelli (1931). XIX,565 pp. 4°
TP 28.1931,149

541. [rev.] R. Pampanini, D. Vinciguerra: Raccolte di piante e di animali. Bologna: Zanichelli (1930). VII,315 pp.,8 pl. 4° (Spedizione italiana de Filippi nell' Himàlaia, Caracorùm e Turchestàn Cinese ‹1913-1914›.II,10.)
TP 28.1931,150

542. [rev.] (Louis Finot, Victor Goloubew:) Le temple d'Angkor Vat. Deuxième partie: La sculpture ornamentale du temple. Paris: Van Oest 1930.18 pp., pl.151-286. 2°
TP 28.1931,150

543. [rev.] Otto Fischer: Die chinesische Malerei der Han-Dynastie. Berlin: Paul Neff 1931. XI,150 pp., 80 pl. 4°
TP 28.1931,150

544. [rev.] K. K. Flug: Očerk istorii Daosskogo kanona (Dao Dzan'a).
Izv. Akad. nauk. 1930,239-250.
TP 28.1931,150-151

545. [rev.] Alfred Forke: Dichtungen der T'ang- und Sung-Zeit, aus dem
Chinesischen metrisch übertragen. Hamburg: Friederichsen 1929.
XII,173; 19,79 pp. 8°
TP 28.1931,151-152
Rev.: *Deutsche Wacht.*17.1931:21, pp.29-31 (E. von Zach)

546. [rev.] W. Sherwood Fox, R. E. K. Pemberton: Passages in Greek
and Latin literature relating to Zoroaster and Zoroastrianism, translated into English. Bombay: D. B. Taraporevala Sons (1928). 145,II
pp. (K. R. Cama Oriental Institute Publication. 4.)
TP 28.1931,152

547. [rev.] Howard Spilman Galt: The development of Chinese educational theory. Shanghai: Commercial Press 1929. VII,180 pp. 8°
TP 28.1931,152-153

548. [rev.] E. Gaspardone: Matériaux pour servir à l'histoire d'Annam.1.
La géographie de Li Wen-fong 李文鳳 From: BEFEO 29.1930,63-
105.
TP 28.1931,153-154

549. [rev.] G. K. Gins: Ètičeskie problemy sovremennogo Kitaja.
Charbin: Russko-Mańčžur. Knigotorg. 1927. 80 pp. 8°
TP 28.1931,154

550. [rev.] Daisy Goldschmidt: L'art chinois. Paris: Garnier 1931. 211
pp. 12°
TP 28.1931,154-155

551. [rev.] René Grousset: Les civilisations de l'Orient. T.1. L'Orient.
Paris: Crès 1929. II,362 pp. 8° T.2. L'Inde. Ibid. 1930. II,371 pp.;
T.3. La Chine. Ibid. 1930. 360 pp. T.4. Le Japon. Ibid. 1930. VIII,
321 pp.
TP 28.1931,155

552. [rev.] Erich Haenisch: Das Ts'ing-shi-kao und die sonstige chine-
     sische Literatur zur Geschichte der letzten 300 Jahre. From: Asia
     major.6.1930,403-444.
     TP 28.1931,155-156

553. [rev.] Erich Haenisch: Sinologie. From: Festschrift Friedrich
     Schmidt-Ott, 262-274.
     Erich Haenisch: Aus ostasiatischen Bibliotheken und Archiven.
     Forschungen und Fortschritte.6.1930,87.
     TP 28.1931,156

554. [rev.] Erich Haenisch: Untersuchungen über das Yüan-ch'ao pi-shi,
     die Geheime Geschichte der Mongolen. Leipzig: S. Hirzel 1931. 100
     pp., large 8° (Abhandlungen der phil.-hist. Kl. der sächs. Akademie
     der Wiss.41, no. 4)
     TP 28.1931,156-157

555. [rev.] C. Hagenauer: Mélanges critiques. Tôkyô 1930. 98 pp., 1
     map. 8° From: Bulletin de la Maison Franco-japonaise.2, no. 3-4.
     TP 28.1931,157-158

556. [rev.] Louis Halphen: La fin du Moyen Age. 1.La désagrégation du
     monde mediéval (1285-1453). Paris: F. Alcan 1931. 569 pp. 8°
     (Peuples et civilisations. Histoire générale.7,1.)
     TP 28.1931,158-159

557. [rev.] E. S. Craighill Handy: The problem of Polynesian origins.
     Honolulu 1930. 27 pp. 8° (Pernice P. Bishop Museum Occasional
     Papers.9, no. 8.)
     TP 28.1931,159

558. [rev.] Olaf Hansen: Zur soghdischen Inschrift auf dem
     dreisprachigen Denkmal von Karabalgasun. Helsingfors 1930. 39
     pp., 1 pl. 8° (Journal de la Société finno-ougrienne. 44,2.)
     TP 28.1931,159-160

559. [rev.] C. Hentze: Beiträge zu den Problemen des eurasischen Tier-
     styles. OZ NF 6.1930, 150-169.
     TP 28.1931,160

560. [rev.] Ho Tchong-han: Code civil de la République de Chine, traduit
     ... Zikawei, Paris 1930. XXX,194 pp. 8°
     TP 28.1931,160

561. [rev.] Hu Shih : Hu Shih wen-ts'un 胡適文存 chi 3. Shanghai: Ya-
     tung t'u-shu-kuan 1930. 4 pen (4,16,1022 pp.)
     TP 28.1931,160-161

562. [rev.] Hu Shih 胡適: Shen-hui ho-shang i-chi 神會和尚遺集.
     Shanghai: Ya-tung t'u-shu-kuan 1930. 5,2,230 pp. 12° (1 pen).
     TP 28.1931,161

563. [rev.] Sung-nien Hsu (Hsü Chung-nien 徐仲年): Po Kyu-yi. From:
     Rev. de l'univ. de Lyon.1930,57-75.
     TP 28.1931,161

564. [rev.] J. Hugon, S.J.: Mes paysans chinois. Paris: Dillen 1930. 206
     pp. 8°
     TP 28.1931,161

565. [rev.] Vincenz Hundhausen: Das Westzimmer. Ein chinesisches
     Singspiel. Peking: Pekinger Verlag 1926. 356 pp.
     TP 28.1931,162

566. [rev.] Vincenz Hundhausen: Die Laute. Von Gau Ming. Ein chine-
     sisches Singspiel. Peking: Pekinger Verlag 1930. 469 pp. 8°
     TP 28.1931,162

567. [rev.] Ikeuchi Kwô 池內宏: Shinkyô-ô no Bôshi junkyô-hi to
     Shiragi no tôhoku kyô 真興王の戊子巡境碑と新羅の東北境.
     Tôkyô 1929. 3,3,97 pp., 1 map, 11 pl. (Koseki chôsa tokubetsu
     hôkoku.6.)
     TP 28.1931,162-163

568. [rev.] Izvestija Juridičeskogo Fakul'teta.6. Harbin 1928. 397 pp. 8°
     7.1929. 477 pp., 2 pl.
     TP 28.1931,163

569. [rev.] C. Ž. Žamcarano: Proizvedenija narodnoj slovesnosti Burjat. 1: Leningrad: Akad. nauk 1930. 166 pp. 8° (Obrazcy nar. slovesn. mong. plemen. Teksty.2.)
TP 28.1931,164

570. [rev.] Arvid Jongchell: Huo Kuang och hans tid. Täxter ur Pan Ku's Ch'ien Han Shu. Göteborg: Elanders boktryckeri 1930. VII,231 pp. 8°
TP 28.1931,164-165

571. [rev.] N. Kano: O fragmente staroj rukopisi «Literaturnogo sbornika» 文選 chranjaščegosja v Aziatskom Muzee Akademii Nauk. (Transl. from the Chinese by J. Ščuckij. From: Izv. Akad. nauk.1930, no. 2, pp.135-144.)
TP 28.1931,165-166

572. [rev.] Kao Lou: Conception d'une fédération mondiale. Paris: Recueil Sirey 1930. 117 pp. 8° (Bibl. de l'Acad. diplom. intern.1.)
TP 28.1931,166

573. [rev.] V. A. Kazakevič: 1.Namogil'nye statui v Darigange. 2. Poezdka v Darigangu. Leningrad 1930. 64 pp., 1 map, 16 pl. 8° (Mater. kom. po issled. mong. i tannu-tuv. nar. respublik i burjat-mong. ASSR.5.)
TP 28.1931,166-168

574. [rev.] Raymond Koechlin: Souvenirs d'un vieil amateur d'art de l'Extrême-Orient. Chalon-sur-Saône: E. Bertrand 1930. 112 pp. 12°
TP 28.1931,168

575. [rev.] Wilhelm Koppers: Tungusen und Miao. Ein Beitrag zur Frage der Komplexität der altchinesischen Kultur. Wien 1930. 4° From: Mitteilungen der Anthropolog. Gesellschaft in Wien.60.1930,306-319.
TP 28.1931,168-169

576. [rev.] P. W. Koppers: Die Frage des Mutterrechts und des Totemismus im alten China. Anthropos.25.1930,981-1002.
TP 28.1931,169-171

577. [rev.] Władysław Kotwicz: Contributions aux études altaïques.1-3.
     Lwów 1930. 105 pp. 8° From: Rocznik oriental.7, pp.130-234.
     TP 28.1931,171-172

578. [rev.] P. K. Kozlov: Kratkij otčet o Mongolo-Tibetskoj ėkspedicii
     gosudarstvennogo Russkogo geografičeskogo obščestva 1923-1926
     gg. Leningrad: Akad. nauk 1928. 47 pp.,11 pl., large 8° (Severnaja
     Mongolija.3.)
     TP 28.1931,172-173

579. [rev.] O. Kümmel: Neun chinesische Spiegel. OZ NF 6, pp.170-
     176.
     B. M. Kupleckij: Predvaritel'nyj otčet geologičeskoj ėkspedicii v
     Severnuju Mongoliju za 1926 god. Leningrad: Akad. nauk 1929. 49
     pp., 4 pl.,1 map. 8° (Mat. kom. po issled. mong. i tannu-tuvin. nar.
     respublik i burjat-mong. ASSR.1.)
     Marcelle Lalou: La version tibétaine des Prajñâpâramitâ. JA
     1929,II,87-102.
     Kenneth Scott Latourette: Chinese historical studies during the past
     nine years. Amer. Historical Review.35.1930,778-797.
     B. Laufer: Methods in the study of domestications. The Scientific
     Monthly.25. 1927,251-255.
     B. Laufer: The prehistory of television. The Scientific Monthly.
     27.1928, 455-459.
     TP 28.1931,174

580. [rev.] B. Laufer: The American plant migration. (From: The Atlantic
     Monthly.28.1929,239-251.)
     B. Laufer: Catalogue of a collection of Chinese paintings in the pos-
     session of Dr. Frederick Peterson. New York 1930. 51 pp. 8°
     TP 28.1931,175

581. [rev.] B. Laufer: The early history of felt. American Anthropo-
     logist.32.1930,1-18.
     TP 28.1931,175-176

582. [rev.] B. Laufer, Wilfrid D. Hambly, Ralph Linton: Tobacco and its
     use in Africa. Chicago: Field Museum 1930. 45 pp. 8°
     TP 28.1931,176

583. [rev.] B. Laufer: A Chinese-Hebrew manuscript, a new source for
     the history of Chinese Jews. American Journal of Semitic languages
     and lit. 44.1930,189-197.
     TP 28.1931,176-177

584. [rev.] B. Laufer: Geophagy. Chicago 1930. 8°
     Louis de La Vallée Poussin: Tathatâ and Bhûtatathatâ. Tôkyô: Taishô
     Univ. 1930. 8° From: Wogihara Commemorative Volume.
     TP 28.1931,177

585. [rev.] Louis de La Vallée Poussin: Notes bouddhiques. Bull. Cl. des
     L. et Sc. m. et p. Ac. R. de Belg.5,16.1930,9-39.
     TP 28.1931,177-178

586. [rev.] Louis de La Vallée-Poussin: Le dogme et la philosophie du
     bouddhisme. Paris: G. Beauchesne 1930. 213 pp. 12°
     Louis de La Vallée-Poussin: Vijñaptimâtratâsiddhi, la Siddhi de
     Hiuan-tsang, trad. et annoté. Paris: Geuthner 1928-1929. 820 pp.
     (Buddhica.I: Mémoires 1.5.)
     TP 28.1931,178

587. [rev.] Bimala Churn Law: A study of the Mahâvastu ... Calcutta,
     Simla: Thacker 1930. X,180 pp.,4 pl. 8°
     (Z. A. Lebedev, B. M. Kupleckij, E. E. Kostyleva, N. M. Pro-
     kopenko, B. B. Polynov, I. M. Krašennikov:) Predvaritel'nye otčety
     geologičeskoj, geochimičeskoj i počvenno-geografičeskoj ėkspedicii
     o rabotach, proizvedennych v 1925 godu. Leningrad: Akad. nauk
     1926. 163 pp., 9 pl., 5 maps 8°
     Li Choen: Le journal de Che Ta-kai 石大開. Episodes de la guerre des
     Taï ping, traduit. Pékin: Impr. de la «Politique de Pékin» 1927. 182
     pp., 1 pl. 8°
     TP 28.1931,179

588. [rev.] Li Tz-hiung: Abolition of extraterritoriality in China, with
     preface by Wei Tao-ming. Nanking: The Internat. Relations
     Committee 1929. IV,86 pp. 8°
     The Library of Congress, Division of Chinese Literature 1929-30.
     Washington 1930. 8°

Liu Fu 劉復: Tun-huang to-so 燉煌掇瑣 (Collection of fragments from Tun-huang). [Pei-p'ing] 2 pen. 4°
TP 28.1931,180-181

589. [rev.] Liu Fu 劉復, Li Chia-jui 李家瑞: Sung Yüan i-lai su-tzu p'u 宋元以來俗字譜 (Repertoire of popular characters since the Sung and Yüan periods). Pei-p'ing 1930. 6,8,137 pp., 2 pp. Errata; large 8°
TP 28.1931,181-182

590. [rev.] A. K. Lu: L'histoire de Fou Sang-siang. Pékin: Impr. de la Politique de Pékin 1928. 43 pp. 8° Chin. binding.
TP 28.1931,182

591. [rev.] Heinrich Lüders: Weitere Beiträge zur Geschichte und Geographie von Ostturkestan. Berlin 1930. 60 pp.,2 pl. 8° (Sitzungsberichte der Preuß. Akademie der Wissenschaften 1930.)
TP 28.1931,182-183

592. [rev.] Heinrich Lüders: Kâtantra und Kaumâralâta. Berlin 1930. 59 pp., 2 pl. 8° (Sitzungsberichte der Preuß. Akademie der Wiss. 1930, pp.482-538.)
TP 28.1931,183

593. [rev.] S. E. Malov: K istorii i kritike Codex Cumanicus (On history and criticism of Codex Cumanicus). Izv. Akad. Nauk 1930,347-375.
TP 28.1931,183-184

594. [rev.] S. E. Malov: Sitâtapatrâ-dhâraṇî v ujgurskoj redakcii (The S. in its Uigur version). Dokl. Akad. Nauk. 1930, no. 5, pp.88-94
TP 28.1931,185

595. [rev.] N. Ja. Marr: Jazyk i piśmo (Language and script). Leningrad 1930. 23 pp. 8° (Izv. Gos. Akad. ist. mat. kul't. VI,6.)
Henri Massé: L'islam. Paris: Armand Colin 1930. 221 pp. 16° (Collection Armand Colin.126.)
L. Massignon: Annuaire du monde musulman. 3e édition (1929). Paris: E. Leroux 1930. 484 pp. 8°
TP 28.1931,185

596. [rev.] N. Matsumoto: La légende de Kogorô le charbonnier. Tôkyô
     1930. 13 pp. 8° (Bull. Maison franco-jap. 2, no. 3-4.)
     Mélanges Charles Diehl. Etudes sur l'histoire et sur l'art de Byzance.
     Paris: E. Leroux 1930. 2 vols., large 4°
     I. I. Meščaninov: Kromlexi. Leningrad 1930. 30 pp. 8°
     TP 28.1931,186-187

597. [rev.] Ming Ch'ing shih-liao 明清史料 (Historical material of Ming
     and Ch'ing), publ. by Kuo-li chung-yang yen-chiu-yüan li-shi yü-
     yen yen-chiu-so. Shanghai 1930. 4 pen, 1 pl. 8°
     V. Minorsky: Tiflis. 1930. 8° From: Encycl. de l'Islâm, livr. M, 791-
     802.
     TP 28.1931,187

598. [rev.] N. D. Mironov: Kuchean studies. I. Indian loan-words in
     Kuchean. Lwów 1929. 81 pp., 2 pp. Addenda et Errata. 8° Rocznik
     oriental. 6, pp.89-169,274-276.
     Missions, séminaires, œuvres catholiques en Chine. 9e année,1928-
     1929. Changhai, Zi-ka-wei 1930. 76 pp. 8°
     Sushil Chandra Mitter: La pensée de Rabindranath Tagore. Paris: A.
     Maisonneuve 1930. 179 pp., 1 portr. 8°
     Jivanji Jamshedji Modi: Cama Oriental Institute Papers. Bombay:
     British India Press 1928. X,254 pp. 8°
     J. J. Modi: Anthropological papers. Pt. 4. Bombay: British India
     Press 1929. XVI,239,XVI pp. 8°
     J. J. Modi: Asiatic papers. Pt. 4. Bombay: Times of India Press
     1929. XIX,337 pp., 1 pl. 8°
     Edvige Toeplitz Mrozowska: La prima spedizione italiana attraverso i
     Pamiri (1929). Roma: R. Soc. Geogr. Ital. 1930. 56 pp., 36 pl., 2
     maps. 8°
     Paul Mus: Etudes indiennes et indochinoises.3: Les balistes du
     Bàyon. BEFEO 29.1929,331-341.
     TP 28.1931,188-189

599. [rev.] Nakao Manzo 中尾万三: Shokuryô honzô no kôsatsu
     食療本草の考察 (Investigation of the Shih-liao pen-ts'ao). Tôkyô:
     Maruzen 1930. 216,6 pp. 8°

Jiujiro Nakaya: Introduction à l'étude des figurines néolithiques au Japon (Résumé). Le Mans 1930. 11 pp. 8° From: Bull. Soc. préhist. franç. 1930, no. 9.
J. Nakaya: Contribution à l'étude de la civilisation néolithique du Japon. Rev. des arts asiatiqes 1930,151-167, 6 pl.
Jiujiro Nakaya: L'âge de pierre au Japon. Formes 4.1930,9-11, 2 pl.
Nan-Ming yeh-shih 南明野史 (Inofficial history of the Southern Ming). Shanghai: Commercial Press 1930. 3 pen. 12°. 2,49,76,95,1 fol.
M. F. Nejburg [Neuburg]: Geologičeskie issledovanija v rajone xr. Batyr-Xairxan (severo-zapadnaja Mongolija) v 1926 g. (Geological investigations in the area of the Batir-Xair-Xan range). Leningrad: Ak. nauk 1929. 29 pp., 1 map, 2 pl. (Mat. kom. po issled. mong. i tannu-tuv. nar. respublik i burjat-mong ASSR.7.)
TP 28.1931,190-191

600. [rev.] J. Németh: Die petschenegischen Stammesnamen. Ungar. Jahrb. 10.1930,27-34.
Németh Gyula: Review on Aurélien Sauvageot: Recherches sur le vocabulaire des langues ouralo-altaïques. Nyelvtud. Közlem. 47. 1930,467-475.
Németh Gyula: A honfoglaló magyarság kialakulása. Budapest 1930. 351 pp. 8°
TP 28.1931,191-192

601. [rev.] Camille Notton: Annales du Siam. 1re partie: Chroniques de Suvaṇṇa Khamdëng, Suvaṇṇa K'ôm Khăm, Siṅhabavati. Paris: Charles Lavauzelle 1926. XXIX,216 pp. 8°
Observatoires de Zi-ka-wei. Calendrier-annuaire pour 1931 (29 année). Zi-ka-wei 1930. IV,106,115 pp., 16 pl., 16°
Panking: Les chevaliers chinois. Roman des mœurs et d'aventures. Traduit. Pékin: La Politique de Pékin 1922. 219 pp. 8°
Panking: Livre de cuisine d'un gourmet poète (Le Brillat-Savarin de la Chine). Traduit. Pékin: La Politique de Pékin 1924. 70 pp. 8°
P. Pasquier: Discours prononcé le 15 octobre 1930 au Grand Conseil des intérêts économiques et financiers de l'Indochine. Hanoi: Impr. d'Extr.-Or. 1930. 124 pp. 8°
TP 28.1931,192-193

602. [rev.] [N. V. Pavlov, Ja. I. Proxanov, N. P. Ikonnikov-Galickij:]
     Predvaritel'nyj otčet botaničeskoj ėkspedicii v Severnuju Mongoliju
     za 1926 god (Preliminary report on the botanical expedition to
     Northern Mongolia, 1926). Leningrad: Ak. Nauk 1929. 131 pp., 14
     pl., 3 maps (Mat. kom. po issled. mong. i tannu-tuvin. nar.
     respublik i burjat-mong. ASSR.2.)
     W. C. Pei: An account of the discovery of an adult Sinanthropus
     skull in the Chou Kou Tien deposit. Peiping 1929. Bull. Geol. Soc.
     of China.8, pp.203-205.
     Paul Pelliot: L'origine des relations de la France avec la Chine: Le
     premier voyage de «L'Amphitrite» en Chine. Paris: Geuthner 1930.
     79 pp. 4° From: Journal des Savants 1928 and 1929.
     Aurelio Peretti: Per la storia del testo di Marco Polo. Florenz: Olschki
     1930. 33 pp. 8° From: Arch. Stor. Ital. VII,13.1930,217-247
     TP 28.1931,193-194

603. [rev.] [B. B. Polynov, V. I. Lisovskij, N. Lebedev, Ju. S. Ne-
     ustruev, A. Krištofovič, I. P. Xomenko:] Predvaritel'nyj otčet po–
     čvenno-geografičeskoj ėkspedicii v Severnuju Mongoliju v 1926
     godu (Preliminary report on the soil science-geographical expedition
     to Northern Mongolia, 1926). Leningrad: Ak. Nauk 1930. 149 pp.,
     9 pl., 2 maps (Mat. kom. po issled. mong. i tannu-tuv. nar.
     respublik i burjat-mong. ASSR.9.)
     [N. N. Poppe, N. B. Bambaev:] Predvaritel'nyj otčet lingvističeskoj
     ėkspedicii v Severnuju Mongoliju za 1926 god (Preliminary report on
     the linguistic expedition ito Northern Mongolia, 1926). Leningrad:
     Ak. Nauk 1929. 74 pp., 2 pl. (Mat. kom. po issled. mong. i tannu-
     tuv. nar. respublik i burjat-mong. ASSR.4.)
     N. N. Poppe: Alarskij govor (The Alar dialect). 1st pt. Leningrad
     1930. 130 pp. 8° (Mater. kom. po issled. mong. i tuvinskoj narodn.
     respublik i burjat-mong. ASSR.11.)
     J. Przyluski: Emprunts anaryens en indo-aryen. Bull. Soc. Ling.
     30.1930,196-201.
     TP 28.1931,194-195

604. [rev.] J. Przyluski: La croyance au messie dans l'Inde et dans l'Iran à
     propos d'un livre récent. 12 pp. From: Rev. hist. des relig. July/
     Aug.1929.

Jean Przyluski: Un ancien peuple du Penjab: les Salva. JA 1929,I, 311-354.
Jean Przyluski: Pre-Dravidian or Proto-Dravidian. Indian historical quarterly. 6.1930,145-149.
J. Przyluski: La théorie des Guṇa. Bulletin of the School of Oriental Studies 6.1930,25-35.
J. Przyluski: Açvaghoṣa et la Kalpanâmaṇḍitikâ. Bull. de la classe des lettres et des sciences morales et pol. de l'Ac. R. de Belgique.V,16.1931,425-434.
Giorgio Pullé: Viaggi a' Tartari di frate Giovanni da Pian del Carpine (Historia Mongalorum). Milano: Ed. «Alpes» 1929. 240 pp. 12°
TP 28.1931,196-197

605. [rev.] Dr. G. R. Rachmati: Zur Heilkunde der Uiguren. Forschungen und Fortschritte.6.1930,436.
Dr. G. R. Rachmati: Zur Heilkunde der Uiguren. Berlin 1930. 25 pp., 2 pl. (Sitzungsberichte d. pr. Akad. d. Wiss., Phil.-hist. Kl. 1930,451-473.)
J. Rahder: Groot-Indië. Utrecht: J. van Druten 1930. 33 pp. 8°
TP 28.1931,198-199

606. [rev.] Salomon Reinach: Amalthée. Mélanges d'archéologie et d'histoire.1. Paris: Leroux 1930. VIII,449 pp.; 2. 502 pp.
Louis Renou: Grammaire sanscrite.2: Le nom, le verbe, la phrase. Paris: A. Maisonneuve 1930, pp. 273-576.
Prof. V. Riasanovsky: Fundamental institutions of Chinese civil law. Harbin: Chin. Eastern Railway 1926. 74 pp. 12°
Prof. V. Rjazanovskij: Mongol'skoe pravo (preimuščestvenno obyc-ˇnoe); istoričeskij očerk. The Mongolian law (with special reference to the customary law). Harbin 1931. 306, 42,II pp. 8°
Dr. Friedrich Risch: Johann de Plano Carpini. Geschichte der Mongolen und Reisebericht 1245-1247, übersetzt und annotiert. Leipzig: Ed. Pfeiffer 1930. XVI,405 pp. (Veröff. des Forschungs-Inst. f. vergleich. Religionsgeschichte an der Univ. Leipzig.II,2.)
TP 28.1931,200-202

607. [rev.] P. Rivet: Sumérien et Océanien. Paris: Champion 1929. 61 pp. 8° (Coll. ling. publiée par la Soc. de Ling. de Paris.24.)

Sir E. Denison Ross: Nomadic movements in Asia. London 1929. 45 pp. 8°

Michel Rostovcev: Le porte-épée des Iraniens et des Chinois. Paris: Paul Geuthner 1930 (L'art byzantin chez les Slaves. 1ʳᵉ recueil),337-346, 2 pl.
TP 28.1931,202-204

608. [rev.] J. Helen Rowlands: La femme bengalie dans la littérature du Moyen Age. Paris: Maisonneuve 1930. VII,243 pp. 8°

L. Sabatier: Palabre du Serment au Darlac. Assemblée des chefs de tribus. 1ᵉʳ janvier 1926. Hanoi 1930. 96 pp. 8°

A. Salmony: Eine neolithische Menschendarstellung in China. IPEK 1929,31-34, 2 pl. 4°

G. Sanžeev: Pesnopenija alarskich Burjat (Songs of the Buriats of Alar). Leningrad 1929. Zap. Kol. Vostokovedov.3, pp.459-552.

G. D. Sanžeev: Fonetičeskie osobennosti govora nižneudinskich Burjat (Peculiarities of the Buriat dialect of Nižne-Udinsk). Leningrad 1930. 11 pp. 8°

G. D. Sanžeev: Darxaty, ětnografičeskij otčet o poezdke v Mongoliju v 1927 godu (The Darxat. Report on a trip to Mongolia, 1927). Leningrad 1930. 64 pp. 8° (Mat. kom. po issled. mong. i tuv. nar. respublik i burjat-mong. ASSR.10.)

La satire chinoise politique et sociale, année 1927. Pékin: Impr. de la Politique de Pékin 1927. 44 pp. 4°

Seu Ring-hai: Autour d'une vie coréenne. 3ᵉ éd. Paris: Agence Korea 1929. 189 pp. 12°
TP 28.1931,204-206

609. [rev.] Sadahiko Shimada 島田貞彦, Sueji Umehara 梅原末活, Tanenobu Aoyagi青柳種信: Studies on the prehistoric sites at Okamoto, Suku in the province of Chikuzen (by Shimada)島田, with: Essay on the ancient mirrors from Suku (by Umehara), and appendix: Illustrated description of ancient objects found at Mikumo Village, Ido-gun in Chikuzen Province (by Aoyagi). Chikuzen Suku shizen iseki no kenkyû 筑前須玖史前遺跡の研究. Kyôto 1930. 8,1,115,36 pp. Japan., 28 pp. Engl., 1 coloured frontisp., 69 pl. (Reports upon archaeol. res. in the Dept. of Lit., Kyôto Imp. Univ. 11.1928/1930.)

S. M. Shirokogoroff: Phonetic notes on a Lolo dialect and consonant
L. Peiping 1930. Bull. of the Nat. Research Inst. of Hist. and Phil.,
Academia sinica.1,2, pp.183-225.
Shôwa shi-nen no kokushi gakukai 昭和四年の國史學界　(Studies
in national history. 1929). Tôkyô 1930. 1,73,42 pp.
TP 28.1931,206-207

610. [rev.] Walter Simon: Tibetisch-chinesische Wortgleichungen. Berlin,
Leipzig: de Gruyter 1930. 72 pp. From: Mitteilungen des Seminars
für Orientalische Sprachen.32.1929, 1.Abt., 157-228.
Jules Sion: Asie des moussons.1-2. Paris: Colin 1928-1929. 548
pp., 96 pl., 2 maps. 8°
Steinilber-Oberlin: Les sectes bouddhiques japonaises. Histoire;
doctrines philosophiques; textes; les sanctuaires. Paris: G. Crès
1930. XVIII,347 pp., 1 frontisp.
Lt.-col. J. Stephenson: The zoological sections of the Nuzhatu-l-
Qulûb of Ḥamdullâh al-Mustaufî al-Qazwînî, edited, translated and
annotated. London 1928. XIX,100,127 pp. 8° (Oriental Translation
Fund.NS 30.)
O. Strauss: Albert von Le Coq† Orient. Literaturzeitung.1930,393-
398.
TP 28.1931,208-210

611. [rev.] Daisetz Teitaro Suzuki: Studies in the Lankavatara sutra.
London: Routledge 1930. XXXII,464 pp., 1 pl. 8°
TP 28.1931,210-212

612. [rev.] W. W. Tarn: Seleucid-Parthian studies. London: Humphrey
Milford [1930]. 33 pp. 8° From: Proceedings of the British
Academy.16.
Ch'en Li 陳澧: Tung-shu tu-shu chi 東塾讀書記. Shanghai: Com-
mercial Press 1930. 1 pen. 8°
Ch'en Chu 陳柱: Lao hsüeh pa p'ien 老學八篇 (Eight articles on
Lao-tzu). Shanghai: Commercial Press 1928. 3,1,151,4 pp. 8°
Ch'en Chu 陳柱 et al.: Ch'ing-ju hsüeh-shu t'ao-lun
清儒學術討論 (Studies on the works of Ch'ing scholars). 1st
series. 2 ch. Shanghai: Commercial Pr. 1930. 3,1,98 pp. 8°
Ch'eng Shu-te 程樹德: Shuo-wen chi-ku p'ien 説文稽古篇. Shang-
hai: Commercial Press 1930. 1 pen. 2,2,3,72,62 pp. 12°

TP 28.1931,212-214

613. [rev.] Tcheou Houan [Chou Huan]: Le prêt sur récolte institué en Chine au XIe siècle par le ministre novateur Wang-Ngan-Che. Paris: Jouve 1930. 150 pp. 8°
TP 28.1931,214-215

614. [rev.] Chung T'ai 鍾泰: Chung-kuo che-hsüeh shih 中國哲學史 (History of Chinese philosophy). Shanghai: Commercial Press 1929. 1,1,3,186,4,175 pp. 8°
Tchou Kia Kien [Chu Chia-chien], Armand Gandon: Ombres de fleurs. Pékin: Nachbaur 1930. 210 pp. 4°
P. Teilhard de Chardin S.J.: Une importante découverte en paléontologie humaine: le Sinanthropus Pekinensis. Louvain 1930. 16 pp. 8° From: Rev. des quest. scient. 1930.
Teilhard de Chardin; C. C. Young: Preliminary report on the Chou Kou Tien fossiliferous deposit. From: Bull. Geol. Soc. of China.8. 1929,173-202.
P. Teilhard de Chardin, C. C. Young: Preliminary observations on the pre-loessic and post-pontian formations in Western Shansi and Northern Shensi. Peiping 1930. 37 pp. Engl., 2,20 pp. Chin., 9 pl. (Geological memoirs [Contin. of Mem. Geol. Survey of China A,8.)
TP 28.1931,215-217

615. [rev.] F. W. Thomas: Tibetan documents concerning Chinese Turkestan.IV: The Khotan region. JRAS 1930,251-300.
Ting Shan 丁山: Shuo-wen chüeh-i chien 説文闕義箋 (Remarks on meanings missing in Shuo-wen.). Peiping: Institute of History and Philology 1930. 4,55 fol. 8° (Chuan-k'an.1.)
Mgr. E. Tisserant: Nestorienne (L'Eglise). In: A. Vacant: Dictionnaire de théol. catholique. fasc. 91/92. Paris: Letouzey 1930,158-288,313-323. 4°
TP 28.1931,217-220

616. [rev.] Tokiwa Daijô, Sekino Tadashi: Buddhist monuments in China. Text. Part 2. Tôkyô: Bukkyô-shiseki kenkyû-kai 1930. 5,142,5 pp. 4°
TP 28.1931,220-221

617. [rev.] F. M. Trautz: Professor Dr. F. W. K. Müller †18.April 1930 in memoriam. Berlin 1930. 7 pp. 4°
N. G. Tretčikov: Bibliografija finansov Kitaja (Bibliography of Chinese finances). Harbin 1930. 70 pp. 8°
Chiang Shan-kuo 蔣善國: Chung-kuo wen-tzu chih yüan-shih chi ch'i kou-tsao 中國文字之原始及其構造 (The origin of the Chinese script and its structure). Shanghai: Commercial Press 1930. 2 pen.
Dr. M. Y. Tsu: Aux lecteurs du «Triple démisme». Liège 1930. 8 pp. 8°
G. Tucci: The Jâtinirâkṛti of Jitâri. Annals of the Bhandarkar Or. Res. Institute [1930?], 54-58.
G. Tucci: The Nyâyamukha of Dignâga, the oldest Buddhist text on logic, after Chinese and Tibetan materials. Heidelberg 1930. 72 pp. 8° (Mat. z. K. d. Buddh. 15.)
TP 28.1931,221-223

618. [rev.] Giuseppe Tucci: Pre-Diṅnâga Buddhist text on logic from Chinese sources. Baroda: Oriental Institute 1929. XXX,40, 32,77, 89,91 pp. 8°
G. Tucci: On some aspects of the doctrines of Maitreya[nâtha] and Asaṅga. Calcutta 1930. 81 pp. 8°
G. Tucci: A fragment from the Pratitya-samutpada-vyakhya of Vasubandhu. JRAS 1930,611-623.
G. Tucci: Bhamaha and Dinnaga. Bombay 1930. 6 pp. 4° From: The Indian Antiquary.59.1930,142-147.
Boris Unbegaun: Catalogue des périodiques slaves et relatifs aux études slaves des bibliothèques de Paris. Avec préface d'André Mazon. Paris: Champion 1929. XIII,223 pp. (Travaux publiés par l'Institut d'études slaves.9.)
TP 28.1931,224-226

619. [rev.] C. S. Usov, Čžen Aj-tan [Cheng Ai-t'ang] 鄭愛堂: Učebnik kitajskogo razgovornogo jazyka (Textbook of the Chinese colloquial language). Harbin [1929-1930]. 4 parts in 9 fasc.
Louis Vanhée: Les séries en Extrême-Orient. Arch. di storia della scienza Archeion.12.1930,117-125.
La vie populaire à Pékin (année 1922). Pékin: La Politique de Pékin 1925. 164 pp.

B. Vladimircov: Kastren-mongolist. O. O. u. J.,87-92. From: Pamjati Kastrena.
B. Ja. Vladimircov, G. I. Borovka: Predvaritel'nye otčety lingvističeskoj i arxeologičeskoj ėkspedicii o rabotach, proizvedennyx v 1925 godu (Preliminary reports on work done in 1925 by the linguistic and archaeological expedition). Leningrad: Ak. Nauk 1927. 88 pp., 1 map, 10 pl. 8° (Severnaja Mongolija.2.)
B. Ja. Vladimircov: Ob odnom okončanii množestvennogo čisla v mongol'skom jazyke (On a plural ending in Mongolian). Dokl. Ak. Nauk 1926,61-62.
B. Ja. Vladimircov: Mongol'skoe nökür (Mongolian *nökür*). Doklady Ak. Nauk 1929,287-288.
B. Ja. Vladimircov: Po povodu drevne-tjurkskogo Ötüken yïš (On Old Turkic Ötüken yïš). Doklady Ak. Nauk 1929,133-136.
TP 28.1931,227-230

620. [rev.] B. Ja. Vladimircov: Geografičeskie imena orxonskich nadpisej, soxranivšiesja v mongol'skom (Geographical names of the Orxon inscriptions, preserved in Mongolian). Doklady Akad. Nauk 1929,169-174.
B. Ja. Vladimircov: Zametki k drevnetjurkskim i staromongol'skim tekstam (Remarks on Old Turkic and old Mongolian texts). Dokl. Ak. Nauk 1929,289-291.
B. Ja. Vladimircov: Mongol'skie tituly *beki* i *begi* (The Mongolian titles beki and begi). Doklady Ak. Nauk 1930,163-167.
B. Ja. Vladimircov: Popravki k čteniju mongol'skoj nadpisi iz Erdeni-dzu (Corrections to the reading of the Mongolian inscription of Erdeni-dzu). Doklady Ak. Nauk 1930,186-188.
TP 28.1931,230-232

621. [rev.] B. Ja. Vladimircov: Gde pjat' xalxaskix pokolenij - Tabun otoɣ xalxa (Where are the «Five Xalxa Tribes»?) Doklady Akad. Nauk 1930,201-205.
B. Ja. Vladimircov: Mongol'skoe ongniɣud - feodal'nyj termin i plemennoe nazvanie (Mongolian ongniɣud, feudal title and tribal name). Doklady Akad. Nauk 1930,218-223.
E. Waldschmidt: Wundertätige Mönche in der ostturkestanischen Hînayâna-Kunst. Ostasiat. Zeitschrift NF 6, pp.3-9.

Ernst und Rose Leonore Waldschmidt: Das Kunstgewerbe Süd- und
Hochasiens. Berlin: Wasmuth [1930] (=Helmuth Th. Bossert: Ge-
schichte des Kunstgewerbes.3, pp.181-344)
A. Waley: Notes on Chinese alchemy (supplementary to Johnson's A
study of Chinese alchemy). 24 pp. 8° From: Bulletin of the School of
Oriental Studies.6.1930.
S. T. Wang: L'histoire anecdotique chinoise sous les Tsing. Pékin:
La Politique de Pékin 1924. 236 pp. 8°
TP 28.1931,232-233

622. [rev.] Y. W. Wong 王雲五: Wong's system for arranging Chinese
     characters, the revised four-corner numerical system. Shanghai:
     Commercial Press 1928. 143 pp.
     Wang Yün-wu ta tz'u-tien 王雲五大辭典 (Large Dictionary by
     Wang Yün-wu). Shanghai: Commercial Press 1930. 3,2,1384,1,45,
     2,53 pp.
     Max Wegner: Ikonographie des chinesischen Maitreya. Berlin: de
     Gruyter 1930. 58 pp., 3 tab., 7 pl. From: Ostasiat. Zeitschr. 1929.
     Friedrich Weller: Kuci-Kuči-Küsän. Asia major 5.1930,319-323.
     Stuart N. Wolfenden: Outlines of Tibeto-Burman linguistic mor-
     phology, with special reference to the prefixes of classical Tibetan
     and the languages of the Kachin, Bodo, Nâgâ, Kuki-Chin and Burma
     groups. London: Royal Asiatic Society 1929. XV,216 pp. 8° (Prize
     Publication Fund.12.)
     TP 28.1931,234-236

623. [rev.] Yabuki Keiki 矢吹慶輝: Meisa yoin 鳴沙餘韻. Rare and
     unknown Chinese manuscript remains of Buddhist literature dis-
     covered in Tun-huang collected by Sir Aurel Stein and preserved in
     the British Museum. Tôkyô: Iwanami 1930. 9 fol., 104 pl., large 2°
     A. Ju. Jakubovskij: Razvaniny Urgenča (The ruins of Urgenč). Le-
     ningrad 1930. 68 pp., 5 pl. 8° (Izv. gos. Ak. ist. mat. kul'tury VI,2.)
     [Yamanaka Company:] Sekai minshû ko-geijutsu hin tenrankai
     世界民眾古藝術品展覽會 (Exhibitions of old specimens of folk art
     of the world). Ôsaka [1930]. 27 pl. and explan., 43 pp.
     TP 28.1931,236-239

624. [rev.] Yanai Watari 箭內互: Môko-shi kenkyû 蒙古史研究 (Researches on Mongolian history). Tôkyô 1930. 45,989,30,1, 117, 50 pp., 8 pl., 1 map. 8°
W. Perceval Yetts: Chinese tomb figures in silver. Ostas. Zeitschrift NF 5, pp. 211-215, 2 pl.
W. Perceval Yetts: A note on the Ying tsao fa shih. Bull. School of Oriental Studies.5.1930,855-859.
TP 28.1931,239-240

625. Nécrologie: Auguste Bonifacy. [† April 3, 1931.]
TP 28.1931,241
   P. Pelliot

626. Nécrologie: Guillaume Capus. [†April 27, 1931.]
TP 28.1931,241-242
   P. Pelliot

627. Nécrologie: Stanislas Chevalier, S. J. [† Oct. 27, 1930.]
TP 28.1931,242
   P. Pelliot

628. Nécrologie: Sir Charles Eliot. [† March 15, 1931.]
TP 28.1931,243-244

629. Nécrologie: Louis Wannieck. [† March 24, 1931.]
TP 28.1931,244
   P. Pelliot

630. Brèves remarques sur l'article de M. Chiu Bien-ming. Par Paul Pelliot.
TP 28.1931,343-345
Re: The phonetic structure and tone behaviour in Hagu (commonly known as the Amoy dialect) and their relation to certain questions in Chinese linguistics. By Chiu Bien-ming, University of Amoy. *TP* 28.1931,245-342

631. Une phrase obscure de l'inscription de Si-ngan-fou.
TP 28.1931,369-378
   Paul Pelliot

632. Sur quelques travaux chinois manuscrits concernant l'époque mon-
     gole.
     TP 28.1931,378-380
       P. Pelliot

     1. Yüan-shih kao 元史稿
     2. Yüan-ch'ao pi-shih shu-cheng 元朝秘史疏證
     3. Yüan-shih hsi-pei ti-li k'ao 元史西北地理考
     4. Ta Yüan sheng-cheng kuo-ch'ao tien-chang 大元聖政國朝典章

633. Une statue de Maitreya de 705.
     TP 28.1931,380-382
       P. Pelliot
     [Against W. Baruch in *Artibus Asiae* 1928/29,245-247.]

634. [rev.] Arthur Waley: A catalogue of paintings recovered from Tun-
     huang by Sir Aurel Stein, K.C.I.E., preserved in the Sub-
     Department of Oriental Prints and Drawings in the British Museum,
     and in the Museum of Central Asian Antiquities, Delhi. London:
     British Museum 1931. LII,328 pp. 4°
     TP 28.1931,383-413
       Paul Pelliot

635. [rev.] Arthur Waley: The travels of an alchemist. The journey of the
     Taoist Ch'ang-ch'un from China to the Hindukush at the summons
     of Chingiz Khan. Recorded by his disciple Li Chih-ch'ang.
     Translated with an introduction. London: Routledge 1931. XI,166
     pp., 1 map. 8° (Broadway Travellers.)
     TP 28.1931,413-428
       Paul Pelliot

636. [rev.] Dr. M. W. de Visser: Ancient Buddhism in Japan. Sûtra and
     ceremonies in use in the seventh and eighth centuries A. D. and their
     history in later times. T. 1. Paris: Geuthner 1931. X,423 pp.
     (Buddhica.I,3.)
     TP 28.1931,428-436
       P. Pelliot

637. [rev.] The Ocean of Story, being C. H. Tawney's translation of Somadeva's Kathâ Sarit Sâgara (or Ocean of streams of story), now edited with introduction, fresh explanatory notes and terminal essay by N. M. Penzer ... in ten volumes. Vol. 6, with preliminary note by A. R. Wright. London: Ch. J. Sawyer 1926. XXIII,332 pp.; Vol. 7, with preliminary note by M. Bloomfield. Ibid. 1927. XXXVII,302 pp.; Vol. 8, with preliminary note by W. R. Halliday. Ibid. 1927. XXXVII,361 pp.; Vol. 9, with preliminary note by Sir Atul Chatterjee. Ibid. 1928. XXIII,335 pp.; Vol. 10. Appendices and index. Ibid. 1928. 368 pp.
TP 28.1931,436-444
Paul Pelliot

638. [rev.] Emil Sieg und W. Siegling: Tocharische Grammatik, in Zusammenarbeit mit Wilhelm Schultze. Göttingen: Vandenhoeck 1931.VI,518 pp. 8°
TP 28.1931,444-450
P. Pelliot

639. [rev.] Edmond Buron: Ymago mundi de Pierre d'Ailly, Cardinal de Cambrai et Chancelier de l'Université de Paris (1350-1420). Paris: Maisonneuve 1930. 828 pp., 36 pl. 8°
TP 28.1931,450-452
P. Pelliot

640. [rev.] Otto Fischer: Die chinesische Malerei der Han-Dynastie. Berlin: Paul Neff 1931. XI,150 pp., 4 pp. ill., 80 pl. 4° Published in 250 copies.
TP 28.1931,452-457
Paul Pelliot

641. [rev.] Hans Reichelt: Die soghdischen Handschriftenreste des Britischen Museums in Umschrift und Übersetzung. 2.Teil: Die nicht buddhistischen Texte und Nachtrag zu den buddhistischen Texten. Heidelberg: Carl Winter 1931.VIII,80 pp., 9 pl. 8°
TP 28.1931,457-463
P. Pelliot

642. [rev.] W. Koppers: Der Hund in der Mythologie der zirkumpa-
     zifischen Völker. Wiener Beiträge zur Kulturgeschichte u. Lin-
     guistik.1.1930,359-399.
     TP 28.1931,463-470
       P. Pelliot

     Livres reçus.
     TP 28.1931,478-514

643. [rev.] Academia sinica. First annual report, 1928-1929
     國立中央研究院十七年度總報告 420 pp. 8°
     TP 28.1931,478-479

644. [rev.] Academia sinica. Second annual report, 1929-1930. 376 pp. 8°
     TP 28.1931,479

645. [rev.] The Academia sinica and its national research institutes. Nan-
     king 1931. 173 pp. 8°
     TP 28.1931,479

646. [rev.] Academia sinica. Bulletin of the National Research Institute of
     History and Philology.1,2-4 (1929); 2,1-2 (1930).
     TP 28.1931,479-491

647. [rev.] 沈刻元典章校補 Shen k'o Yüan tien-chang chiao-pu. By
     Ch'en Yüan 陳垣. Peiping: Sinolog. Institute of the National Univer-
     sity of Peiping 1931. 5 pen. 8°
     TP 28.1931,491-492

648. [rev.] Chinese chronological charts with index. Harvard-Yenching
     Institute Sinological Index Series. Supplement 1. Peking 1931.
     22,V,2 pp. 2°
     TP 28.1931,492-493

649. [rev.] Haneda Tôru 羽田亨: A propos des Ta-yue-tche 大月氏 et des
     Kouei-chouang 貴霜. Shigaku zasshi. 40, pp.1025-1054.
     TP 28.1931,493-495

650. [rev.] Haneda Tôru 羽田亨: Fragments de vœux de Manichéens en ouigour, trouvés à Turfan. 24 pp., 1 pl. From Kuwabara Festschrift.
TP 28.1931,495

651. [rev.] Haneda Tôru: A propos d'un rouleau fragmentaire d'une description de Cha-tcheou 沙州 et de Yi-tcheou 伊州 écrit la 1re année kouang-k'i des T'ang (885, ou plus précisément le 9 février 886). 22 pp., 1 pl. Offprint from Shigaku chirigaku ronsô, Ogawa Festschrift.
TP 28.1931,495-496

652. [rev.] Yoshita Harada 原田淑人: Lo-lang. A report on the excavation of Wang Hsü's tomb in the «Lo-lang» province of ancient Chinese colony in Korea, in cooperation with Kingo Tazawa 田澤金吾 and an appendix on bones, teeth, and hair by K. Kiyono. Tokyo: The Toko-Shoin 刀江書院 1930. Separate pagin. 4°
TP 28.1931,496-497

653. [rev.] William Hung 洪業: Indexing Chinese books. (1931). 13 pp., 2 pl. 8°
TP 28.1931,497-501

654. [rev.] Kuo-li Pei-p'ing t'u-shu-kuan yüeh-k'an 國立北平圖書館月刊. Bulletin of the National Library of Peiping.3.1929-4.1930.
TP 28.1931,501-502

655. [rev.] An-yang fa-ch'üeh pao-kao 安陽發掘報告 No 2. Peiping 1930. No 3. 1931.
TP 28.1931,503-507

656. [rev.] Osvald Sirén: Chinese and Japanese sculptures and paintings in the National Museum, Stockholm. London: E. Goldston 1931. 48 pp., 63 pl. 4°
TP 28.1931,507-508

657. [rev.] Hsü Hsü-sheng hsi-yu jih-chi 徐旭生西遊日記. Peking 1930. 3 pen. 8°
TP 28.1931,508-510

658. [rev.] B. Vladimircov: Arabskie slova v mongol'skom. Zap. Koll.
     Vostokovedov.5.1930,73-82.
     TP 28.1931,510-511

659. [rev.] Voctočnye zapiski.1. Leningrad 1927. 328 pp., 1 pl. 8°
     TP 28.1931,511-512

660. [rev.] Yin-te 引得. No. 1. Harvard-Yenching Institute Sinological
     Index Series. No. 1: Shuo-yüan yin-te 説苑引得. Peking 1931.
     VI,58 pp. 8°
     TP 28.1931,512-513

661. [rev.] Yin-te 引得. No. 2. Harvard-Yenching Institute Sinological
     Index Series. No. 2: Po-hu t'ung yin-te 白虎通引得. Peking 1931.
     XVI,33 pp. 8°
     TP 28.1931,513-514

662. Raymond Koechlin (Nécrologie). [† Nov. 9, 1931.]
     TP 28.1931,515
       Paul Pelliot

663. Albert Pouyanne. (Nècrologie.)[† Dec. 28, 1931.]
     TP 28.1931,516
       Paul Pelliot

664. Boris Jakovlevič [here: Yakovlovič] Vladimircov. (Nécrologie.) [†
     Aug. 17, 1931.]
     TP 28.1931,516
       P. P.

1932
665. Sceaux-amulettes de bronze avec croix et colombes provenant de la
     boucle du Fleuve jaune.
     Revue des arts asiatiques 7.1931/32,1-3, 8 pl.
       Paul Pelliot

666. [rev.] Otto Kümmel: *Jörg Trübner zum Gedächtnis*. Ergebnisse
     seiner letzten chinesischen Reisen. Berlin: Klinkhardt & Biermann
     1930. 148 pp., 84 pl., 1 portrait. 4° 300 copies.

Revue des arts asiatiques 7.1931/32,120
  P. Pelliot

667. Le vrai nom de «Seroctan». Par Paul Pelliot.
TP 29.1932,43-54
[Giovanni de Piano Carpini mentions a Christian Kerait woman, the
widow of Tului, under the name of Seroctan, the mother of the Great
Xans Möngke and Chubilai as well as the founder of the Moghul
dynasty in Persia, Hülägü. The correct form, according to Pelliot, is
Soryoqtani-bägi.]
Rev.: *Deutsche Wacht.*19.1933:5, p. 32 (E. von Zach)

668. Sur quelques manuscrits sinologiques conservés en Russie.
TP 29.1932,104-109
   Paul Pelliot
P. briefly describes the following manuskripts:
1. Moscow, Collection Skačkov Mss. 565 (51). 3 fasc. of *Yung-lo
ta-tien* 雍樂大典, containing the section *chan-ch'e'* jamči (mail
system), ch.19416-19423.
2. Ibid., Mss. 787 Liu-t'iao cheng-lei 六條政類. = *Yung-lo ta-tien*
ch.19423, perhaps 19421-19423.
3. Ibid., Mss. 787: *Copy of Yung-lo ta-tien* 雍樂大典 ch.17595.
4. Ibid. Mss. 323: *Yüan Shang-tu i-ch'eng k'ao* 元上都驛程考.
Quoted after Palladius' manuscript, see Bretschneider: *Recherches
archéologiques sur Pékin*, pp.88-89.
5. Ibid., Mss.213: Collection of memorials by the office of trans-
lators.
6. Ibid., Mss. 79: *Hsi-yü Lun-t'ai i-chi* 西域輪臺遺蹟.
7. Ibid., Mss. 187: *Chin-shih pu* 金史補, by Hang Shih-chün (1696-
1772). Unpublished.
8. Ibid., Mss. 1250: Includes *Hsi-hsia t'u* 西夏圖, from *Fan Wen-
cheng-kung chi* (Works of Fan Chung-yen, 989-1052).
9. Ibid., Mss. 562 (42): *Ku-chin ching-t''en chien* 古今敬天鑒,
author's preface 1707 Apparently a work of Father Joachim Bouvet
S.J. Cf. Pfister 561.
10. Leningrad, Coll. Lixačev: Ms. *O-lo-szu fan-i chieh-yao ch'üan-
shu* 俄儸斯繙譯捷要全書 (Manchu, Chinese and Russian).
Preface by Fulohe who translated the Russian grammar in cooperation with Larion Rossoxin and Aleksej Leont'ev.

669. Trois noms chinois de missionnaires sous K'ang-hi.
     TP 29.1932,109-111
       P. Pelliot
     [Regarding contributions by Ch'en Yüan and S. Kuwabara (*Shirin*
     11.1926,442-451), which deal with two documents from the imperial
     palace; they list the Chinese names of 18 missionaries, who had been
     ordered by the K'ang-hsi emperor to appear at audience on Dec. 17,
     1720. P. identifies three names that had remained obscure: An T'ai -
     Etienne Rousset; Hsü Ta-sheng - Jacques-Philippe Simonelli; Ni
     T'ien-chüeh - Jean-Baptiste Gravereau.]

670. Une liasse d'anciens imprimés chinois des Jésuites retrouvée à
     Upsal.
     TP 29.1932,114-118
       P. Pelliot
     1. João Soeiro: 天主聖教約言 Hangchou? 1650?
     2. Adam Schall: 進呈書像 Hangchou 1661?
     3. 論釋氏之非 Hangchou 1661.
     4. 關輪迴非理之正 Hangchou s. d.
     5. Without title. [Christian work on filial piety.] Hangchou?

671. [rev.] Masaharu Anesaki: A concordance to the history of Kirishitan
     missions (Catholic missions in Japan in the sixteenth and seventeenth
     centuries). Tokyo: Imp. Academy 1930. 225 pp., 1 map. 8° (Pro-
     ceedings of the Imperial Academy. Supplement to vol. 6.)
     TP 29.1932,122-125
       P. Pelliot

672. [rev.] Hans Fürstenberg: Kaiser Kien-lung's französisches Kup-
     ferstichwerk. Philobiblon.4.1931,371-377.
     TP 29.1932,125-127
       P. Pelliot

673. [rev.] Esson M. Gale: Discourses on Salt and Iron. A debate on state
     control of commerce and industry in ancient China, chapters I-XIX.
     Trad., avec introd. et notes. Leide 1931. LVI,165 pp. 8° (Sinica
     Leidensia.2.)
     TP 29.1932,127-130
       P. Pelliot

674. [rev.] Arthur W. Hummel: The autobiography of a Chinese historian,
     being a preface to a symposium on ancient Chinese history (Ku shih
     pien). Trad. et annotée. Leide: Brill 1931. XLII,199 pp. 8° (Sinica
     Leidensia.1.)
     TP 29.1932,130-135
     P. Pelliot

675. [rev.] Hans Jörgensen: Vicitrakarṇikâvadânoddhṛta. A collection of
     Buddhist legends. Nevârî text, edited and translated. London: Royal
     Asiatic Society 1931. 344 pp. 8° (Oriental Translation Fund. NS 31.)
     TP 29.1932,135-136
     P. Pelliot

676. [rev.] Quatre esquisses détachées relatives aux études orientalistes à
     Leiden. Leiden: Brill [1931]. 44 pp., 5 (not 6!) pl. 12°
     TP 29.1932,136-138
     P. Pelliot

677. [rev.] P. Johann Weig, SVD: Die chinesischen Familiennamen nach
     dem Büchlein Po-chia-hsing, nebst Anhang enthaltend Angaben über
     berühmte Persönlichkeiten der chinesischen Geschichte. Tsingtau:
     Missionsdruckerei 1931. X,1,285 pp. 8°
     TP 29.1932,138-140
     P. Pelliot

     Livres reçus:
678. [rev.] N. Adriani: Spraakkunst der Bare'e-Taal. Bandoeng: A. C.
     Nix 1931. VII,481 pp. 4° (Verhandelingen van het Koninklijk Bat.
     Genootschap van Kunsten en Wetenschappen.70.)
     V. M. Alekseev: Predposylki k latinizacii kitajskoj piśmennosti. Vest-
     nik Akademii Nauk.1931, no. 4, col.1-6.
     TP 29.1932,141

679. [rev.] Andreas Alföldi: Die geistigen Grundlagen des hochasiatischen
     Tierstiles. Forschungen und Fortschritte.7.1931,278-279.
     Andreas Alföldi: Die theriomorphe Weltbetrachtung in den hoch-
     asiatischen Kulturen. Arch. Anzeiger.1931, col. 393-418.
     L'annam. Hanoi: Imprimerie d'Extrême-Orient 1931. 227 pp. 8°
     TP 29.1932,141-142

680. [rev.] Annual report of the Imperial Household Museums Tokyo &
     Nara for the year 1930. Tôkyô: Imperial Household Museum 1931.
     9,180,3 pp. Japan., 10 pp. Engl. 8°
     TP 29.1932,142-143

681. [rev.] Hjalmar Appelgren-Kivalo: Alt-Altaische Kunstdenkmäler.
     Briefe und Bildermaterial von J. R. Aspelins Reisen in Sibirien und
     der Mongolei 1887-1889. Helsingfors 1931. IX,47 pp., 71 pl.,1
     add. pl., 1 map. 4°
     T. G. Aravamuthan: Portrait sculpture in South India. Introduction
     by A. K. Coomaraswamy. London: The India Society 1931.
     XVI,100 pp., 34 pl. 8°
     TP 29.1932,143-144

682. [rev.] H. d'Ardenne de Tizac: La sculpture chinoise. Paris: Van Oest
     1931. 51 pp., 64 pl. 4°
     G. Aymé: Monographie du Ve Territoire militaire. Hanoi: Imprimerie
     d'Extrême-Orient 1931. 178 pp., 53 ill., 6 sketch-maps. Preface by
     Lt.-Col. Bonifacy.
     TP 29.1932,144-145

683. [rev.] P. C. Bagchi: On some Tântrik texts studied in ancient Kam-
     buja. I-II. Indian historical review.5.1929,754-769; 6.1930,97-107.
     P. C. Bagchi: The Sandhâbhâṣâ and Sandhâvacana. Indian historical
     review. 6.1930,389-396.
     P. C. Bagchi: Sâdhanamâlâ. Indian historical review.6.1930,576-
     587.
     P. C. Bagchi: Śulika, Cûlika and Cûlika-paiśacî. Journal of the De-
     partment of Letters, University of Calcutta.21.1930. 10 pp.
     P. C. Bagchi: On foreign elements in the Tantra. Indian historical re-
     view. 7.1931,1-16.
     TP 29.1932,145-148

684. [rev.] Eugenjusz Banasiński: Japonja Mandżurja. Studjum politycz-
     no-ekonomiczne. Warschau: Instytut Wschodni 1931. 3,171 pp., 3
     maps. 8°
     TP 29.1932,148-149

685. [rev.] W. Bang, A. von Gabain: Türkische Turfan-Texte.5. Berlin
     1931. 36 pp., 2 pl. 8° (Sitzungsberichte der Preuß. Akademie der
     Wissenschaften, Phil.-hist. Kl. 14.1931,323-356.)
     W. Bang, A. von Gabain: Analytischer Index zu den fünf ersten
     Stücken der Türkischen Turfan-Texte. Berlin 1931. 59 pp.
     (Sitzungsberichte der Preuß. Akademie der Wissenschaften, Phil.-
     hist. Kl. 17.1931,461-517.)
     TP 29.1932,149-151

686. [rev.] K. J. Basmadjian: Les inscriptions arméniennes d'Ani, de
     Bagnaïr et de Marmachên, recueillies sur place et publiées avec leurs
     traductions françaises. Paris: Didot 1931. 246 pp., 15 pl. 8° Edition:
     100 copies.
     Siegfried Behrsing: Das Chung-tsi-king des chinesischen Dîrghâ-
     gama, übersetzt und annotiert. Leipzig: Asia Major 1930. 150 pp.
     Thesis, University of Leipzig.
     TP 29.1932,151-153

687. [rev.] E. Benveniste: Noms sogdiens dans un texte pehlevi de Tur-
     fan. Journal asiatique 1930,II,291-296.
     E. Benveniste: Le texte du Draxt asûrîk et la versification pehlevie.
     Journal asiatique.1930,193-225.
     E. Benveniste: Deux notes iraniennes. Bulletin de la Société de la
     linguistique.32.1931,86-91.
     TP 29.1932,153-154

688. [rev.] Bibliographie bouddhique.II, Mai 1929 - Mai 1930. Rétro-
     spective: L'œuvre de Léon Féer. Paris: Geuthner 1931. IX,97 pp. 4°
     Alfred Bohner: Wallfahrt zu zweien. Die 88 heiligen Stätten von
     Shikoku. Tôkyô 1931. VII,160 pp., 1 map, 51 pl. 8° (Mitteilungen
     der OAG. Suppl. 12.)
     Oberstleutnant Bonifacy: A propos d'une collection de peintures
     chinoises représentant divers épisodes de la guerre franco-chinoise de
     1884-1885 et conservées à l'Ecole française d'Extrême-Orient. Hanoi
     1931. 42 pp., 16 pl., 1 map. 8°
     G. Bouillard: Le temple des lamas. Temple lamaiste de Yung Ho
     Kung 雍和宮 à Peking. Descriptions, plans, photos, cérémonies.
     Pékin: A. Nachbaur 1931. 128 pp., 9 pl. and plans. 8°

G. Bouillard: Les tombeaux impériaux, Ming et Tsing. Historique, cartes, plans. Pékin: Nachbaur 1931. 225 pp., 15 pl. a. maps, mostly in colour; small 8°
TP 29.1932,154-156

689. [rev.] C. R. Boxer: Jan Compagnie in Japan, 1672-1674. Anglo-Dutch rivalry in Japan and Formosa. Transactions of the Asiatic Society of Japan. NS 7.1931,138-202, 5 pl.
TP 29.1932,156-159

690. [rev.] Catholic University of Peking. Bulletin 1.1926 - 7.1930.
TP 29.1932,159

691. [rev.] Chôsen Shina bunka no kenkyû 朝鮮支那文化の研究. Keijô (Seoul) 1929. 1,603 pp.
TP 29.1932,159-160

692. [rev.] La Cochinchine. Publié sous le patronage de la Société des études indochinoises. Saigon: Gastaldy 1931. 168 pp., numerous pl. a. maps. 8°
Committee on the promotion of Chinese studies of the American Council of Learned Societies: Progress of Chinese studies in the United States of America. Bulletin 1 (Mai 1931). Washington 1931. 102 pp.
TP 29.1932,160-161

693. [rev.] A. Conrady: Zu Lao-tze cap. 6. Asia Major.7.1931,150-156.
A. Conrady: Yi-king-Studien, hrsg. von Ed. Erkes. Asia Major. 7. 1931,409-468.
TP 29.1932,161-162

694. [rev.] Ananda K. Coomaraswamy: Yakṣas. Part II. Washington 1931. 84, 50 pp. (Smithsonian Institution, Freer Gallery of Art. Publication 3059.)
TP 29.1932,162-163

695. [rev.] Henri Courbin: Grammaire élémentaire du sanskrit classique.
1ʳᵉ partie: Grammaire; 2ᵉ partie: Exercices. Paris: Adrien Maisonneuve 1931. 128,119 pp. 8° Autogr.
TP 29.1932,163

696. [rev.] Judson Daland: The evolution of modern printing and the discovery of movable metal type by the Chinese and Koreans in the
fourteenth century. Journal of the Franklin Institute. 212.1931,209-
234.
J. Deny: Tughra. Encyclopédie de l'Islâm. Livr. M bis. 1930, 865-
869, 6 pl.
Kai Donner: Über sprachgeographische Untersuchungen und ihre
Ausführung in Finnland. 23 pp. From: Finno-ugrische For-
schungen.21.
Kai Donner: M. A. Castrén's memory in Russia. Marginal notes to
Pamyati M. A. Castrena. 1931. 15 pp. (Journal de la Société finno-
ougrienne.45,1.)
Kai Donner; Martti Räsänen: Zwei neue türkische Runeninschriften.
1931. 7 pp. (Journal de la Société finno-ougrienne.45,2.)
TP 29.1932,164-165

697. [rev.] A. Dragunov: Binoms of the type 尼卒 in the Tangut-Chinese
Dictionary. Doklady Akademii Nauk. 1929,145-148.
A. Dragunov: The hPhags-pa script and ancient Mandarin. Izvestija
Akademii Nauk. 1930,627-647,775-797.
A. Dragunov: A Persian transcription of ancient mandarin. Izvestija
Akademii Nauk.1931,359-375.
TP 29.1932,165-168

698. [rev.] Gustav Ecke: Atlantes and Caryatides in Chinese architecture.
42 pp. From: Bulletin of the Catholic University of Peking. 7.1930.
TP 29.1932,168-169

699. [rev.] Ecole française d'Extrême-Orient: Inventaire du fonds chinois
de la Bibliothèque de l'Ecole française d'Extrême-Orient. T. I, fasc.
2. Hanoi 1931. VIII,321-644, II pp.
L'Ecole française d'Extrême-Orient. Hanoi: Impr. d'Extrême-Orient
1930. 59 pp., 16 pl. 8°

Ed. Erkes: Die Götterwelt des alten China. 10 pp., 4 ill. From: Der Weltkreis 2.1931.
TP 29.1932,169-170

700. [rev.] Jean Escarra: La législation maritime chinoise. Paris 1931. 46 pp. From: Revue de droit maritime comparé.23.
Jean Escarra: La codification du droit de la famille et du droit des successions (livres IV et V du Code civil de la Republique chinoise). Rapport présenté au Conseil législatif du Gouvernement national. Zikawei 1931. II,89 pp. 8°
Jean Escarra: La Chine et le droit international. Préface de Marcel Sibert. Paris: A. Pedone 1931. XX,419 pp.
TP 29.1932,170-173

701. [rev.] Ferrand: Les grands rois du monde. Bulletin of the School of Oriental Studies 6.1931,329-339.
TP 29.1932,173-174
[With refernce to Quatre fils du ciel.]

702. [rev.] Hans Findeisen: Kunstgewerbe nordasiatischer Grenzlande. Geschichte des Kunstgewerbes, hrsg. von H. Th. Bossert. Bd 4, pp.21-47.
Hans Findeisen: Reisen und Forschungen in Nordsibirien. Skizzen aus dem Lande der Jenissejostjaken. Berlin: Author 1929. 47 pp. 8°
Hans Findeisen: Das mongolische Ständewesen, mit Anhang von W. A. Unkrig. Mitteilungen des Seminars für Orientalische Sprachen.32. 1929,130-146.
Hans Findeisen: Neue Untersuchungen und Materialien zum Problem der westasiatischen Altasiaten sowie über den Ursprung der Altasiaten überhaupt. Zeitschrift für Ethnologie.59.1927,281-290.
Hans Findeisen: Die Fischerei im Leben der «altsibirischen» Völkerstämme. Berlin 1929. 73 pp. From: Zeitschrift für Ethnologie. 1928.
Hans Findeisen: Der älteste Mensch in Nord-Asien und seine Kultur. Der Weltkreis.1929/30,95-123.
Hans Findeisen: Landkarten der Jenissejer (Ketó). Zeitschrift für Ethnologie. 62.1930,215-226.

Hans Findeisen: Viehzüchter und Jägervölker am Baikalsee, im Fluß-
gebiet der Bureja und im Amurlande. 29 pp. From: Baessler-Archiv
14.1930.
TP 29.1932,174-178

703. [rev.] Shang-Ling Fu 傅尚霖: One generation of Chinese studies in
      Cambridge. An appreciation of Professor H. A. Giles. 1931. 14 pp.
      8° From: Chinese Social and Political Science Review. 1931.
      Fu-jen hsüeh-chih 輔仁學誌. Series sinologica. T. I, fasc. 2 (Sept.
      1929); T. II, fasc. 1 (Jan. 1930).
      TP 29.1932,178-179

704. [rev.] A. Foucher: De Kâpiśî à Pushkarâvatî. Bull. of the School of
      Oriental Studies.6, pp. 341-348.
      TP 29.1932,179-180

705. [rev.] Everard D. H. Fraser: Index to the Tso Chuan, revised and
      edited by James Haldane Stewart Lockhart. Oxford Univ. Press
      1930. X,430 pp. 4°
      TP 29.1932,180-181

706. [rev.] Toyohachi Fujita: 1.Sur Yeh-t'iao 葉調, Szu-t'iao 斯調 et
      Szu-hê-t'iao 私訶條. 2.Li-hsüan 黎軒 et Ta-ch'in 大秦. Taihoku
      Imperial University 1929. 75 pp. (Memoirs of the Faculty of
      Literature and Politics, Taihoku Imp. University.1,1.)
      TP 29.1932,181-184

707. [rev.] Esson M. Gale: Historical evidences relating to early Chinese
      public finance. 15 pp. From: Proceedings of the Pacific Coast Branch
      of the American Historical Association. 1929.
      Marie Gallaud: La vie du Bouddha et les doctrines bouddhiques.
      Paris: Maisonneuve frères 1931. 220 pp., 21 pl.
      TP 29.1932,184

708. [rev.] Geimun 藝文 22th year, no. 3. 283 pp.
      Herbert Giles (Chai Li-szu 翟理斯): Han-wen ts'ui-chen 漢文萃珍
      (Gems of Chinese literature). Shanghai: Commercial Press 1927.
      1,9,198 pp.

S. Goto, M. Prunier: Episodes du Heiké monogatari, traduits, avec avant-propos de S. Lévi. Paris: E. Leroux (1931). 148 pp. 8°
Pierre Gourou: Le Tonkin. [Macon] 1931. 360 pp., 30 pl., 4 maps.
Guillaume Grandidier: Gallieni. Paris: Plon 1931. 259 pp. 12° (Les grandes figures coloniales.3.)
TP 29.1932,184-186

709. [rev.] Georges Groslier: L'enseignement et la mise en pratique des arts indigènes au Cambodge (1918-1930). Paris 1931. 44 pp., 4 pl. 8° From: Bulletin de l'Académie des sciences coloniales.16.
Georges Groslier: Les collections khmères du musée Albert Sarraut à Phnom-Penh. Avec préface de George Cœdès. Paris: Van Oest 1931. 129 pp., 50 pl. 4° (Ars asiatica.16)
René Grousset: Les philosophies indiennes. Les systèmes. Avec avant-propos d'Olivier Lacombe. Paris. Desclée 1931. 2 vols.: XIX,344; 416 pp.
TP 29.1932,186-187

710. [rev.] J. Hackin: La sculpture indienne et tibétaine au Musée Guimet. Paris: Leroux 1931. 24 pp., 51 pl. 4°
E. Haenisch: Die Rachepflicht. Ein Widerstreit zwischen konfuzianischer Ethik und chinesischem Staatsgefühl. Zeitschrift der Deutschen Morgenländischen Gesellschaft.10. 1931,69-92.
Erich Haenisch: Lehrgang der chinesischen Schriftsprache.II. Leipzig: Asia Major 1931. XI,235 pp. 8°
TP 29.1932,187-189

711. [rev.] C. Haguenauer: Notions d'archéologie japonaise. Tôkyô 1931. IV,68 pp., 6 pl., 2 folded maps. From: Bulletin de la Maison franco-japonaise.3.
C. Haguenauer: Une nouvelle tentative pour prouver que le Lieou-k'ieou kouo du Souei chou désigne Formose. Bulletin de la Maison franco-japonaise.3,2.1931,pp.1-3.
C. Haguenauer: Relations du royaume des Ryûkyû avec les pays des mers du Sud et la Corée. Bulletin de la Maison franco-japonaise.III,2.1931,4-16.
C. Haguenauer: La danse rituelle dans la cérémonie du Chinkonsai. JA 1930,I,299-350.

C. Haguenauer: Note sur l'existence d'un culte du coq à Silla. Bulletin de la Maison franco-japonaise.III,2.1932,17-18.
C. Haguenauer: Two lectures on prehistoric and proto-historic Japanese civilization. Tôkyô: Maison Franco-Japonaise (1931). 13, 12 pp.
TP 29.1932,189-191

712. [rev.] L. Halphen, Ph. Saignac: La fin du Moyen Age. 2ᵉ partie: L'annonce des temps nouveaux (1453-1492). Paris: F. Alcan 1931. 324 pp. 8°
J. E. Heeres: Corpus diplomaticum Neerlando-indicum. 2ᵉ partie: 1650-1675. La Haye: Nijhoff 1931. XXIV,625 pp. (Bijdragen tot de Taal-, Land en Volkenkunde van Nederlandsch-Indie.87.)
Albert Herrmann: Lou-lan. China, Indien und Rom im Lichte der Ausgrabungen am Lobnor, mit Vorwort von Sven Hedin. Leipzig: Brockhaus 1931. 160 pp., 7 maps, 1 frontispiece, 30 pl. 12°
C. Hooykaas: Tantri Kâmandaka. Een Oudjavaansche Pañtjatantra-bewerking, edited and translated. Bandoeng: A. C. Nix 1931. 213 pp., 64 ill. on 32 pl. 8° (Bibliotheca javanica.2.)
TP 29.1932,191-193

713. [rev.] Paul Houo-Ming-Tse 霍明志 [Huo Ming-chih]: Preuves des antiquités de Chine. Pékin 1930. 676,35,2 pp. 2°
Indochine française. Service géographique de l'Indochine. Son organisation, ses méthodes, ses travaux. Hanoi: Impr. d'Extrême-Orient 1931. 35 pp., 5 maps. 8°
Ishiyama Juntarô: Manshû-go yaku Dai-zô-kyô (Sur la traduction du Kanjur en mandchou). Continuation. 22 pp. From: Shomotsu no shumi 書物の趣味 No. 6.
Ishiyama Juntarô: Tôkyô teikoku daigaku shozô Môbun Tanjur ki 京都帝國大學所藏蒙文丹殊爾記 Notice sur le Tanjur mongol conservé à l'Université impériale de Kyôto.
TP 29.1932,193-195

714. [rev.] P. Jabouille, J. H. Peyssonnaux: Musée Khai-Dinh (Hué). Historique du Musée. Sélection d'objets d'art et de meubles conservés au Musée Khai-Dinh et notices les concernant. [Hué] 1931. 12 pp., 66 pl. mostly in colour. 8°

Henry F. James: China. Philadelphia 1930. VI,431 pp., 1 map, 1 pl.
(The annals of the American Academy of Political and Social
Sciences.152)
TP 29.1932,195-196

715. [rev.] Olov Janse: Notes sur quelques épées anciennes trouvées en
Chine. The Museum of Far Eastern Antiquities. Bulletin 2.1930,67-
134, 21 pl.
Olov Janse: Quelques antiquités chinoises d'un caractère halstattien.
The Museum of Far Eastern Antiquities. Bulletin 2.1930,177-183, 4
pl.
TP 29.1932,196-197

716. [rev.] Jaw Yuanrenn 趙元任 [Chao Yüan-jen]: Phonetics of the Yao
folk-songs 廣西猺歌記音 (Kuang-hsi Yao-ko chi yin). Peking
1930. 2,187 pp. 8° (Academia sinica, Institute of History and
Philology. Monograph series. A,1.)
Jan Jaworski: La section de la nourriture dans le Vinaya des
Mahîsâsaka. Rocznik Orjentalistyczny.7.1930,53-124.
Jan Jaworski: Rozdział o ordynacji mnichów w Vinaya Mûlasar-
vâstivâdinów. La section de l'ordination dans le Vinaya des Mûla-
sarvâstivâdin. Warschau 1931. 48 pp. From: Comptes-rendus de la
Société des sciences et des lettres de Varsovie.23.1930.
Jan Jaworski: Historija Chin. [From an unidentified work.] pp.239-
311.
TP 29.1932,197-198

717. [rev.] Jung Yüan 容媛: Chin-shih shu mu-lu 金石書錄目 [Biblio-
graphy of epigraphical works]. Peking 1930. 8°
Kanô Jihei 金石書錄目: Hakkaku-jô 白鶴帖. I, with preface by
Naitô Torajirô and Hamada Seiryô. 1931. 13 fol., 75 pl.; II. with
preface by Izumoji Tsûjirô. 1930. 4 fol., 44 pl.; III. Preface by
Nagao Kô; 8 fol., 91 pl.: IV.1931, 3 fol.,60 pl.; V.1931, 6 fol., 75
pl.
TP 29.1932,198-200

718. [rev.] O. Karlbeck: Notes on the archaeology of China. The Museum
of Far Eastern Antiquities. Bulletin 2.1930,193-207, 8 pl.

B. Karlgren: Shang-ku Chung-kuo yin tang-chung-ti chi-ko wen-t'i 上古中國音當中的幾個問題. Peking 1930 (Translation of problems in archaic Chinese, by Chao Yüan-jen).
Bernhard Karlgren: Chinese books in Swedish collections.I. Göteborg: Elanders 1931. 26 pp.
TP 29.1932,200-202

719. [rev.] Chi Ming T'ai-wan Cheng-shih wang shih 記明臺灣鄭氏亡事 [Fall of the Cheng family (of Coxinga) from Formosa]. Peiping 1930.
Raymond Koechlin: Gaston Migeon et le Louvre. Paris: Lahure 1931. 20 pp. 8°
M. Kokin, G. Papajan: Czin-tjań, agrarnyj stroj drevnego Kitaja (The *Ching-t'ien* agricultural system of old China). With preface by L. Mad'jar. Leningrad 1930. LXIV,184 pp. (Izd. Leningradskogo Vostočnogo Instituta.38)
P. Wilh. Koppers: Weltgeschichte der Steinzeit. Anthropos.26.1931, 223-243.
TP 29.1932,202-204

720. [rev.] Kuo-hsüeh lun-ts'ung 國學論叢/ Chinese classical review. 2,2. 302 pp.
Kuo Mo-jo 郭沫若: Chia-ku wen-tzu yen-chiu 甲骨文字研究. s.l. 1931. 2 vols.
TP 29.1932,204-209

721. [rev.] Mme. Y. Labrouste-Dammann: Etude historique de la séismicité en Chine et principalement dans les provinces septentrionales. Bulletin de la section de géographie du Comité des travails historiques et scientifiques.44.1929,147-168.
TP 29.1932,209-210

722. [rev.] Marcelle Lalou: Catalogue du fonds tibétain de la Bibliothèque Nationale. 4e partie: I. Les mDo-man. Paris: Geuthner 1931. 110 pp. autograph. 8° (Buddhica. 2e série: Documents.4.)
Marcelle Lalou: Iconographie des étoffes peintes (paṭa) dans le Mañjuśrîmûlakalpa. Paris: Geuthner 1930. 119 pp., 7 pl. 8°
TP 29.1932,210-211

723. [rev.] B. Laufer: The domestication of the cormorant in China and
     Japan. Chicago 1931. Field Museum of Natural History. Anthro-
     pological series.18, pp. 205-262, pl.13-16.
     TP 29.1932,211-212

724. [rev.] Louis de La Vallée Poussin: Documents d'abhidharma. 1-2.
     BEFEO 30.1930,1-80.
     Paul Le Boulanger: Histoire du Laos français, essai d'une étude
     chronologique des principautés laotiennes. Preface by J. Bosc, ill. by
     Mme A. Hava des Hautschamps. Paris: Plon 1931. VIII,381 pp. 8°
     Sylvain Lévi: Indochine. Paris: Société d'éditions géographiques
     1931. 232,215 pp., 24 pl., 4 colour pl. 4°
     TP 29.1932,213-214

725. [rev.] R. Lingat: Review of Commentaire des lois sur les époux, par
     le Pha:ja Vinăisŭnthon (1930). Journal of the Siam Society.24.1930,
     211-219.
     R. Lingat: L'esclavage privé dans le vieux droit siamois (avec une
     traduction des anciennes lois siamoises sur l'esclavage). Paris:
     Dumat-Montchrestien 1931. XI,395 pp. 8°
     Lo Ch'ang-p'ei 羅常培: Hsia-men yin-hsi 廈門音系 [Phonetics of
     the Amoy dialect. Peking 1930. XIV,278 pp., numer. tables.
     (Academia sinica. Institute of History and Philology. Monograph
     series. A,4.)
     Lo Chen-yü 羅振玉: Pen-ch'ao hsüeh-shu yüan-liu kai-lüeh
     本朝學術源流概略 [Sketch of the history of sciences under the
     present dynasty]. Dairen: Chinese-Japanese Culture Society 1930.
     4,27 pp.
     TP 29.1932,215-217

726. [rev.] J. Courtenay Locke: The first Englishmen in India. London
     1930. XVI,229 pp., 8 pl., 2 maps. 8°
     Maejima Shinji 前島信次: Les royaumes au Sud de la Mer Caspienne
     et leurs relations avec les T'ang. Offprint, pp.1272-1305, from an
     unidentied journal.
     H. Mansuy: La préhistoire en Indochine. [Macon] 1931. 26 pp., 3
     pl.

A. V. Marakuev: Mery i vesy v Kitae. Weights and measures in China. Vladivostok: Izd. Dal'ne-Vost. Kraev. Naučno-issled. Inst. 1930. 152 pp. 8°
TP 29.1932,217-220

727. [rev.] Roland Meyer: Le Laos. Hanoi: Impr. d'Extrême-Orient 1930. 113 pp., numer. pl. and maps 8°
Thomas F. Millard: The end of exterritoriality in China. Shanghai: A.B.C. Press 1931. 278 pp. 8°
Ming Ch'ing shih-liao 明清史料 [Historical material of the Ming and Ch'ing]. Shanghai 1931. Fasc. 5-7 (fol. 401-700)
V. Minorsky: Tûrân. Encyclopédie de l'Islâm. Livr. N. 1931. 6 pp.
V. Minorsky: Essai de bibliographie des travaux de J. Markwart. Journal asiatique. 1930,II,313-324.
Missions, séminaires, œuvres catholiqes en Chine. 10th year, 1929-1930. Zikawei 1931. 99 pp. 8°
TP 29.1932,220-222

728. [rev.] M. Miyasaki, C. Haguenauer: Le gisement préhistorique d'Ichiôji, près de Korekawa (Préfecture d'Aomori). Zeitschrift für Prähistorie / Shizengaku zasshi.2.1930, 337-357, 5 pl.
R. von Moellendorff: P. G. von Moellendorff, ein Lebensbild. Leipzig: Harrassowitz 1930. VIII,166 pp. 8°
A. Monfleur: Monographie de la province du Darlac (1930). Hanoi: Impr. d'Extrême-Orient 1931. 65 pp., pl., maps.
René Morizon: Monographie du Cambodge. Hanoi: Impr. d'Extrême-Orient 1931. 284 pp., numer. pl., maps. 8°
TP 29.1932,222-224

729. [rev.] A. Mostaert, A. de Smedt: Le dialecte monguor parlé par les Mongols du Kansu occidental. 1re partie: Phonétique. Anthropos.24. 1929,145-165,801-815; 25.1930,657-669,961-973, 2 pl., 1 map.
F. W. K. Müller: Uigurica.IV. Posthum herausg. von A. von Gabain. Berlin 1931. 55 pp. 8°
TP 29.1932,224-226

730. [rev.] N. A. Nevskij: Očerk istorii tangutovedenija (Historical sketch of Hsi-hsia studies). Izvestija Akademii Nauk.1931,7-22.
TP 29.1932,226-229

731. [rev.] Nguyên-văn-Khoan: Essai sur le đinh et le culte du génie tutélaire des villages au Tonkin. BEFEO 30.1930,107-139.
Muḥammad Niẓámu'd-Dín: Introduction to the Jawámi'u'l-Ḥikáyát wa Lawámi'u'r-Riwáyát. London: Luzac 1929. XXIII,313 pp.
[Ôtani Daigaku Toshokan:] 西藏研究論文總目錄　Seizô kenkyû rombun sô-mokuroku [Bibliography of critical works on Tibet], Japanese works, 1930. 11 pp. 8°
Paul Pelliot: La Haute Asie. [Paris 1931.] 37 pp., 1 pl.
Raffaele Pettazzoni: La confession des péchés, trad. par R. Monnot. 1ʳᵉ partie, vol.1: Primitifs, Amérique ancienne. Paris: E. Leroux 1931. XI,306 pp., 1 pl.
Hartmut Piper: Der gesetzmäßige Lebenslauf der Völker Indiens. Leipzig: Th. Weicher 1931. XVI,232 pp. (Piper: Die Gesetze der Weltgeschichte.2,2.)
TP 29.1932,229-231

732. [rev.] J.-M. Planchet: Les missions de Chine et du Japon. Neuvième année. Pékin: Impr. des Lazaristes 1931. 782 pp. 12°
TP 29.1932,231

733. [rev.] N. N. Poppe: Alarskij govor [The Alar dialect]. 2nd pt. Leningrad: Akademija Nauk 1931. 216 pp. 8°
N. N. Poppe: Praktičeskij učebnik mongol'skogo razgovornogo jazyka (Xalxaskoe narečie) [Practical textbook of the Mongolian colloquial, the Xalxa dialect]. Leningrad 1931. VIII,180 pp.
Jean Przyluski: Une étoffe orientale, le kaunakes. Journal of the Royal Asiatic Society 1931,339-347.
Jean Przyluski: Le nom du blé. Rocznik Orjentalistyczny.7, pp.125-129.
Jean Przyluski: Un dieu iranien dans l'Inde. Rocznik Orjentalistyczny.7, pp.1-9.
W. Radloff: Suvarṇaprabhâsa (Das Goldglanz-Sûtra). Aus dem Uigurischen ins Deutsche übersetzt. Fasc. 1-3. Leningrad 1930. II,256 pp. (Bibliotheca Buddhica.27.)
Johannes Rahder, Shinryû Susa: The Ḍaśabhûmika sûtra (gâthâ portion). II,23 pp. 8° From: Eastern Buddhist.5, no. 4 (Juli 1931).
J. Rahder: Japanologische verkenningen. Leiden: S. C. van Doesburgh 1931. 30 pp. 8°
TP 29.1932,231-233

734. [rev.] H. G. Rawlinson: Captain Basil Hall, Travels in India, Ceylon and Borneo. London 1931. 272 pp., 4 pl.
Hans Reichelt: Beiträge zur soghdischen Grammatik. Studia Indo-Iranica. Ehrengabe für W. Geiger. Leipzig: Harrassowitz 1931,248-260.
Louis Renou: Bibliographie védique. Paris: Adrien-Maisonneuve 1931. V,339 pp. 8°
Aldo Ricci: The travels of Marco Polo. Translated from the text of Prof. L. F. Benedetto, with introduction and index by Sir E. Denison Ross. London: G. Routledge 1931. XVIII,439 pp., 11 pl., map.
TP 29.1932,233-235

735. [rev.] J. N. Roerich: The animal style among the nomad tribes of Northern Tibet. Prag: Seminarium Kondakovianum 1930. 42 pp., 5 pl. 4°
F. Rosenberg: Notes sogdiennes. Izvestija Akademii Nauk 1931, 627-635.
E. Denison Ross: Körösi Csoma Sándor. Körösi Csoma Archivum. 2.1930,333-345.
G. D. Sanžeev: Darxatskij govor i fol'klor [Dialect and folklore of the Darxat]. Leningrad: Akademija Nauk 1931. 112 pp. 8°
Aurélien Sauvageot: Recherches sur le vocabulaire des langues ouralo-altaiques. Budapest 1929. XLII,143 pp.
F. M. Savina: Histoire des Miao. 2e édition. Hongkong: Impr. des Miss. Etrangères 1930. XXII,303 pp. 8°
TP 29.1932,235-237

736. [rev.] P. Dorotheus Schilling OFM: Das Schulwesen der Jesuiten in Japan (1551-1614). Teilausgabe. Münster: Regensberg 1931. XXVIII,86 pp.
Fr. Schjöth: The currency of the Far East. The Schjöth Collection at the Numismatic Cabinet of the University of Oslo, Norway. London, Oslo 1929. 88 pp., 131 pp., ill., small 2°
Heinrich Schmidt: Der zweite Internationale Kongreß persischer Kunst im Januar 1931 in London. ZDMG 10.1931,93-102.
P. W. Schmidt: Methodologisches und Inhaltliches zum Zweige-schlechterwesen. Anthropos.26.1931,55-98.

Ali Akbar Siassi: La Perse au contact de l'Occident. Etude historique et sociale. Paris: E. Leroux 1931. 273 pp. 12°
Walter Simon: Yen-wen-dui-dschau 言文對照 und Kokuyaku-Kanbun 國譯漢文, eine bibliographische Zusammenstellung. Mitteilungen des Seminars für Orientalische Sprachen.33.1930, Ostas. Studien, 155-181.
TP 29.1932,237-239

737. [rev.] Th. Stcherbatsky: Buddhist logic. Vol.2: Containing a translation of the short treatise of logic by Dharmakîrti and of its commentary by Dharmottara, with notes, appendices and indices. Leningrad: Academy of Sciences 1930. VI,468 pp.
F. I. Ščerbatskoj: Tibetskij perevod Abhidharmakoçakârikâh i Abhidharmakoçabhâṣyam, sočinenij Vasubandhu.II. Leningrad: Akademija Nauk 1930. pp.97-192. 8° (Bibliotheca Buddhica.20,2.)
Josef Strzygowski: Asiens bildende Kunst in Stichproben, ihr Wesen und ihre Entwicklung. Augsburg: Benno Filser 1930. XXII,779 pp., 658 ill.
TP 29.1932,239-245

738. [rev.] Taguchi Minoru: Les noms des lieux habités par les chinois en Mandchourie. Paris: Jouve 1931. 108 pp. 8°
Chao Wan-li 趙萬里: Chiao-chi Sung Chin Yüan jen tz'u 校輯宋金元人詞 [Tz'u by Sung, Chin and Yüan authors, collected and collated]. Peking 1931. 5 pen.
Ting Fu-pao 丁福保: Shuo-wen chieh-tzu ku-lin 説文解字詁林 [«Forest of Glosses» to Shuo-wen chieh-tzu]. 64 pen. 8°
Ting Tso-tchao: La douane chinoise. Paris: Geuthner 1931. 214 pp. 8°
TP 29.1932,245-246

739. [rev.] 東方學報 Tôhô gakuhô. No. 1. Tôkyô 1931. 1,237 pp. 8°
Tôhô gakuhô. No. 1. Kyôto 1931. 1,305 pp.
TP 29.1932,246-250

740. [rev.] 從征實錄 Ts'ung-cheng shih-lu, by Yang Ying 楊英, *hu-kuan* 戶官 of the prince of Yen-p'ing. Peiping 1931. 26,156 fol.
TP 29.1932,250-251

741. [rev.] Giuseppe Tucci: Linei di una storia del materialismo indiano.
Roma 1929. Rendiconti dell'Accademia nazionale dei Lincei. Ser.
VI, vol. 2, pp.667-713.
G. Tucci: Note indologiche. Revista degli studi orientali.12.1930,
408-427.
G. Tucci: Notes on the Nyâya-praveśa by Śaṅkarasvâmin. Journal of
the Royal Asiatic Society.1931,381-413.
TP 29.1932,251-252

742. [rev.] Umehara Sueji 梅原末活: 筑前國井原發見鏡片の複原
Chikuzen no kuni Ihara hakken kyô-hen no fukugen. 21 pp. From:
Shirin.16, No. 3.
Umehara Sueji: Kôkogaku-jô yori kantaru Kandai bumbutsu no sai-
zen 考古學上より觀たる漢代文物の西漸 [The spread of Han
culture towards the West, from the archaeological point of view]. 24
pp. 8° From: Ogawa hakushi kanreki kinen shigaku chirikagaku
ronsô.
Umehara Sueji: Kan Sankoku Rokuchô kinen kyô shûroku
漢三國六朝紀年鏡集錄 [Collection of dated mirrors of the Han,
Three Kingdoms and Six Dynasties]. Tôkyô 1931. 1,2,49,5 pp., 6
pl.
Umehara Sueji: 歐米に賣された日本出土の古鏡 [Old mirrors
from Japanese tombs, seen in Europe and America] Shigaku.9,
pp.27-38
TP 29.1932,252-253

743. [rev.] Umehara Sueji 梅原末活: 亞米利加で觀た唐鏡の三四に就
[On three or four T'ang mirrors seen in America]. Shigaku.9,
pp.587-601, 2 pl.
Umehara Sueji: 亞米利加の博物館に於ける支那の古美術 [On
old Chinese art works in American museums.]. 1st pt. 13 pp., 8 pl.
From: Bukkyo bijutsu. No. 16.
Umehara Sueji: Toronto hakubutsukan no Shina kodai no hi to riki
no nisan [On a horse bit and two or three cutting tools 利器 from
old China in the museum of Toronto]. Rekishi to chiri. Vol. 25, pp.
457-470.
Umehara Sueji: Sur un bassin de bronze à scènes de chasse
incrustées conservé à la Freer Gallery en Amérique. Mélanges

d'histoire extrême-orientale offerts pour l'anniversaire du professeur
Kuwabara. 23 pp., 2 pl.
Umehara Sueji: Epées de bronze et pointes de flèches en bronze
trouvées récemment en Corée et objets apparentés. Jinrui-gaku zas-
shi.45.1930,301-318.
Umehara Sueji: Tarumi Utashiki-yama kofun 垂水歌敷山古墳. s.1
s.d. 26 pp., 12 pl.
TP 29.1932,254-255

744. [rev.] Giovanni Vacca [u.a.]: Cina. Enciclopedia italiana. 10.1931,
     257-318, pl.43-82.
     L. van Hée: Le précieux miroir des quatre éléments. Asia Major.7,
     pp.242-270.
     B. A. Vasil'ev: Drevnie istočniki Ljao-čžaja [The old sources of the
     Liao-chai]. Izvestija Akademii Nauk 1931,23-52.
     M. W. de Visser: The bodhisattva Âkâśagarbha (Kokûzô) in China
     and Japan. Amsterdam 1931. 47 pp. 8° (Verhandelingen d. Konink-
     lijke Akademie van Wetenschappen te Amsterdam, Afd. Letterkunde,
     NR 30,1.)
     B. Ja. Vladimircov: L. Ja. Šternberg kak lingvist. Akademija Nauk.
     Očerki po istorii znanij.7, pp.37-49.
     TP 29.1932,255-257

745. [rev.] Watanabe Ryôkichi 渡邊良吉: Recherches sur l'origine de
     l'expression de «tissu de Canton». 24 pp. 8° From: Tokuun 德雲.
     Vol. 2, No. 3.
     Wei Yung 韋榮: The cult of Dr. Sun (Sun Wen hsüeh shuo)
     孫文學説; translated. Shanghai: The Independent Weekly 1931.
     II,230,XX pp. 12°
     Yrjö Wichmann: Volksdichtung und Volksbräuche der Tscheremis-
     sen. Helsinki 1931. XVI,479 pp.
     J. V. S. Wilkinson: The Shâh-nâmah of Firdausî, with 24 illustrat-
     ions from a XVth cent. mss. formerly in the Imperial Library, Delhi,
     and now in the possession of the Royal Asiatic Society. With
     introduction by L. Binyon. London: The India Society 1931. XX,93
     pp., 24 pl., 7 of which in colour.
     TP 29.1932,257-259

746. [rev.] U. Wogihara, Th. Stcherbatsky: Sphûṭârthâ Abhidharma–koçavyâkhyâ, the work of Yaçomitra, second koçasthâna. Leningrad 1931. 96 pp. 8° (Bibliotheca Buddhica.21,2.)
Monpeng Wou 吳孟班 [Mlle Wu Meng-pan]: L'évolution des corporations ouvrières et commerciales dans la Chine contemporaine. With preface by Kao Lou. Paris: Geuthner 1931. 299 pp. 8°
Lawrence G. Wroth, Gertrude L. Annam: Acts of French royal administration concerning Canada, Guiana, the West Indies and Louisiana, prior to 1791. New York: The New York Public Library 1930. 151 pp. 8°
Wu Ging-ding 吳金鼎 [Wu Chin-ting]: Shan-tung jen t'i-chih chih yen-chiu 山東人體質之研究 [Anthropometrical study of the population of Shantung]. Peiping 1931. 132 pp., 1 tab. 8° (Academia sinica, National Research Institute of History and Philology. Monograph 7.)
Yang Chien: The Communist situation in China. Nanking 1931. 11 pp. 8°
TP 29.1932,259-260

747. [rev.] 燕京學報 Yen-ching hsüeh-pao. Yen-ching journal of Chinese studies. No. 8 (Dec. 1930).
The same, no. 9 (June 1931). pp.1661-1954.
TP 29.1932,260-272

748. [rev.] W. Perceval Yetts: Problems of Chinese bronzes 1931. 4 pp. 8° From: Journal of the Royal Central Asiatic Society.18, No. 3.
Yu Dawchyuan 于道泉 [Yü Tao-ch'üan]: Love songs of the sixth Dalailama Tshangs-dbyangs rgya-mtsho, translated into Chinese and English with notes and introduction by Yu Dawchyuan and transcribed by Dr. Jaw Yuanrenn [Chao Yüan-jen]. Peking 1930. XI,204 pp., 1 pl. (Academia sinica, Institute of History and Philology. Monograph series A,5.)
I. I. Zarubin: K izučeniju beludžkogo jazyka u fol'klora [On the study of Beluchi language and folklore]. Leningrad: Akademija Nauk 1930. From: Zapiski Kollegii Vostokovedov.5, pp.653-679.
I. I. Zarubin: Pamirskaja ėkspedicija 1928 g. [The Pamir expedition 1928]. Works of the expedition, part 6: Linguistics. Leningrad: Akademija Nauk 1930. VIII,108 pp., 1 map.
TP 29.1932,272-275

749. Shuo-fu k'ao 説郛考.
Po-hsi-ho chuan 伯希和撰, Feng Ch'eng-chün i 馮承鈞譯.
Bulletin of the National Library of Peiping.6.1932:6, pp.19-39

750. Po-hsi-ho chuan 伯希和撰, Feng Ch'eng-chün i 馮承鈞譯.
Mou-tzu k'ao 牟子考.
Bulletin of the National Library of Peiping.6.1932:3, pp.29-48
(=287-306)
[Meou-tseu ou les doutes levées, Chinese translation.]

751. Po-hsi-ho chuan 伯希和撰, Feng Ch'eng-chün i 馮承鈞譯.
Chung-Ya shih-ti i-ts'ung 中亞史地譯叢.
Fu-jen hsüeh-chih.3.1932:1, pp.1-37
[Neuf notes, Chinese translation.]

751a.[Ch'ien-tzu-wen k'ao] 千字文考. Po-hsi-ho P. Pelliot chuan
伯希和撰, Feng Ch'eng-chün i 馮承鈞譯.
T'u-shu-kuan-hsüeh chi-k'an.6.1932,67-86

752. Les plaques de l'empereur du ciel. Par Paul Pelliot.
BMFEA 4.1932,115-116, 1 pl.

753. Trois termes des Mémoires de Hiuan-tsang. Par Paul Pelliot.
*Etudes d'orientalisme publiées par le Musée Guimet à la mémoire de
Raymonde Linossier*. Paris: Leroux 1932,423-431
Contents:
1. 宿麥 sou-ma.
2. 亟縛犀 ki-fou-si.
3. Les hérétiques 計多 ki-to.

1933
754. Les Nestoriens en Chine après 845.
JRAS 1933,115-116
 P. Pelliot
Cf. A. C. Moule: The Nestorians in China. *JRAS* 1933,116-120.

755. [Preface] Bibliothèque nationale, Département des Manuscrits:
Répertoire du Tanjur d'après le catalogue de P. Cordier. Par Marcelle
Lalou. Avec une préface de M. Paul Pelliot.

Paris 1933. VIII,239 pp.
VI, Préface, gez.: Paul Pelliot, membre de l'Institut.

756. Pâpîyân > Po-siun 波旬. Par Paul Pelliot.
TP 30.1933,85-99
Cf. E. von Zach: *Sinologische Beiträge.*3.1936,171

757. Les grands voyages maritimes chinois au début du XVe siècle. Par
Paul Pelliot.
TP 30.1933,237-452
Re: J. J. L. Duyvendak: *Ma Huan re-examined.* Amsterdam 1933. 74
pp. large 8° (Verhandelingen der Kon. Akademie van Wetenschap-
pen, Afd. Letterkunde, NR 32,3.)
Cf. E. von Zach: *Sinologische Beiträge.*3.1936,171

758. Le plus ancien possesseur connu du «Kou K'ai-tche» du British
Museum.
TP 30.1933,453-455
P. Pelliot

1934
759. Mongoli.
*Encyclopedia italiana.*23.1934,661-666
P. Pel.

760. Mongolia, missione ed esplorazione.
*Encyclopedia italiana.*23.1934,667-668
P. Pel.

761. Mongolia, storia.
*Enciclopedia italiana.*23.1934,672-674
P. Pel.

762. Les bronzes chinois de l'Orangerie.
Le Temps. June 8, 1934
Paul Pelliot

763. Les bronzes chinois. Par Paul Pelliot, de l'Institut.
Beaux Arts 73.1934:75 (8 juin),1

764. *Bronzes chinois; conférence au Musée de l'Orangerie le 8 juin 1934.*
Musée de l'Orangerie 1934. 21 pp.
[Not seen.]

765. Les bronzes chinois de l'Orangerie.
*Revue archéologique.*VI,4.1934,64-67
Paul Pelliot
Voir également les articles de G. Salles dans *L'Illustration* du 7 juillet 1934, p. 331-333 et *The illustrated London News* du 23 juin 1934, p. 1030-1031.

766. Les bronzes chinois de l'Orangerie des Tuileries.
L'Asie française 1934, 221-224
Paul Pelliot

767. Les déplacements de fresques sous les T'ang et les Song.
Revue des arts asiatiques 8.1934,201-228
Paul Pelliot, Membre de l'Institut

768. Tokharien et koutchéen. Par Paul Pelliot.
Journal asiatique 224.1934,23-106
Re: Sten Konow: War «Tocharisch» die Sprache der Tocharer? (*Asia major* IX,455-466) and Sylvain Lévi: Le «Tocharien» (*JA* 1933,I, 1-30).

769. La civilisation chinoise.
*Cahiers de Radio-Paris.*5.1934, no. 9,857-863
[Not seen.]

1935

770. L'art chinois à l'exposition de Londres. Par Paul Pelliot.
*Renaissance.*18.1935,127

771. Sur un passage du Cheng-wou ts'ing-tcheng lou [!]. Par Paul Pelliot.
Ch'ing-chu Ts'ai Yüan-p'ei hsien-sheng liu-shih-wu sui lun-wen-chi (Studies presented to Ts'ai Yuan-p'ei on his 65th birthday).
Peking: Kuo-li Chung-yang yen-chiu-yüan 1933/35,907-938
聖武親征錄
慶祝蔡元培先生六十五歲論文集

772. Un ouvrage sur les premier temps de Macao. Par Paul Pelliot.
     TP 31.1935,58-94
     Re: T'ien-tsê Chang: *Sino-Portuguese trade from 1514 to 1644*. A
     synthesis of Portuguese and Chinese sources. Leiden: E. J. Brill
     1934. VIII,157 pp. 8°

773. Michel Boym. Par Paul Pelliot.
     TP 31.1935,95-151
     Re: Robert Chabrié: *Michel Boym jésuite polonais et la fin des Ming
     en Chine (1646-1662)*. Contribution à l'histoire des missions d'Ex-
     trême-Orient. Paris: Pierre Bossuet 1933. 283 pp.,1 pl.

774. [rev.] R. P. Fr. Severiano Alcobendas O.F.M.: Las misiones Fran-
     ciscanas en China. Cartas, informes y relaciones del Padre Buena-
     ventura Ibáñez (1650-1690). Con introducción, notas y apéndices.
     Madrid: Estanislao Maestre 1933. XLVI,334 pp. (Bibliotheca
     Hispana Missionum.5.)
     TP 31.1935,152-157
     Paul Pelliot

775. [rev.] E. Haenisch: Die letzten Feldzüge Cinggis Han's und sein Tod
     nach der ostasiatischen Überlieferung. Asia Major 10.1933,503-551.
     TP 31.1935,157-167
     Paul Pelliot

776. [rev.] Sir E. Denison Ross: Sir Anthony Sherley and his Persian ad-
     venture, including some contemporary narratives relating hereto.
     London: G. Routledge 1933. XXXVIII,293 pp., 2 maps, 8 pl.
     (Broadway travellers.)
     TP 31.1935,167-172
     Paul Pelliot

777. [rev.] Edward J. Thomas: The history of Buddhist thought. London:
     Kegan Paul 1933. XVI,314 pp., 4 pl. 8°
     TP 31.1935,172-176
     Paul Pelliot

778. [rev.] G. J. Ramstedt: Die Palatalisation in den altaischen Sprachen.
     Ann. Acad. Scient. Fennicae. Ser. B, vol. 27.1932,239-251.

TP 31.1935,176-178
  Paul Pelliot

779. [rev.] Alfons Väth: Johann Adam Schall von Bell S.J., Missionar in
     China, Kaiserlicher Astronom und Ratgeber am Hofe von Peking
     1592-1666. Ein Lebens- und Zeitbild. Unter Mitwirkung von Louis
     van Hée S.J. Köln: J. P. Bachem 1933. XX,380 pp. 8° (Veröff. des
     Rheinischen Museums in Köln.2.)
     TP 31.1935,178-187
       Paul Pelliot

780. Notes additionnelles sur Tcheng Houo et sur ses voyages. Par Paul
     Pelliot.
     TP 31.1935,274-314
     The Addenda, pp.308-314 refer to a new publication:
     Cheng Ho's expeditions to the South Sea under the Ming dynasty
     鄭和の西征, by T. Yamamoto. *Tôyô gakuhô* 21.1934,374-404,
     506-556.

781. Paul Pelliot: Letter to the editor.
     Monumenta serica 1. 1935/36,192
     Dated: Peiping, 3 juin 1935. Paul Pelliot

1936
782. L'exposition chinoise de Londres.
     Revue archéologique.VI,7.1936,133-135
       Paul Pelliot
     (*Le Temps*, feuille du 7 janvier 1935.)

783. Après l'exposition d'art chinois à Londres. Remarques et con-
     clusions. Opinions de MM. P. Pelliot et J. Hackin.
     Revue de l'art ancien et moderne [Paris].69.1936,176-179
       J. Hackin, Conservateur du Musée Guimet

784. L'exposition d'art chinois à Londres.
     L'Asie française 1936,57-59
       Paul Pelliot, de l'Institut

785. Le prétendu album de porcelaines de Hiang Yuan-pien. Par Paul Pelliot.
TP 32.1936,15-58
Re: *Noted porcelains of successive dynasties* with comments & illustrations by Hsiang Yüan-pien revised and annotated by Kuo Pao-ch'ang and John C. Ferguson. Peiping: Chih Chai Publishing Co. 1931. 19 fol., 83 pl., 83 fol. explan. 2°
Sir Percival David: Hsiang and his album. *Transactions of the Oriental Ceramic Society* 1933/1934. London 1934,22-47, pl. X-XXII.
Cf. J. C. Ferguson: Review of a review. *Journal of the North China Branch of the Royal Asiatic Society* 67.1936,200-204

786. [rev.] The Kâçyapaparivarta. A Mahâyânasûtra of the Ratnakûṭa class edited in the original Sanskrit in Tibetan and in Chinese by Baron A. von Staël-Holstein. Shanghai: Commercial Press 1926. XXVI,234 pp., large 8°
A commentary to the Kâçyapaparivarta edited in Tibetan and in Chinese by Baron A. von Staël-Holstein. Peking: The National Library of Peiping, The National Tsinghua University 1933. XXIV, 340 pp.
Index to the Tibetan translation of th Kâçyapaparivarta. By Friedrich Weller. Cambridge, Mass.: Harvard-Yenching Institute 1933. VI,252 pp. 4° (Harvard Sino-Indian series.1.)
TP 32.1936,68-76
P. Pelliot

787. [rev.] Urban T. Holmes: French words of Chinese origin. Language.10.1934,280-285.
TP 32.1936,76-79
P. Pelliot

788. [rev.] Dr. Friedrich Risch: Wilhelm von Rubruk. Reise zu den Mongolen 1253-1255, übersetzt und erläutert. Leipzig 1934. VIII,336 pp. (Veröffentlichungen des Forschungsinstituts für vergleichende Religionsgeschichte an der Universität Leipzig. 2.Ser.,13.)
TP 32.1936,79-80
P. Pelliot

789. [rev.] Henri Bernard S.J.: Le Frère Bento de Goes chez les musulmans de la Haute Asie (1603-1607). Tientsin: Hautes Etudes 1934. 166 pp. 8°
TP 32.1936,80-81
  P. Pelliot

790. [rev.] E. Backhouse, J. O. P. Bland: Les empereurs mandchous. Mémoires de la Cour de Pékin. Trad. par Mlle L. M. Mitchell; préface de Henri Maspero. Paris: Payot 1934. 329 pp. 8°
TP 32.1936,81
  P. Pelliot

791. [rev.] Roswell S. Britton: The Chinese periodical press 中國報紙. Shanghai: Kelly & Walsh 1933. VIII,151 pp., 24 pl.
TP 32.1936,81-82
  P. Pelliot

792. [rev.] Comte de Semallé: Quatre ans à Pékin, août 1880 - août 1884. Le Tonkin. Paris: G. Enault (1933). 277 pp., 7 pl.
TP 32.1936,82-83
  P. Pelliot

793. [rev.] D. G. E. Hall: The Dalhousie-Phayre correspondence 1852-1856. London: Oxford Univ. Press 1932. LXXII,426 pp., 3 pl., 1 map.
TP 32.1936,83-84
  P. Pelliot

794. Brèves remarques sur le phonétisme dans l'écriture chinoise. Par Paul Pelliot.
TP 32.1936,162-166

795. Encore à propos des voyages de Tcheng Houo. Par Paul Pelliot.
TP 32.1936,210-222

796. Les relations du Siam et de la Hollande en 1608. Par Paul Pelliot.
TP 32.1936,223-229

797. Sao-houa, sauγa, sauγat, saguate. Par Paul Pelliot.
     TP 32.1936,230-237
     Re: an article by Wang Kuo-wei: *Kuan-t'ang chi-lin* 16 / 19a-b. Cf.
     TP 1928/29,130.

798. A propos du «tokharien». Par Paul Pelliot.
     TP 32.1936,259-284

799. Le Chao-hing ki-kou lou 紹興稽古錄.
     TP 32.1936,345-346
     P. Pelliot

800. [rev.] Mehmed Fuad Köprülü: Les origines de l'empire ottoman.
     Avec préface de S. Charléty. Paris: de Boccard 1935. 146 pp. 8°
     (Etudes orient. de l'Institut fr. d'archéologie de Stamboul.3.)
     TP 32.1936,353
     P. Pelliot

801. [rev.] Lucien Gibert: Dictionnaire historique et géographique de la
     Mandchourie. Hongkong: Soc. des Miss. Etr. 1934. XX,1040 pp. 8°
     TP 32.1936,354-355
     P. Pelliot

802. [rev.] Erich Haenisch: Mangḥol un niuca tobca'an (Yüan-ch'ao pi-
     shi). Die Geheime Geschichte der Mongolen, aus der chinesischen
     Transkription (Ausgabe Ye Têh-hui) im mongolischen Wortlaut wie-
     derhergestellt. Leipzig: Asia Major 1935. XII,124 pp.
     TP 32.1936,355-359
     P. Pelliot

803. [rev.] Albert Herrmann: Die Gobi im Zeitalter der Hunnenherrschaft.
     Geografiska Annaler 1935, dedicated to Sven Hedin, pp.130-143.
     TP 32.1936,359-360
     P. Pelliot

804. [rev.] Albert Herrmann: Die älteste türkische Weltkarte (1076 n.
     Chr.). Imago Mundi 1935,21-28.
     TP 32.1936,361-363
     P. Pelliot

805. [rev.] Albert Herrmann: Historical and commercial atlas of China. Cambridge, Mass.: Harvard Univ. Press 1935. 112 pp., small 2° (Harvard-Yenching Institute monograph series.1.)
TP 32.1936,363-372
P. Pelliot

806. [rev.] Rudolf [not: Richard] Kelling: Das chinesische Wohnhaus. Tô-kyô 1935. IX,128 pp., 107 ill., 3 pl.; Anhang: Bauwörterbuch. 27 pp. (Mitteilungen der Deutschen Gesellschaft f. Natur- und Völker-kunde Ostasiens. Supplementband 13.)
TP 32.1936,372-374
P. Pelliot

807. [rev.] Ed. Horst von Tscharner: Der mitteldeutsche Marco Polo nach der Admonter Handschrift. Berlin: Weidmann 1935. LII,102 pp., 1 pl. 8° (Deutsche Texte des Mittelalters.40.)
TP 32.1936,374-375
P. Pelliot

808. [rev.] G. J. Ramstedt: Kalmückisches Wörterbuch. Helsinki 1935. XXX,560 pp. 8° (Lexika Soc. Fenno-ugricae.3.)
TP 32.1936,375-379
P. Pelliot

809. [rev.] P. Anastasius van den Wyngaert OFM: Sinica Franciscana.3. Avec la collaboration du P. Fabiano Bollen. Quaracchi 1936. XXVIII,883 pp., 1 map. 8°
TP 32.1936,379-384
P. Pelliot

810. [rev.] Olov Jansé: Briques et objets céramiques funéraires de l'époque des Han appartenant à C. T. Loo et Cie. Paris: Ed. d'art et d'histoire 1936. 40 pp., 32 pl. 4°
TP 32.1936,384-386
Paul Pelliot

811. Les documents mongols du Musée de Teherân. [With illustration of 3 documents.]

Athâr-é Irân [Haarlem] 1.1936,37-44
  Paul Pelliot, membre de l'Institut de France

1937
812. The royal tombs of An-yang.
Independency, convergence & borrowing. Harvard centenary.
Cambridge, Mass.1937, 265-272, 4 pl.
[Not seen.]

812a.*Brahma et Bouddha. Les religions de l'Inde dans leur evolution historique* / H. v. Glasenapp. Préf. de Paul Pelliot. Trad. de l'allemand
d'Oreste Toutzevitch.
Paris: Payot 1937. 304 pp., 24 pp. of pl.

812b.Laure Morgenstern: *Esthétique d'Orient et d'Occident.* Avec une
préface de M. Paul Pelliot. Introduction de M. René Grousset.
Vendôme, Paris: Presses Universitaires de France, Paris: E. Leroux
1937. VIII,283 pp., portrait

813. Le Dr. Ferguson et l'album dit de Hiang Yuan-pien.
TP 33.1937,91-94
  Paul Pelliot
Re Ferguson in *Journal of the North China Branch of the Royal
Asiatic Society* 1936,200-204.

1938
814. The royal tombs of An-yang. By Professor Paul Pelliot.
Studies in Chinese art and some Indian influences. (Lectures de-
livered in connection with the International Exhibition of Chinese Art
at the Royal Academy of Art) by J. Hackin, Osvald Sirén, Langdon
Warner, Paul Pelliot. With a foreword by Sir William Llewellyn, P.
R. A. London: The India Society (1938),51-59, 8 pl.
«Lecture delivered in connection with the International Exhibition of
Chinese Art in the hall of the Royal Society on January 6,1936. I
have delivered a lecture on the same subject at Harvard during the
Harvard Tercentenary Conference in September, 1936, and the

present publication is, to some extent, a combined text of both
lectures.»
Rev.:*OLZ* 1939,252-256 (L. Bachhofer)
Revue des arts asiatiques 1938,127-128

815. Prof. Paul Pelliot (Paris): Remarques sur l'itineraire de Marco Polo.
*Actes du XXe Congrès international des Orientalistes, Bruxelles 5-10
Septembre 1938.* Louvain 1940,216

816. Marco Polo: *The description of the world.* [Translated & annotated
by] A. C. Moule & Paul Pelliot. 1-2.
London: G. Routledge & Sons 1938. 595 pp., CXXXI pp. 4°
Vol.2: A transcription of Z. The Latin codex in the Cathedral Library
at Toledo by A. C. Moule. Printed March 1935.
[A 3rd volume «Notes», by Pelliot and comprising appr. 400 pages
was projected. It is probably the posthumously published material, v.
i. Pelliot's share in the 1938 volumes is not clear.]
Rev.: *TP* 34.1938,246-248,334-340 (J. J. L. Duyvendak)
Tôa mondai 21.1940, p.30-39 (Iwamura Shinobu)

817. *Les arts de l'Iran, l'ancienne Perse et Bagdad.* Catalogue rédigé par
Henry Corbin, Rémy Cottevieille-Giraudet, Jean David-Weill,
Eustache de Lorey et Georges Salles. Avec une préface de Paul Pel-
liot, membre de l'Institut.
Paris: Bibliothèque nationale 1938. VII,207 pp., 16 pl.
Préface, III-VII, gez.: Paul Pelliot, membre de l'Institut, professeur
au College de France

818. Le nom du xwârizm dans les textes chinois. Par Paul Pelliot.
TP 34.1938,146-152

819. Les Franciscains en Chine au XVIe et au XVIIe siècle. Par Paul
Pelliot.
TP 34.1938,191-222
Re: P. Anastasius van den Wijngaert OFM: *Sinica Franciscana*.2.
Relationes et epistolas Fratrum Minorum saeculi XVI et XVII
collegit, ad fidem codicum redegit et adnotavit. Quaracchi: Coll. S.
Bonaventura 1933. LVI,662 pp. 8°

820. Henri Boucher, S.J. (Nécrologie.) [† Febr. 18, 1939]
TP 34.1938,413
    P. Pelliot

821. L'exposition des arts de l'Iran à la Bibliothèque nationale. – L'art
iranien.
Cahiers de Radio-Paris.9.1938, no 8, 747-752
    Paul Pelliot

822. [rev.] Fox, Ralph: Genghis Khan. London: John Lane, The Bodley
Head 1936. XV,285 pp., 8 ill., 2 maps. 8°
Bespr. von P. Pelliot, Paris
OLZ 1938,48-49

823. [rev.] Lüders, Heinrich: Textilien im alten Turkistan. Berlin: Verlag
der Akademie der Wissenschaften in Komm. bei W. de Gruyter &
Co. 1936. 38 pp. (Abhandlungen der Preuß. Akademie der Wiss. Jg.
1936. Phil.-Hist. Klasse No. 3.)
Bespr. von P. Pelliot, Paris
OLZ 1938,184-188

1939
824. Die Jenseitsvorstellung der Chinesen. Von Paul Pelliot.
Eranos-Jahrbuch.7.1939,61-82

1940
825. Marco Polo.
JRAS 1940,200-201
    P. Pelliot
Re: *JRAS* 1939,628-644 (Benedetto)

826. *Prens Kalyanamkara ve Papamkara hikâyesinin Uygurcası.*
(Hazırlıyan) Hüseyin Namik Orkun.
Istanbul: A. Kiral Basimevi 1940. 118 pp. 8°
Soghdian and Turkish. Text from *Le Sûtra des causes des effets du
bien et du mal.*
[Not seen.]

827. Deux lacunes dans le texte mongol actuel de l'Histoire secrète des
     Mongols. Par Paul Pelliot.
     Journal asiatique 232.1940,1-18
     1. Les enfants de Čaraqai-Lingqu.
     2. La mère de Bälgütäi.
     3. Les enfants de Bartan-ba'atur.

828. Le «Cheynam» de Marco Polo. Par M. Paul Pelliot, membre de
     l'Institut.
     Cahiers de l'EFEO, suppl. A (Paris 1940/41),3-5

828a. *Chinese Jews. A compilation of matters relating to the Jews of
      K'aifeng Fu.* By William Charles White in collaboration with Ronald
      James Williams. Part 3: Genealogical.
      Toronto: University of Toronto Press 1942. XIII, S. 4°
      Contains: The Jew Ai. Father Matteo Ricci's source of information.
      By Paul Pelliot (Translated from the French, Le Juif Ngai. T'oung
      pao.20.1920/21, p.38, by A. E. H. Petrie.) S.16-19

1944
829. *La découverte de la Chine par les Portugais au XVIème siècle et la
     cartographie des Portulans.* Par Albert Kammerer. Avec des notes de
     toponymie chinoise, par Paul Pelliot. Avec **XXIII** planches et trois
     tableaux dont un en grand format.
     Leiden: E. J. Brill 1944. IX,260 pp.
     (T'oung Pao. Supplément au vol. 39.)

830. Une tribu méconnue des Naiman: Les Bätäkin. Par Paul Pelliot.
     TP 37.1944,35-72

831. Les formes avec et sans q- (k-) initial en turc et en mongol. Par Paul
     Pelliot.
     TP 37.1944,73-101

832. Širolγa - Širalγa. Par Paul Pelliot.
     TP 37.1944,102-113

833. Le terme «kereksur». Par Paul Pelliot.
     TP 37.1944,114-124

834. Les caractères de transcription 斡 *wo* ou *wa* et 白 *pai*. Par Paul
     Pelliot.
     TP 37.1944,125-134

835. Qubčiri-qubčir et qubči'ur-qubčur. Par Paul Pelliot.
     TP 37.1944,153-164

836. Tämgrim > tärim. Par Paul Pelliot.
     TP 37.1944,165-185

837. [rev.] Spuler, Berthold: Die goldene Horde. Die Mongolen in
     Rußland 1223-1502. Leipzig: Harrassowitz 1943. XVI,556 pp., 2
     Tab., 1 map, large 8° (Das mongolische Weltreich. Quellen und
     Forschungen, hrsg. v. E. Haenisch u. H. H. Schaeder.2.)
     Bespr. v. P. Pelliot, Paris
     OLZ 1944,14-21

1945

838. Les études chinoises. Par Paul Pelliot†
     Renaissance.2/3.1944/45,258-264
     Conférence prononcé à l' Ecole libre des hautes études le 26 janvier
     1945.

839. *Le chapitre CVII du Yuan che*. Les généalogies impériales mongoles
     dans l'histoire chinoise officielle de la dynastie mongole. Par Louis
     Hambis. Avec des notes supplementaires par Paul Pelliot. Avec 71
     tableaux dont 10 hors-texte.
     Leiden: E. J. Brill 1945.

840. *Address by Paul Pelliot, delivered at a meeting of the Chinese Art
     Society of America*. The Metropolitan Museum of Art Lecture Hall,
     January 25, 1945.
     (New York: The Chinese Art Society of America?) 1945. 15 pp. 8°

841. Orientalists in France during the war. / Paul Pelliot. Address deliver-
     ed at a meeting of the Chinese Art Society of America, January 25th,
     1945.
     Chinese Art Society of America. Archives.1.1945/46,14-25

842. Henri Maspero.
     Fraternité 18 mai 1945,4
       Paul Pelliot, membre de l'Institut

1948
843. *Les influences européennes sur l'art chinois au XVIIe et au XVIIIe
     siècle.* [Conférence faite au Musée Guimet le 20 février 1927.]
     Paris: Imprimerie nationale 1948. 28 pp., 8 pl. 8°
       Paul Pelliot

844. Le Hõja et le Sayyid Ḥusain de l'Histoire des Ming. Par Paul Pelliot†
     TP 38.1948,81-292
     Offprint: Leiden: E. J. Brill 1948. [81]-292 pp. 8°

1949
845. Un rescrit mongol en écriture «'Phags-pa». Par Paul Pelliot.
     G. Tucci: *Tibetan painted scrolls.* Roma: Libreria dello Stato 1949,
     621-624

846. *Œuvres posthumes de Paul Pelliot.* Publiées sous les auspices de
     l'Académie des inscriptions et belles-lettres et avec le concours du
     Centre national de la recherche scientifique.
     Paris: Librairie d'Amérique et d'Orient Adrien-Maisonneuve 1949-
     1961.
     1. Histoire secrète des Mongols. 1949.
     2. Notes sur l'histoire de la Horde d'Or. 1950.
     3. Mémoires sur les coutumes du Cambodge de Tcheou Ta-Kouan.
        1951.
     4. Les débuts de l'imprimerie en Chine. 1953.
     5. Histoire ancienne du Tibet. 1961.
     6. Notes critiques d'histoire kalmouke.1960.

847. *Histoire secrète des Mongols.* Restitution du texte mongol et
     traduction française des chapitres I à VI.
     Paris: Librairie d'Amérique et d'Orient Adrien-Maisonneuve 1949.
     [III],196 pp. 8°
     (Œuvres posthumes de Paul Pelliot.1.)
     Pref.: Paris, le 5 juillet 1947. L. Hambis

848. *Notes sur l'histoire de la Horde d'or; suivies de Quelques noms turcs d'hommes et de peuples finissant en «ar».*
Paris: Adrien-Maisonneuve 1949 [jacket: 1950]. 292 pp. 8°
(Œuvres posthumes de Paul Pelliot.2.)
Pref.: Paris, le 20 mai 1947. Pour le comité de publication: Louis Hambis.

1951

849. *Mélanges sur l'époque des Croisades.* Par Paul Pelliot.
Paris: Imprimerie nationale 1951. 97 pp. 8°
Extrait des Mémoires de l'Institut national de France. Académie des inscriptions et belles-lettres, tome 44.
Contents:
1. Le synode d'Antioche de 1140, le Concile de Jérusalem de 1141, l'avènement du roi Amaury 1er en 1163, l'évêque Hugues de Ga bala. 1-
2. Jean du Plan-Carpin en Pologne. 43-
3. Sur quatre passages de Guillaume de Rubrouck. 48-
4. Habent falcones girfaus Erodios in magna multitudine, quos omnes portant super manum dextram. 65-
5. Deux passages de la prophétie de Hannan, fils d'Issac. 73-97

849a. *Mémoires sur les coutumes du Cambodge* de Tcheou Ta-kouan. Version nouvelle suivie d'un commentaire inachevé.
Paris: Imprimerie nationale, Librairie d'Amérique et d'Orient 1951. 178 pp. 8°
(Œuvres posthumes de Paul Pelliot.3.)
Avertissement, p.6, signed:
Octobre 1949. G. Cœdès, P. Demiéville

850. *Histoire des campagnes de Gengis Khan. Cheng-wou ts'in-tcheng lou* [聖武親征錄]. Traduit et annoté par Paul Pelliot et Louis Hambis. Tome 1.
Leiden: E. J. Brill 1951. XXVII,485 pp.
473-477: Collation du Chouo Fou [説郛]
Avant-propos, p.VIII, dated: Pékin, le 15 mai 1948.
[rev.] *Tôyôgakuhô* 33:3/4.1951,148 (Murayama Shichirô 村山七郎)

1953

851. *Les début de l'imprimérie en Chine.*
Paris: Imprimerie nationale, Librairie d'Amérique et d'Orient 1953.
VIII,138 pp. 8°
(Œuvres posthumes de Paul Pelliot.4.)
121-138: Appendice:
Notes additionnelles sur les éditions imprimés du Canon bouddhique,
par Paul Demiéville.
Contents:
1.   Le texte du *Li tai san pao ki*
2.   Les image à légende soit-disant imprimée en 607 de notre ère
3.   La prétendue «dhâraṇî des Souei»
4.   Une prétendue édition bouddhique de 655
5.   Les feuillets du *K'ai yuan tsa pao*
6.   Les chou-pen des Six Synasties et des T'ang
7.   Le texte du pélerin Yi-tsing (692)
8.   La réplique de l'inscription de la montagne Yi
9.   Le texte de Lieou Yu-si
10.   Le million de dhâraṇî imprimées au Japon en 764-770
11.   La préface de Yuan Tchen aux œuvres de Po Kiu-yi
12.   Le rapport de Fong Sieou
13.   Le texte du *Yun k'i yeou yi*
14.   La préface des instructions familiales de Lieou P'ien
15.   Le texte de Sseu-k'ong T'ou
16.   Le texte du prétendu *Kouo che tche* et celui de Tchou Yi
17.   Le texte du *Yun sien san lou*
18.   Le *King kang king* imprimé en 868
19.   Le rouleau imprimé de Paris
20.   Le rouleau de Londres de 975
21.   Les éditions du Kouo-tseu-kien au temps de Fong Tao
22.   Les classques gravés sur pierre au Sseu-tch'ouan
23.   Les éditions xylographiques de Wou Tchao-yi
24.   L'édition du *Kouang cheng yi* de Tou Kouang-t'ing et celles
        des collections littéraires de Kouan-hieou et de Houo Ning
25.   Les premières éditions des Song
26.   Les premières éditions du *Canon bouddhique* et du *Canon
        taoïque*
27.   Les estampages et les reproductions d'autographes

1955

852. Pelliot 著: Chiao-kuang Yin-tu liang-tao k'ao 交廣印度兩道考.
[Transl.:] Feng Ch'eng-chün i 馮承鈞譯.
Peking: Chung-hua shu-chü 中華書局 1955. 2,6,158 pp.
Translator's pref. signed: 1931

1957

853. T'u-huo-lo yü k'ao 吐火羅語考. Po-hsi-ho, Lieh-wei [Sylvain Lévi]
chu, Feng Ch'eng-chün i 伯希和烈維著馮承鈞譯.
(Shanghai:) Chung-hua shu-chü (1957). 156 pp.

853a. Reconnaissance en Haute Asie par cinq envoyés ouigours au XVIIIe
siècle, par Jacques Bacot. [Avec des notes de Paul Pelliot.]
Paris: Société asiatique 1957. 19 pp.
(Manuscrits de Haute Asie conservés à la Bibliothèque nationale de
Paris (Fonds Pelliot).4.)
From *JA* 244/2.1956

1959

854. Paul Pelliot: *Notes on Marco Polo*. Ouvrage posthume publié sous
les auspices de l'Académie des inscriptions et belles-lettres et avec le
concours du Centre national de la recherche scientifique.1-3.
Paris: Imprimerie nationale, Librairie Adrien-Maisonneuve 1959-
1973. 4°
1. 1959. XII,611 pp. Preface: Paris, le 20 mars 1958. Louis Hambis
2. 1963. pp.613-885, XII, [II]
3. Index. 1973
Rev.: *OLZ* 1961,191-195 (P. Kahle)
OLZ 72.1977,413-416 (H. Franke)
Tôyô gakuhô 43.1961:3, p.92-94 (Enoki Kazuo)

1960

855. *Notes critiques d'histoire kalmouke.*
Paris: Librairie d'Amérique et d'Orient, Adrien-Maisonneuve 1960.
VI,235 pp., 4 genealog. pl.
(Œuvres posthumes de Paul Pelliot.6.)
Contents:
   1. Les noms donnés aux Kalmouks.

2. Notice historique de l'ensemble des tribus dzoungar par l'em
    pereur K'ien-loung.
3. Les Dzoungars jusqu'au début du XVIIe siècle.
4. La notice des Dzoungar du Kökä-nôr dans le Piao tchouan.
5. La généalogie du Dzoungar Batûr-Khontaiji.
6. Notice générale des Turghut au chapitre 101 du Piao tchouan.
7. Keraït et Turghut.
8. Le retour des Turghut de la Volga en 1771.
9. Les Qazaq dans les textes chinois.
10. Les généalogies des princes qazaq.
Notes
Index.
[The genealogical tables form the second volume.]
[rev.] *Tôyôshi kenkyû* 20:2.1961,100-101 (Haneda Akira 羽田
明)

1961

856. *Histoire ancienne du Tibet.*
Paris: Librairie d'Amérique et d'Orient Adrien-Maisonneuve 1961.
II,168 pp. 8°
(Œuvres posthumes de Paul Pelliot. Publiées sous les auspices de
l'Académie des Inscriptions et Belles-Lettres et avec le concours du
Centre national de la recherche scientifique.5.)
Avertissement, gez.: Paris, le 1er décembre 1956. Louis Hambis.

Contents:
Histoire ancienne du Thibet:
Kieou T'ang Chou, chapitre 196A
Kieou T'ang Chou, chapitre 196B
Sin T'ang Chou, chapitre 216A
Sin T'ang Chou, chapitre 216B
Itinéraire vers Lhasa:
Sin T'ang Chou, chapitre 40, 6v°-7r°
Manuscrit Pelliot 2762:
Lexique sino-tibétain.
Index général

Occasioned by Bushell: The early history of Tibet. *JRAS*.NS12.
1880,435-541

1967

856a.*Les origines de l'astronomie chinoise*, par Léopold de Saussure. A
new edition with the book review by Alexander Pogo (Isis 1932, 17:
267-271) and the list of writings by Paul Pelloit [!] (T'oung Pao
1926, 24: 298-230 [!]).
Taipei: Ch'eng-wen Publ. Co. 1967. XIV,601 pp.
Pelliot's contribution on pp. 599-601.

1971

856b.Le juif Ngai, informateur du P. Mathieu Ricci.
Studies of the Chinese Jews. Selections from journals East and West.
Compiled with preface and introductions by Hyman Kublin.
New York: Paragon 1971,93-100

857. Paul Ratchnevsky: *Un code des Yuan*. II. Préface de P. Pelliot.
Paris: Presses Universitaires de France 1972. XI,197 pp. large 8°
(Bibliothèque de l'Institut des hautes études chinoises.4.)

857a. Hsi-yü nan-hai shih-ti k'ao-cheng i-ts'ung. Vol. 1-5.
西域南海史地考證譯叢 (Translated by Feng Ch'eng-chün.)
T'ai-pei: T'ai-wan shang-wu yin-shu-kuan 1971.
(Jen-jen wen-k'u.1861-1870.)

1973

858. Paul Pelliot: *Notes on Marco Polo*. III. Index. Publié sous les
auspices de l'Académie des inscriptions et belles-lettres et avec le
concours du Centre national de la recherche scientifique.
Paris: Imprimerie nationale, Librairie Adrien-Maisonneuve 1973.
II,305 pp. 4°
Preface signed: Paris, le 10 août 1973. Louis Hambis

859. *Recherches sur les chrétiens d'Asie centrale et d'Extrême-Orient*. I.
En marge de Jean du Plan Carpin; II.Guillaume de Rubrouck; III.Màr
Ya(h)bhallàhâ, Rabban Sàumâ et les princes Öngüt chrétiens.
Paris: Imprimerie nationale 1973. IV,307 pp.
(Œuvres posthumes de Paul Pelliot.)
Edited by Jean Dauvillier and Louis Hambis.
pp.298-307: Index

1981

860. *Grottes de Touen-houang*. Carnet de notes de Paul Pelliot.
[1] Inscriptions et peintures murales. Grotte 1 à 30.
Paris: Collège de France, Instituts d'Asie, Centre de recherche sur l'Asie centrale et la Haute Asie 1981. XIII,129 pp., 64 pl.
(Mission Paul Pelliot. Documents conservés au Musée Guimet.11.)
Avant-propos de Nicole Vandier-Nicolas.
Notes préliminaires de Monique Maillard.
2. Grottes 31 à 72. 1983. XIV,76 pp., pl. 65-128
3. Grottes 72 à 111a. XVI,97 pp., pl. 129-192
4. Grottes 112a à 120n. 1984. XVII,108 pp., pl. 193-256
5. Grottes 120n à 146. 1986. XVIII,151 pp., pl. 257-320
6. Grottes 146a à 182. 1992. XV,101 pp., pl. 321-376

1984

861. *La stèle de Si-ngan-fou* / Paul Pelliot.
Paris: Editions de la Fondation Singer-Polignac (1984). X,105 pp., 10 pl.
(Recherches sur les chrétiens d'Asie centrale et Extrême-Orient.2,1.)
(Œuvres posthumes de Paul Pelliot.)
Préface, par Thérèse de Sonneville-David.
Avant-propos, par Jean Dauvillier.
1. L'inscription chinoise de la stèle de Si-ngan-fou. Présentation par Jean Dauvillier.
Traduction par Paul Pelliot.
2. Inscriptions syriaques de la stèle de Si-ngan-fou, par Jean Dauvillier.
Texte revu et complété par Antoine Guillaumont.

1991

862. *La croisière jaune: expédition Citroën Centre-Asie* / George Le Fèvre; La Haute Asie / Paul Pelliot. Avant-propos V. Eliséev; préface André Citroën. Introduction Louis Audouin-Dubreuil.
Paris: L'Asiathèque 1991. 343 pp.

1993

862a. *The customs of Cambodia* [Chen-la feng-t'u chi] 真臘風土記. By Chou Ta-kuan 周達觀 (Zhou Daguan). Translated into English from

the French version by Paul Pelliot of Chou's Chinese original by J. Gilman d'Arcy Paul. Third edition.
Bangkok: The Siam Society 1993. XIX,77 pp.
ISBN 974-8298-25-6

1996

863. Paul Pelliot: *L'inscription nestorienne de Si-ngan-fou*. Edited with supplements by Antonino Forte.
Kyoto: Scuola di Studi sull'Asia Orientale; Paris: Collège de France. Institut des Hautes Études Chinoises. 1996. XXI,540 pp., pl.
(Italian School of East Asian Studies. Epigraphical series.2.)
(Collège de France. Œuvres posthumes de Paul Pelliot.)

VII-XII	Foreword, signed: Antonino Forte
XIII-XIX	Avant-propos, signed: Antonino Forte
XX-XXI	Acknowledgements, signed: A. F.
2	Avertissement, signed: A. F.

Notes editoriales
Suppléments

349-	The edict of 638 allowing the diffusion of Christianity in China
375-	On the so-called Abraham from Persia. A case of mistaken identity
411-	Appendix A: On the original name of Aluohan
415-	Appendix B: Mainland China's recent interest in the Axis of the Sky
429-	The Chongfu-si in Chang'an. A neglected Buddhist monastery and Nestorianism
455-	Appendix: The Chongfu Monastery in Chang'an. Foundation and name changes
473-	A literal model for Adam. The Dhûta Monastery inscription
489-	Additional remarks
497-	The Chinese inscriptions on the stele of 781
505-	Index of proper names and titles
540-	List of illustrations

1998

864. Marco Polo: *Le devisement du monde. Le livre des merveilles*. Tome 1-2. Texte intégral établi par A. C. Moule et Paul Pelliot. Version française de Louis Hambis. Introduction et notes de Stéphane Yerasimos.
(Paris:) La Découverte (1998). 554 S.
(La découverte / Poche.45.)
La présente édition reprend intégralement celle publiée en 1980 dans la collection «La Découverte» des Éditions François Maspero.

Two Japanese additions to the bibliography

865. Chôjô sei 長城[生
      [A brief record of the expedition to Hsin-chiang by Paul Pelliot. Paul
      Pelliot no Shinkyô tanken ryakki.]
      ポール.ペリオの新疆探檢略記
      Enjin 44.1911,8-14

866. Sakaki Ryôsaburô 榊亮三郎 (transl.)
      [Les influences iraniennes au Asie centrale et en l'Extrême-Orient.
      Iran gozoku no minshû ga Chûô Ajia narabi ni kyoku-tô chi ni
      oyoboseru eikyô.]
      イラン語族の民眾が中央亞細亞並に極東の地に及
      ぼせる影響
      Geibun 4:8. 1912,1-38

R = review
Chinese names have been standardised, whenever possible, according to the Wade/Giles system, Russian names according to the international system, except for a few well-known names, e.g. Minorsky, and Shirokogoroff.

The Jew Ai 828a
Jörg Trübner zum Gedächtnis. Ergebnisse seiner letzten chinesischen Reisen (Kümmel) 666
Jörg Trübner. (Nécrologie.)[† Febr. 7, 1930.] 453
Johann Adam Schall von Bell S.J., Missionar in China, Kaiserlicher Astronom und Ratgeber am Hofe von Peking 1592-1666 (Väth) 779
Johann de Plano Carpini. Geschichte der Mongolen und Reisebericht 1245-1247 (Risch) 606
Josef Markwart (Marquart). (Nécrologie.)[1864-1930.] 448
Journal asiatique 1920 224. 240
Le journal d'André Ly, prêtre chinois, missionnaire et notaire apostolique, 1746-1763 332
Le journal de Che Ta-kai 石大開 (Li Choen) 587
Journal of the North China Branch of the Royal Asiatic Society 224
Journal of the Royal Asiatic Society 1920 224. 240
Ju-Tao-Fo 儒道佛 Die religiösen und philosophischen Systeme Ostasiens (Krause) 296
Le juif Ngai 艾, informateur du P. Ricci 218. 856b
K istorii i kritike Codex Cumanicus (On history and criticism of Codex Cumanicus) (Malov) 593
K izučeniju beludžkogo jazyka u fol'klora [On the study of Beluchi language and folklore] (Zarubin) 748
K značeniju slov jigür-ê aɣulɣan v piśme il-chana Arguna k Filippu Krasivomu (Bogdanov) 505
Kâçyapaparivarta. A Mahâyânasûtra of the Ratnakûṭa class edited in the original Sanskrit in Tibetan and in Chinese by Baron A. von Staël-Holstein 786
Kaiser Kien-lung's französisches Kupferstichwerk (Fürstenberg) 672
Kalmückisches Wörterbuch (Ramstedt) 808
Kan Sankoku Rokuchô kinen kyô shûroku 漢三國六朝紀年鏡集錄 [Collection of dated mirrors of the Han, der Three Kingdoms and Six Dynasties] (Umehara) 742
Kao-tch'ang, Qočo, Houo-tcheou et Qâra-Khodja 154
De Kâpiśî à Pushkarâvatî (Foucher) 704
Karman. Ein buddhistischer Legendenkranz (Zimmer) 391
Kaschgar und die Kharoṣṭhî (Franke, Pischel) 53. 66
Kastren-mongolist (Vladimircov) 619
Kâtantra und Kaumâralâta (Lüders) 592
亟縛犀 ki-fou-si 753
Le Kin kou k'i kouan 今古奇觀 324
Les kökö-däbtär et les hou-k'eou ts'ing-ts'eu 戶口青冊 440
Körösi Csoma Sándor (Ross) 735
Kokei no kenkyû (Tomioka) 221

This is an auxiliary tool only as it is expected that most searches will be done by the chronological arrangement of the publications, and by the name and title indices. Especially with regard to the many short review notes, no effort has been made in the present index to be comprehensive. The focus is on key-words that the other indices do not contain, and that may be useful for pinpointing a publication.

woman: Bengal 608R
world map, oldest Turkish 804R
world politics 572R
Xalxa dialect 733R
Xwârizm, name of 818
yakṣas 694R
yam (post station) 439
Yang-tzu: travel 102R. 104R
Yao folksongs: phonetic 716R
yeh-t'iao 706R
Yen-ching hsüeh-pao 747R
Yen-t'ieh lun 673R
yin-ch'i («de façon cachée s'élever») 299

yü-lan-p'o 8R
yü-lan-pen 8R
Yüan dynasty: history 632
Yüan tien-chang 647R
Yüan-ch'ao pi-shih 441. 554R. 802R. 827. 847
Yüan-shih 839
Yüeh-shih 649R
Yung-ho-kung 688R
Yünnan: aborigines 112R
Zach, Erwin von 417. 421
Zikawei: observatory 601R
zodiac: Turks 419
zoology: Qazwînî 469
Zoroastrianism 546R

LITERATURE ON PELLIOT

1. *Études sinologiques.* Par Fernand Farjenel.
   Chang-hai s.d. 7,5 pp. [Offprint from *Echo de Chine*, Shanghai]
   Contains: IV. Les procédés de M. Pelliot.

2. Les «mandarins» de Paris en perdition, par Jean Ajalbert [polémique
   sinologique entre MM. Chavannes, Farjenel et Pelliot].
   L'Avenir du Tonkin.1910: Nov. 4, 19 and 23

3. Réponse à M. Pelliot, par M. Farjenel.
   La depêche, journal de démocratie, Toulouse. Oct. 18, 1910

4. [Lettre de M. E. Blochet, bibliothécaire à la Bibliothèque nationale
   (polémique avec M. Pelliot).]
   La dépêche, Toulouse. Oct. 20, 1910

5. La guerre des sinologues. Lettre de M. Ajalbert.
   L'Echo de Tientsin. Dec. 17, 1910

6. La guerre des sinologues. Réponse de M. Pelliot à M. Jean Ajalbert.
   L'Echo de Tientsin. Dec. 18 and 21, 1910

7. L'EFEO et les études sinologiques. Les manuscrits de la mission
   Pelliot. Lettre de M. Farjenel.
   La revue indigène. Paris. 5.1910:56, pp. 689-713

8. Haneda Toru 羽田亨
   [P. Pelliot's exploration into Central Asia: His discovery of manu-
   scripts in Tunhuang stone caves. Pelliot shi no Chûô ajia ryokô –
   Tonkô sekijitsu isho hakken no shidai.]
   ペリオ氏の中央亞細亞旅行 - 敦煌石室遺書發見の次第
   Geibun 1:4.1910,107-114

9. *Autour d'une chaire du Collège de France. Les documents de la
   Mission Pelliot.* Par MM. P. Malingre, F. Farjenel, cap. Roux etc.
   Paris: Marcel Rivière 1911. 48 pp. 8°

10. A propos de la controverse Pelliot-Farjenel.
    Revue indochinoise. No. 4. Avril 1911

11. Mueller, Herbert: Die Manuskripte von Tunhuang. Wissenschaftliche
    Beleuchtung der Ohrfeigenszene zwischen Prof. Paul Pelliot und
    seinem Widersacher Farjenel.
    Vossische Zeitung 330: 7.7.1911

12. Petrucci, Raphaël: The Pelliot Mission to Chinese Turkestan.
    Burlington Magazine 19.1911,211-218

13. Takahashi Setsuko 高橋節子
    [Pelliot's account of his expedition to Tunhuang: The great discovery
    of ancient Buddhist images and sutras. Butsujin Pelliot no Shina
    Tonkô kikôbun – ko butsuzô ko shakyô no dai hakken.]
    佛人ペリオの支那敦煌紀行文– 古佛像古寫經の大發見
    Shoga to kenkyû.1:5. 1917,23-31

14. Documents de la Mission Pelliot (exposés au Musée Guimet). Décrits
    par J. Hackin.
    Asie centrale et Tibet. Missions Pelliot et Bacot. (Documents exposés
    au Musée Guimet.)
    Paris, Bruxelles: G. van Oest 1921,9-20
    (Bulletin archéologique du Musée Guimet.2.)

15. Oldenburg, S. [et al.]: Zapiska ob učenych trudach Polja Pellio.
    IAN VI,16.1922,56-57

16. Hentze, Carl: Réponse à la lettre ouverte de M. Paul Pelliot.
    Anvers: De Sikkel 1930. 32 pp. 4°

17. *Bibliographie bouddhique*.4/5. mai 1931 - mai 1933. Rétrospective:
    L'œuvre de M. le Prof. Paul Pelliot, par Marcelle Lalou.
    Paris: Librairie d'Amérique et d'Orient, Adrien-Maisonneuve 1934,1-
    29

18. Aoki Tomitarô 青木富大郎
    [Paul Pelliot's arrival in Japan. Pelliot shi iyoiyo raichô.]
    ペリオ氏いよいよ來朝

Shigaku zasshi 46.1935:8, p.87-88
Rekishigaku kenkyû 4:2.1935,64

19. Thomas, F. W.: Professor Paul Pelliot.
    Indian art and letters. NS 19.1945,81-85

20. Lods, Adolphe: Nécrologie: La collaboration de Paul Pelliot au
    Journal des Savants.
    Journal des Savants 1945,150-155

21. Robequain, Charles: Paul Pelliot.
    *Académie des sciences coloniales. Comptes rendus mensuels des
    séances.* 1945,539-546

22. Filliozat, Jean: Paul Pelliot, 1878-1945, honneur de la sinologie
    française.
    France-Orient 53.1945,43-49

23. *Paul Pelliot.*
    Paris: La Société asiatique 1946. 80 pp.
    Georges Salles, Edmond Faral: Paroles prononcées le 31 octobre 1945
    devant le cercueil de Paul Pelliot. 1-7, 8-12
    Jean Filliozat: Paul Pelliot, honneur de la sinologie française, 1878-
    1945. Publié dans *France-Orient*. 13-20
    Louis Vaillant: Paul Pelliot, chef de mission. Lu le 8 février 1946 à la
    Société asiatique. 21-28
    Paul Demiéville: La carrière scientifique de Paul Pelliot et son œuvre
    relative à l'Extrême-Orient. Allocution prononcée à la Société
    asiatique le 9 novembre 1945. 29-54
    Jean Deny: Paul Pelliot et les études altaïques. Lu le 9 novembre
    1945, à la Société asiatique. 55-68
    L. Hambis: Paul Pelliot et les études mongoles. 69-77
    L. Hambis: Fonds Pelliot [au Musée Guimet]. 78-79

24. Deydier, H.: Paul Pelliot.
    Bulletin de la Société des études indochinoises NS 21.1946,13-15

25. Bernard, Henri: Paul Pelliot, un maître de la sinologie française.
    Bulletin de l'Université l'Aurore III,7.1946,123-138

26. Auboyer, Jeannine: Paul Pelliot (1878-1945).
    Artibus Asiae 9.1946,141-143

27. Eberhard, Wolfram: Paul Pelliot.
    *Ankara Üniversitesi Dil Tarih ve Coğrafya Fakültesi dergisi.*4.
    1946,232-236

28. Elisséeff, Serge: Paul Pelliot, 1878-1945.
    Archives of the Chinese Art Society of America. 1.1945/46,11-13

29. Des Rotours, Robert: Paul Pelliot (28 mai 1878 - 26 octobre 1945).
    Mélanges chinois et bouddhiques 8.1946,227-234

30. Fazy, Robert: Paul Pelliot.
    *Mitteilungen der Schweizerischen Gesellschaft für Ostasiatische
    Kunst.*8. 1946,96-97

31. Umehara Sueji 梅原末治
    [Scholars who made Central Asian expeditions. 2: Prof. P. Pelliot.
    Sei-iki tanken no gakusha-tachi. Pelliot kyôju no tsuioku]
    西域探檢の學者達 2.ペリオ教授の追憶
    Chikei 知慧 2.1947:6, p. 56-64; 3.1948:4, p. 57-64

32. Des Rotours, Robert: Paul Pelliot, 28 mai 1878 - 26 octobre 1945.
    Monumenta serica 12.1947,266-276

33. Musées nationaux, Département des Arts Asiatiques. Musée Guimet:
    *Manuscrits et peintures de Touen-houang. Mission Pelliot 1906-
    1909. - Collections de la Bibliothèque Nationale et du Musée Guimet.*
    (Paris:) Éditions des Musée nationaux 1947. 41 pp., 1 map.
    Preface signed, p.12: Louis Hambis

34. Duyvendak, J. J. L.: Paul Pelliot† (May 28th 1878 - October 26th
    1945).
    TP 38.1947/48, 1-18

35. Konow, Sten: Paul Pelliot.
    *Acta Orientalia.*20.1948,161-164

36. Lévy, Paul: Nécrologie de Paul Pelliot.
    Dên Viêt Nam 1.1948,55-61

37. Haneda Toru 羽田亨
    [L'orientalisme dans notre pays et le Professeur Pelliot. Waga kuni no
    tôhôgaku to Pelliot kyôju.]
    わが国の東方学とペリオ教授
    Tôyôshi kenkyû 10:3. 1948,46-57

38. Kanda Kiichirô 神田喜一郎
    [On the publication of the posthumous manuscripts of Prof. Pelliot.
    Ko-Pelliot kyôju no ikô kankô ni tsuite.]
    故ペリオ教授の遺稿刊行について
    Tôkô. 東光 6.1948,63

39. Fazy, Robert: Les œuvres posthumes de Paul Pelliot.
    Asiatische Studien 3.1949,53-55

40. Renou, Louis: Notice sur la vie et les travaux de M. Paul Pelliot,
    membre de l'Académie. Lu dans la séance du 21 avril.
    Paris: Institut de France, Académie des inscriptions et belles-lettres
    1950. 19 pp.

41. Hambis, Louis: Paul Pelliot (1878-1945). Historien et linguiste.
    Revue historique 203.1950,30-40

42. Haenisch, Erich: Paul Pelliot.
    Zeitschrift der Deutschen Morgenländischen Gesellschaft 101 (NF
    26). 1951,9-10

43. Akiyama Terukazu 秋山光和
    [Paul Pelliot's travels to Tunhuang (archaeology). Pelliot no Tonkô
    kikô (Tonkô no iseki).]
    ペリオの敦煌紀行 (敦煌の遺蹟)
    Geijutsu shinchô 藝術新潮 4.1953:4, p.114-116

44. Akiyama Terukazu 秋山光和

[Itinerary of the Pelliot mission in Central Asia and its archaeological findings. Pelliot chôsa kuni no chûô Ajia ryotei to sono kôkogaku-teki seika.] ペリオ調査國の中央アジア旅程とその考古
學的成果
Bukkyô geijutsu 佛教藝術 19/29.1953, (1-5, 1-), 82-96,56-70

45. Vaillant, Louis Auguste André Marie: *Rapport sur les travaux géographiques faits par la Mission archéologique d'Asie centrale (Mission Paul Pelliot, 1906-1909).*
Paris: Impr. nat. 1956. Pp. 77-162
From: Bulletin de la section de géographie du Comité des travaux historiques et scientifiques. 1955.

46. Paul Pelliot: *Carnets de Pékin, 1899-1901.* [Avant-propos de L. Hambis.]
Paris: Impr. nationale 1976. III,74 pp., 8 pl., 4 maps
(Documents inédits du Collège de France.1.)

47. Naitô Torajirô 内藤虎次郎
[A letter to Dr. P. Pelliot. Yo Haku Ki Wa kansenrin.]
與伯希和翰旋林
Naitô Konan zenshû 14. Tôkyô 1976,267

48. Séguy, Marie-Rose: Trésors de Chine et de Haute Asie. Centième anniversaire de Paul Pelliot.
*Bulletin de la Bibliothèque nationale.*4.1979,110-119

49. *Trésors de Chine et de Haute Asie.* Centième anniversaire de Paul Pelliot.
Paris: Bibliothèque nationale 1979. XX,113 pp., incl. 8 colour pl.
13-28: Paul Pelliot, explorateur et savant

50. Hopkirk, Peter: *Foreign devils on the silk road. The search for the lost cities and treasures of Central Asia.*
(Oxford:) Oxford University Press (1984). X,252 pp.
On Pelliot esp. pp.177-189,211-216

51. Etiemble: «Je fus ébloui par Pelliot....»

Marie-Claire Bergère, Angel Pino [eds.]: *Un siècle d'enseignement du chonois à l'Ecole des langues orientales, 1840-1945*. Paris: L'Asiathèque 1995,168-172
[Reprint, with additions, of an article from *Alexandrie*, no.4, 1946.]

52. Pino, A.: Pelliot, Paul.
Deux siècles d'histoire de l'Ecole des langues orientales. Textes réunis par Pierre Labrousse. (Paris:) Hervas (1995),292-293

53. *Les arts de l'Asie centrale. La collection Paul Pelliot du musée national des arts asiatiques - Guimet*. Sous la direction de Jacques Giès. Par Jacques Giès, Conservateur en chef du patrimoine, Michel Soymié, Directeur d'études à l'Ecole pratique des Hautes Etudes, Jean-Pierre Drège, Directeur d'études à l'Ecole pratique des Hautes Etudes, Danielle Eliasberg, Chargée de recherches au Centre national de la Recherche scientifique, Richard Schneider, Ingénieur d'études à l'Ecole pratique des Hautes Etudes. [vol. 2: and] Paul Magnin, Directeur de recherches au Centre national de la Recherche scientifique, Krishna Riboud, Chargée de mission au musée Guimet, Terukazu Akiyama, Professeur honoraire à l'Université de Tokyo, avec la collaboration de Keiko Omoto, Bibliothécaire au musée Guimet. 1-2.
Paris: Réunion des Musées Nationaux (1995-1996). 372, 446 pp.

Contents:
Avant-propos par Jean-François Jarrige
La mission Pelliot, par Jacques Giès
Le langage pictural à Dunhuang par Jacques Giès
Table analytique des pigments par Jean-Paul Rioux
Deux peintures inédites du fonds Paul Pelliot, provenant de Dunhuang par Jacques Giès
Table des planches en coleurs
Planches en couleur
Figures monochromes
Notice sur les planches en coleur par Michel Soymié, Jean-Pierre Drège, Danielle Eliasberg, Paul Magnin et Richard Schneider.
Index analytique

Les sites et les œuvres d'Asie centrale à la lumière des trouvailles faites par la mission Pelliot par Jacques Giès
Les soieries de Dunhuang par Krishna Riboud
Liste des planches en couleurs
Notes sur les planches en couleurs:
Peintures et bannières de Dunhuang au musée Guimet par Michel Soymié, Jean-Pierre Drège, Danielle Eliasberg, Paul Magnin, Richard Schneider
Tissus de Dunhuang par Krishna Riboud
Sculptures, peintures murales et autres œuvres archéologiques provenant des sites d'Asie centrale et de Dunhuang, par Jacques Giès avec la collaboration de Keiko Omoto (les textes des planches 132, 181, 182, 183, 184 ont été rédigés par Terukazu Akiyama)
Index
Bibliographie générale
Table de concordance des œuvres et des planches

English version / abstract:
The arts of Central Asia. The Pelliot collection in the Musée Guimet.
General editor: Jacques Giès. Translated by Hero Friesen, in collaboration with Roderick Whitfield.
London: Serindia Publications (1996). 235 pp.
Contents:
The Pelliot expedition, by Jacques Giès
The pictorial language of Dunhuang, by Jacques Giès
Analytical table of pigments, by Jean-Paul Rioux
Two unpublished paintings from Dunhuang in the Pelliot collection, by Jacques Giès
Captions to the colour plates: Volume 1.
Notes to Part 1.
Central Asian sites and works of arts in the light of the discoveries made by the Pelliot expedition, by Jacques Giès
The silks of Dunhuang, by Krishna Riboud
Captions to the colour plates: Volume 2.
Notes to Part 2.

SOME FURTHER PUBLICATIONS ON THE MISSION PELLIOT

Mission Pelliot en Asie Centrale. Série petit in-octavo

54. R. Gauthiot: *Essai de grammaire sogdienne.* Avant-propos de A.
Meillet. Première partie: Phonétique.
Paris: Paul Geuthner 1914-1923. 183 S., 1 planche d'écritures, 2 cartes
(Mission Pelliot en Asie Centrale. Série petit in-octavo.1.)

55. *Formulaire sanscrit-tibétain du Xe siècle.* Édité et traduit par Joseph
Hackin, conservateur du Musée Guimet.
Paris: Paul Geuthner 1924. IX,130 S.
(Mission Pelliot en Asie Centrale. Série petit in-octavo.2.)

56. N. P. Chakravarti: *L'Udânavarga sanskrit.* Texte sanscrit en transcription, avec traduction et annotations, suivi d'une étude critique et de
planches. T.1. (chapitres I à XXI).
Paris: Paul Geuthner 1930. 272 pp. 8°
(Mission Pelliot en Asie Centrale. Série petit in-octavo.4.)

Mission Pelliot en Asie centrale. Série in-quarto

Pelliot: Les grottes de Touen-houang.
(Mission Pelliot en Asie centrale. Série in-quarto.1)
-> 179

Gauthiot / Pelliot: Le Sûtra des causes et des effets du bien et du Mal.
(Mission Pelliot en Asie centrale. Série in-quarto.2.)
-> 209

57. *Textes sogdiens*, édités, traduits et commentés, par E[mile] Benve-
niste. Paris: Paul Geuthner 1940. IX,284 pp. 4°
(Mission Pelliot en Asie centrale. Série in-quarto.3.)
[Dedication:] A la mémoire de Robert Gauthiot.

58. *Codices Sogdiani.* Manuscrits de la Bibliothèque nationale (Mission
    Pelliot) reproduits en fac-similé, avec une introduction par E. Benve-
    niste.
    Copenhague: E. Munksgaard 1940. XIII,213 pp.
    (Monumenta linguarum Asiae Maioris.3.)

59. *Vessantara Jâtaka.* Texte sogdien édité, traduit et commenté par E.
    Benveniste. [Vign.]
    Paris: Paul Geuthner 1946. X,136 pp. 4°
    (Mission Pelliot en Asie centrale. Série in-quarto.4.)
    [Dedication:] A la mémoire de Paul Pelliot

60. *Sâriputra et les six maîtres d'erreur.* Facimilé du manuscrit chinois
    4524 de la Bibliothèque nationale, présenté par Nicole Vandier-
    Nicolas, chargée de cours à l'Institut des hautes études chinoises. Avec
    traduction et commentaire du texte. Ouvrage publié avec le concours
    du Centre national de la Recherche scientifique.
    Paris: Imprimerie nationale 1954. 32 pp. 2 pp. Chin. text. 4°; and
    folder with plates.
    (Mission Pelliot en Asie centrale. Série in-quarto.5.)

Mission Paul Pelliot. Documents conservés à la Bibliothèque nationale

61. 本際經 *Pen-tsi king (Livre du terme originel).* Ouvrage taoiste inédit
    du VIIe siècle. Manuscrits retrouvés à Touen-houang reproduits en
    facsimilé. Introduction par Wu Chi-yu.
    Paris: Centre national de la recherche scientifique 1960. 50,208 pp. 4°
    (Mission Paul Pelliot. Documents conservés à la Bibliothèque natio-
    nale.1.)

62. 燉煌曲 *Airs de Touen-houang (Touen-houang k'iu).* Textes à chanter
    des VIIIe-Xe siècles. Manuscrits reproduits en fac-similé. Avec une
    introduction en chinois par Jao Tsong-yi, Professeur à l'Université de
    Singapore. Adaptée en français avec la traduction de quelques textes
    d'airs par Paul Demiéville, membre de l'Institut, Professeur honoraire
    au Collège de France.
    Paris: Editions du Centre national de la recherche scientifique 1971.
    184,182,58 pp. 4°

(Mission Paul Pelliot. Documents conservés à la Bibliothèque nationale. 2.)
Préface [signed:] Noël 1968. Paul Demiéville

63. *Manuscrits ouigours de Touen-houang.* Le conte bouddhique du bon et du mauvais prince en version ouigoure. Texte établi, traduit et commenté par James Russell Hamilton.
Paris: Editions du Centre national de la recherche scientifique 1971. 204 pp. 8°
(Mission Paul Pelliot. Documents conservés à la Bibliothèque nationale. 3.)
[Dedication:] To Eunice Eittreim Hamilton, for rare courage and understanding
[Ms. Pelliot chinois 3509.]

Mission Paul Pelliot. Documents archéologiques, publiés sous les auspices de l'Académie des inscriptions et belles-lettres [subtitle varies: Documents conservés au Musée Guimet et à la Bibliothèque Nationale. Documents archéologiques.]

64. *Toumchouq.* Planches. Édité avec le concours de l'Académie des inscriptions et belles-lettres (Fondations Benoît-Garnier, Fontane et Senart), du Centre national de la recherche scientifique et de l'Institut des hautes études chinoises sous la direction de Louis Hambis.
Paris: Adrien Maisonneuve 1961. 5 pp., 155 pl., 1 colour pl., 11 (partly folded) plans.
(Mission Paul Pelliot. Documents archéologiques, publiés sous les auspices de l'Académie des inscriptions et belles-lettres.1.)

65. *Toumchouq.* Par M[adeleine] Paul-David, M[adeleine] Hallade et L. Hambis. Édité avec le concours de l'Académie des inscriptions et belles-lettres (Fondations Benoît-Garnier, Fontane et Senart), du Centre national de la recherche scientifique et de l'Institut des hautes études chinoises sous la direction de Louis Hambis.
Paris: Imprimerie nationale 1964. XXXIII, 450 pp., 13 pl., 538 Ill.
(Mission Paul Pelliot.2.)
Contents:

Hambis: Sites et monuments de la région de Kachgar et de Toum-
chouq.
Hallade: Sculptures et objets divers
Paul-David: Céramique.
Simone Gaulier, Marie-Rose Lotéron: Catalogue descriptif.
Paul Pelliot: Notes de voyage (pp.421-440)

66. *Douldour-Âqour et Soubachi*. Planches. Edité avec le concours de
l'Académie des inscriptions et belles-lettres (Fondation Dourlans), du
Centre national de la recherche scientifique et de l'Institut des hautes
études chinoises sous la direction de Louis Hambis.
Paris: Adrien Maisonneuve 1967. 17 pp., 124 pl., 11 plans, 8+5
dessins
(Mission Paul Pelliot.3.)

67. *Douldour-Âqour*. Texte. Madeleine Hallade, Simone Gaulier avec la
participation de Liliane Courtois / Centre de Recherche sur l'Asie
centrale et la Haute-Asie, Instituts d'Asie, Collège de France.
Paris: Editions Recherche sur les civilisations 1982. 448 pp.
(Mission Paul Pelliot.4.)
(Mémoire.9.)
Contents:
Les sites
Les documents archéologiques
Catalogue descriptif / Collection du Musée Guimet
31-38: Paul Pelliot: Notes de voyage (extraits).

Temples rupestres (Koutcha). Planches.
(Mission Paul Pelliot.5.)
«en préparation.»

Temples rupestres (Koutcha). Texte.
(Mission Paul Pelliot.6.)
«en préparation.»

Peintures relevées au trait (Koutcha).
(Mission Paul Pelliot.7.)
«en preparation.»

68. *Koutcha. Sites divers de la région de Koutcha.* Épigraphie koutché-
    enne. Par Chao Huashan, Simone Gaulier, Monique Maillard, Georges
    Pinault. Ouvrage publié avec le concours du Centre National de la
    Recherche Scientifique.
    Paris: Collège de France, Instituts d'Asie, Centre de Recherche sur
    l'Asie centrale et la Haute Asie (1987). IX,204 pp., XCVI pl.
    (Mission Paul Pelliot.8.)
    1a: 4 89508-8

    Grottes de Touen-houang. Carnet de notes de Paul Pelliot. 1-6.
    Paris: Collège de France, Instituts d'Asie, Centre de recherche sur
    l'Asie centrale et la Haute Asie 1981-1992.
    (Mission Paul Pelliot. Documents conservés au Musée Guimet.11.)
    ->860

    *Bannières et peintures [de Touen-houang]. Études stylistiques et
    iconographiques.*
    (Mission Paul Pelliot.12.)
    «en préparation.»

69. *Tissus de Touen-houang conservés au Musée Guimet et à la
    Bibliothèque nationale.* Par Mme Krishna Riboud et M. Gabriel Vial
    avec le concours de Mlle Madeleine Hallade. Edité avec le concours
    de l'Académie des inscriptions et belles-lettres (Fondation Dourlans),
    du Centre national de la recherche scientifique et de l'Institut des
    hautes études chinoises sous la direction de Louis Hambis.
    Paris: Imprimerie nationale 1970. XLI,443 pp.
    (Mission Paul Pelliot.13.)

70. *Bannières et peintures de Touen-houang conservées au Musée
    Guimet.* Par Mme Nicolas-Vandier [!] avec le concours de Mmes
    Gaulier, Leblond et Maillard et M. Jera-Bezard. Edité avec le con-
    cours de l'Académie des inscriptions et belles-lettres (Fondation
    Dourlans), du Centre national de la recherche scientifique et de
    l'Institut des hautes études chinoises sous la direction de Louis
    Hambis.
    Paris: Imprimerie nationale 1974. XXIII,431 p., 18 pl.
    (Mission Paul Pelliot. Documents conservés au Musée Guimet.14.)
    Contents:

Buddha
Bodhisattva
Divinités gardiennes et êtres surnaturels
Moînes éminents
Divers

71. *Bannières et peintures de Touen-houang conservées au Musée Guimet.* Planches. Edité avec le concours du Centre national de la recherche scientifique et du Centre de recherche sur la l'Asie centrale et la Haute Asie du Collège de France sous la direction de Louis Hambis.
Paris 1976. 133 pp. ill. = 216 ill.
(Mission Paul Pelliot. Documents conservés au Musée Guimet.15.)

Bannières et peintures. Inscriptions et cartouches.
(Mission Paul Pelliot.16.)
«en préparation.»

72. *A catalogue of the Sanskrit manuscripts brought from Central Asia by Paul Pelliot preserved in the Bibliothèque nationale (preliminary).* Edited by Taijun Inokuchi, Professor of Ryukoku University, in collaboration with Takashi Irisawa, Naozumi Azuma, Ekyou Uno, Norisato Aohara.
Kyôto: Ryukoku University, Institute of Buddhist Cultural Studies 1989. XI,490 S.

Catalogue des manuscrits chinois de Touen-houang (Fonds Pelliot chinois)

73. Bibliothèque nationale, Département des manuscrits: *Catalogue des manuscrits chinois de Touen-houang (Fonds Pelliot chinois).* Vol. 1: Nos. 2001-2500. Publié avec le concours de la Fondation Singer-Polignac.
Paris: Bibliothèque nationale 1970. XXIX,405 S., 24 Taf.
Ce catalogue a été établi d'après les notes de Paul Pelliot ... et de Wang Tchong-min ... par Jacques Gernet ... et Wu Chi-yu.
[rev.:] *Okayama shigaku* 26.1973,73-77 (Obuchi Ninji 大淵忍爾)

74. Bibliothèque nationale, Département des manuscrits: *Catalogue des manuscrits chinois de Touen-houang (Fonds Pelliot chinois)*. Vol. 3: Nos. 3001-3500.
Paris: Bibliothèque nationale 1983. XX,482 S.
(Editions de la Fondation Singer-Polignac.)
... rédigé sous la direction de Michel Soymié.

75. *Catalogue des manuscrits chinois de Touen-houang*. Fonds Pelliot chinois de la Bibliothèque nationale. IV. Nos. 3501-4000.
Paris: EFEO 1991. XX,558 pp.
Catalogue rédigé sous la direction de Michel Soymié par Jean-Pierre Drège, Danielle Eliasberg, Paul Magnin, Richard Schneider, Eric Trombert et Michel Soymié.

75a.*Catalogue des manuscrits chinois de Touen-houang*. Fonds Pelliot chinois de la Bibliothèque nationale. V. Nos. 4001-6040.
Paris: EFEO 1995. XXXI,740 pp. (2 volumes)

76. M. Lalou: *Inventaire des manuscrits tibétains de Touen-houang conservés à la Bibliothèque nationale (Fonds Pelliot tibétain)*. 1. Nos. 1-849.
Paris: Librarie d'Amérique et d'Orient 1939. VII,186 S.
2. Nos. 850-1282. Paris: Bibliothèque nationale 1950. VII,97 S.
3. Nos. 1283-2216. 1961. LV,XIX,220 S.

77. Kabutogi, Shôkô: *Descriptive catalogue of the Miao-fa-lien-hua-ching from Tunhuang collected by Aurel Stein and Paul Pelliot*. With forewords by K. B. Gardner and B. Frank. I-II. Tôkyô: The Reiyûkai 1978. 34, XVII,351 pp., 54 pl., 8 colour pl.; 253 pp., 2 pl. 4°

78. *Revendications des fonctionnaires du Grand Tibet au VIIIe siècle*. Par Marcelle Lalou.
Paris: Société asiatique 1956. 42 S., 2 Taf.
(Manuscrits de Haute Asie conservés à la Bibliothèque nationale de Paris (Fonds Pelliot).3.)
Journal asiatique 1955 (T. CCXLIII-2), publié avec le concours du Centre national de la Recherche scientifique.

Unpublished catalogues:

79. *Inventaire sommaire des rouleaux Pelliot chinois.*
    Ms. s.d. Nos. 2000-3511, 4500-4521
    135 fol.
    BN: Bureau F° 8

80. Wang Chung-min: *Catalogue de la collection Pelliot du fonds
    d'estampages.*
    Ms. 1938. 420 pp.
    BN: Bureau 4° K 2

81. *Chinois. Catalogue des collections Pelliot A et B* rédigé par Wang
    Tchong-min, 1935-1939.
    Ms. 2 vols. 4°
    BN: Bureau 4° K 1

Three lecture manuscripts in the library of the Musée Guimet

82. *Rapport sur sa mission en Chine en 1933.* Commission du Pacifique,
    26 juin 1933.
    Carbon. 28 pp.

83. Conférence de M. Paul Pelliot, membre de l'Institut, Professeur au
    Collège de France.
    Les premiers relations entre la Chine et l'Orient gréco-romain
    [Conférence au Musée Guimet le 15 mars 1931.]
    Carbon. 34 pp.

84. The China Society. The following lecture by M. Pelliot was delivered
    before the above Society at the Oriental School of Studies, Finsbury
    Circus E.C. on Friday, November 19th, 1926.
    Carbon. 20 pp.

Some Japanese studies on manuscripts from the Pelliot Collection

85. Kanaoka Shôkô 金岡照光
敦煌出土文學文獻分類目錄[Tonkô shutsudo bungaku bunken bunrui mokuroku. Classified catalogue of literary and popular works in Chinese in Tunhuang documents: From Stein and Pelliot collections.]
Tôkyô 1971. VII,251,5 p.

86. Akiyama Terukazu 秋山光和
[Pien-wen and picture scrolls: The *Xiangmo bian tujuan* brought back by Paul Pelliot. Henbun to emaki Pelliot shôrai kôma henzu maki ni tsuite]
變文と繪卷 一 ペリオ将来降魔變圖卷
文化史懇談會報 32.1955

87. Akiyama Terukazu 秋山光和
[A scroll painting illustrating the Pien-wen: *The magic competition between Sâriputra and Raudrâksa* brought back by Paul Pelliot from Tunhuang. Tonkô hon kôma hen (Rôdo satô shôhen) gaken ni tsuite]
敦煌本降魔變 (牢度叉鬥聖變) 畫卷について
Bijutsu kenkyû 187.1957,43-77

88. Akiyama Terukazu 秋山光和
[The three wooden caskets from Subashi in the Kucha region, brought back by the Pelliot mission. Pelliot shôrai no Subashi shutsudo mokusei shari yôki sanshu]
ペリオ将来のスバシ出土木製舍利容器三種
Bijutsu kenkyû 191.1957,266-287

89. Akiyama Terukazu 秋山光和
[Paintings in the manuscripts acquired in Tunhuang by Paul Pelliot. Pelliot shûshû Tonkô shahon no ega shiryô.]
ペリオ收集敦煌寫本の繪畫資料
Bukkyô geijutsu 佛教藝術 96.1974,p.99-100

90. Akiyama Terukazu 秋山光和

[*Lao-to ch'a-tou sheng-pien pai-miao fen-pen* (Pelliot Tibétain 1293) and the wall paintings of Tunhuang. *Rôdo satô shôhen hakubyô funpon* to Tonkô hekiga.]
牢度叉鬥聖變白描粉本 (Pelliot Tibétain 1293) の敦煌壁畫
Tôkyô daigaku bungakubu bunka kôryû kenkyû shisetsu kenkyû kiyô 2/3.1979, 1-28

91. Fujieda Akira 藤枝晃
[The processing of photocopying the Pelliot Collection. Pelliot collection fukusha shimatsu-ki]
ペリオコレクシヨン複寫始末記
Tosho 201.1966,8-11

92. Hirano Kenshô 平野顯照
[A commentary on *Shun-tzu pien-wen*, Stein No. 4654 and Pelliot No. 2721. Shunshi henbun kaidoku hôkoku.]
舜子變文 解讀報告
Shinagakuhô 3.1958,10-17

93. Ishihama Juntarô 石濱純太郎:
[Three Tunhuang documents brought back by Paul Pelliot. Haku Ki Wa shûshû Tonkô isho naka no 3 hen.]
白希和蒐集敦煌遺書中 3 篇
Hattori sensei koki shukuga kinen ronbunshû. Tôkyô 1936, 117-120

94. Kimura Ryûtoku 木村隆德: [A study of the Pelliot Tibetan manuscript no. 116. Tonkô Chibetto-bun shahon Pelliot no 116 kenkyû]
敦煌チベット文寫本 Pelliot no 116 研究
Indogaku Bukkyôgaku kenkyû 23:2.1975,281-284 (778-781)

95. Kimura Ryûtoku 木村隆德: Une lacune dans le manuscrit tibétain de Touen-houang, Pelliot tibétain 116.
Indogaku Bukkyôgaku kenkyû.26:1.1977,23-28 (489-484)

96. Mishima Hajime 三島一
[The publication of the Manuscrits de Touen-houang conservés à la Bibliothèque nationale de Paris. Tonkô isho no kankô.]
敦煌遺書の刊行
Shigaku zasshi.38:3.1927,88

97. Mizuhara Ikô 水原渭江: [A study on explication of score of
     dancing discovered at Tunhuang, China (note V). Mission Pelliot no
     Touen-houang (Tonkô) yori hakken no bufu 1.]
     Mission Pelliot の Touen-houang (敦煌)より發見の舞譜
     (1)
     Ôtani joshi daigaku kiyô 16:1.1981,37-48

98. Mizuhara Ikô 水原渭江: [A study on explication of score of
     dancing (Huan Xi Sha) and (Feng Kuei Yün) discovered at Tun-
     huang, China. Mission Pelliot no Touen-houang (Tonkô) yori hakken
     no bufu 3.]
     Mission Pelliot の Touen-houang (敦煌)より發見の舞譜
     (3)
     Ôtani joshi daigaku kiyô 16:2.1981,21-31

99. Mizuhara Ikô 水原渭江: [A study on explication of score of
     dancing discovered at Tunhuang by Paul Pelliot. Mission Pelliot no
     Touen-houang (Tonkô) yori hakken no bufu 2.]
     Mission Pelliot の Touen-houang (敦煌)より發見の舞譜
     (2)
     *Ôtani joshi daigaku kiyô.*17:1.1982,101-110

100. Niida Noboru 仁井田陞
     [Some legal historical source materials discovered at Tunhuang by
     the Pelliot expedition. Toroban shutsudo no Tôdai hôritsu shiryô
     sûshu.]
     吐魯番出土の唐代法律史料數種
     Kokka gakkai zasshi 50:10.1936,109-130

101. Niida Noboru 仁井田陞:
     [Some legal historical materials brought back from Tunhuang by Sir
     Aurel Stein and Paul Pelliot. Stein-Pelliot ryôshi Tonkô shôrai
     hôritsu shiryô sûshu.]
     スタイン. ペリオ兩氏敦煌将来法律史料數種
     Tôhô gakuhô (Tôkyô) 9.1939,91-122

102. Niida Noboru 仁井田陞
     [Re-examination of the T'ang ling fragments collected by Paul
     Pelliot at Tunhuang. Pelliot Tonkô shûshû no Tôrei no saigimmi.]

ペリオ敦煌收集の唐令の再吟味
Shigaku zasshi 73:12.1964,81

103. Niida Noboru 仁井田陞
[A re-examination of the fragments of the T'ang ling discovered by
Pelliot at Tunhuang: The fragments of the Gongshi ling. Pelliot
Tonkô hakken no Tôrei no saigimmi - toku ni kôshiki ryô dankan.]
ペリオ敦煌發見の唐令の再吟味 一 とくに公式令
断檢
Tôyô bunka kenkyûjo kiyô 35.1965,1-15, I-IV

104. Niida Noboru 仁井田陞
[Reexamination of the fragments of the T'ang chih-yüan ling discovered by Pelliot at Tunhuang. Pelliot Tonkô hakken Tô shokuin
rei no saigimmi]
ペリオ敦煌發見唐職員令の再吟味 (牢度叉鬥聖變)
Ishida hakushi shôju kinen tôyôshi ronsô
石田博士頌壽記念東洋史論叢 Tôkyô 1965,339-353

105. Ôtani Shôshin 大谷勝真
[Tunhuang mss, Pelliot No. 2696. Tô kisô shaga kankyô shi daisha
bun ni tsuite.]
唐僖宗車駕還京師大赦文について
Seikyû gakusô 青丘學叢 2.1930, p.1-20

106. Sakai Ken'ichi 坂井健一
[A comparative study on the difference of phonological notes between Chuang-tzu of the Mss (Pelliot 3602) discovered in Tunhuang
and Ching-tien shih-wen. Tonkô shutsudo Sôshi ongi shahon zanken
(Pelliot 3602) to kyôten shakubun ongi to no hikaku kôsatsu.]
敦煌莊子音義寫本殘卷 (ペリオ 3602)と經典釋文音義 と
の比較考察
Nihon daigaku jimbun kagaku kenkyûjo kenkyû kiyô 15.1973,13-24

107. Yamamoto Tatsurô 山本達郎
[Ten documents concerning the family and land registration system
discovered at Tunhuang and brought back by Oldenburg and Pelliot.
Tonkô hakken Oldenburg oyobi Pelliot shôrai kosei densei kanseki
bunsho 10 shu.]

敦煌發見オルデンブルグ及ペリオ將来戸製
田製關系文書10 種
Shigaku zasshi 69:12.1960,90-91

108. Yoshida Yutaka 吉田豊
[The Sogdian formula for receiving the eight commandments: Pelliot
Sogdian 5 and 17. Sogdo-go no Ju hachi sai kaigi.]
ソグド語の收八齋戒儀
Indogaku Bukkyôgaku kenkyû 印度學佛教學研究 33:1.1984,313-
310 (104-106)

109. Yoshida Yutaka 吉田豊: On the Sogdian formula for receiving
the eight commandments: Pelliot Sogdian 5 and 17.
*Orient.*20.1984,157-172

And de Jong's paper in a Japanese *festschrift*:

110. J. W. de Jong: Fond Pelliot Tibétain No. 610 et 611.
Yamaguchi hakushi kanreki kinen Indogaku Bukkyôgaku ronsô.
山口博士還曆記念印度學佛教學論叢 Tôkyô 1955,58-67

Addenda

111. *Die Dreizehn und die Zwölf im Traktat Pelliot. (Dogmen in Zahlen-
formeln.)* Ein Beitrag zu den Grundlagen des Manichäismus. Von
Luise Troje.
Leipzig: Pfeiffer 1925. 174 pp.
(Veröffentlichungen des Forschungsinstituts für vergleichende Reli-
gionsgeschichte an der Universität Leipzig. 2,1.)

112. *Rituel bon-po des funérailles royales (Fonds Pelliot tibétain 1042).*
Par Marcelle Lalou.
Paris: Société asiatique 1953. 24 S.
(Manuscrits de Haute Asie conservés à la Bibliothèque nationale de
Paris, Fond Pelliot 1.)

113. *Fragments sanskrits de Haute Asie (Mission Pelliot).* [Edited by]
Bernard Pauly.

Paris: Société asiatique 1958. 27 pp., V pl.
(Manuscrits de Haute Asie.5.)
From *JA* 245.1957:3.

114. *Fragments sanskrits de Haute Asie (Mission Pelliot).* [Edited by]
Bernard Pauly.
Paris: Société asiatique 1960. 47 pp. V pl.
(Manuscrits de Haute Asie.7.)
From *JA* 247.1959:2.

115. *Fragments sanskrits de Haute Asie (Mission Pelliot).* [Edited by]
Bernard Pauly.
Paris: Société asiatique 1961. 46 pp. XI pl.
(Manuscrits de Haute Asie.9.)
From *JA* 248.1960:2.

116. *Fragments sanskrits de Haute Asie (Mission Pelliot).* [Edited by]
Bernard Pauly.
Paris: Société asiatique 1962. 30 pp. IV pl.
(Manuscrits de Haute Asie.11.)
From *JA* 248.1960:4.

117. *Fragments sanskrits de Haute Asie (Mission Pelliot).* [Edited by]
Bernard Pauly.
Paris: Société asiatique 1962. 78 pp. XI pl.
(Manuscrits de Haute Asie.12.)
From *JA* 249.1961:3.

118. *Fragments sanskrits de Haute Asie (Mission Pelliot).* [Edited by]
Bernard Pauly.
Paris: Société asiatique 1965. 95 pp. XXIV pl.
(Manuscrits de Haute Asie.13.)
From *JA* 252.1964:1.2.

119. Ariane Macdonald: Une lecture des Pelliot Tibétain 1286, 1287,
1038, 1047 et 1290. Essai sur la formation et l'emploi des mythes
politiques dans la religion royale de Sroṅ-Bcan Sgam-Po.
Études tibétaines. 1971, 190-391

[rev.] *Tôyôgakuhô* 54:4.1972,78-87 (Yamaguchi Zuihô 山口
瑞鳳)

120. *Einige Gedichte von Wang Fan-chih.* Übersetzungen von Texten aus
Fonds Pelliot Chinois Ms. 3833 von Dorothée Tafel-Kehren.
Bonn 1982. IX, 169 pp.
Diss., University of Bonn 1984.

121. *Udanavarga de Subasi.* Edition critique du ms. sanskrit sur bois
provenant de Subasi. Bibliothèque nationale de Paris, Fonds Pelliot.
Par H. Nakatani.
Paris: De Boccard 1987-88. 108 pp.; 21 ll. pl.
(Publications de l'Institut de civilisation indienne.53-54.)

122. *Un traité tibétain de Dhyana chinois (chan).* Ms. de Dunhuang Pel-
liot tibétain 116, folios 119-170 / Guilaine Mala, Kimura Ryûtoku.
Tokyo: Maison Franco-Japonaise 1988. V,103 pp.
(Bulletin de la Maison Franco-Japonaise.NS 11,1.)

123. *Choix de documents tibétains conservés à la Bibliothèque Nationale,*
complété par quelques manuscrits de l'India Office et du British
Museum / Mission Paul Pelliot. Présentés par Ariane Macdonald et
Yoshiro Imaeda. Préf. de R.-A. Stein. Introd. par Marie-Rose Séguy.
Paris: Bibliothèque nationale 1978-1979, 1990.
1.1978. 25 pp., 304 pl.
2.1979. 31 pp., pl. 305-640
3.1990. Corpus syllabique, par Yoshiro Imaeda. XIV,59,1009 pp.
[rev.] *Tôyôgakuhô* 61:1/2.1979,181-185 (Yamaguchi Zuihô 山
口瑞鳳)

Further additions on Pelliot, the scholar

124. V. M. Alekseev: *Pis̆ma k Èduardu S̆avannu i Polju Pellio.* Sostavi-
tel' I. E. Ciperovič.
Sankt-Peterburg: PB 1998. 230 pp.

125. Remembering Paul Pelliot, 1878-1945.
*Journal of the American Oriental Society.*119.1999,467-472
Indiana University. Denis Sinor